RELIGIOUS AFFECTIONS

BY
JONATHAN EDWARDS

ABRIDGED AND
UPDATED BY
ELLYN SANNA

CHRISTIAN BOOK CLUB
Since 1948, The Book Club You Can Trust®

RELIGIOUS
AFFECTIONS

CONTENTS

Introduction

In today's world, if we are familiar with Jonathan Edwards at all, we are apt to connect him with the sort of hellfire-and-damnation message that he preached in his most famous sermon, "Sinners in the Hands of an Angry God." However, this sermon was not really typical of Edwards, for far more often he described God's love and joy and the sweetness of Christian life. As a preacher, he spoke quietly, without any gestures, relying on the effectiveness of his thoroughly thought-out logic. All of his words revealed a deep and unmoving confidence in a living God, a God who loves and heals human beings' entire being—heart, mind, and body. This confidence is at the heart of *Religious Affections.*

Historical Background

Jonathan Edwards lived in New England in the years before the Revolutionary War. The colony had been settled by the Puritans a hundred years before, and the colonists' sense of their religious history was important to their identity. Originally, they had seen themselves as a "righteous remnant" that was fleeing persecution from the established Church of England. Nominal Christianity did not exist in their community, for their congregation was made up of believers who were committed enough to leave their homes and families.

But as the years went by, as they became settled and secure in the New World, the colonists now became an established church rather than a persecuted one. New England was basically a safe little world, and the Puritans' strong work ethic made most of them prosper there. Almost none of them were poor, and most of them were relatively well-educated. Many people were now more interested in material blessings rather than spiritual ones. Nominal Christianity became a reality that more and more New England churches faced.

On top of this, New England Christians were influenced by what historians refer to as the "Age of Reason" in Europe. Many European thinkers were rejecting the idea of sinful humanity living under the judgment of a wrathful God; instead, they saw humanity as basically good, especially when guided by human reason. As a result, in many New England churches, strict Calvinism gave way to a Christianity that emphasized the human capacity for good.

Christian leaders began to pray for a revival—and in 1734, this revival was sparked to life in Jonathan Edwards's congregation in Northampton, Massachusetts. It swept through the American colonies for the next sixteen years, gaining momentum as it went, a religious movement so widespread that historians call it the "Great Awakening."

Up until now, Puritan preachers had been mostly concerned with doctrine, but during the Awakening, they appealed more to the emotions. A conversion *experience* became vitally important, a point of inward change in a person's heart. Individuals needed to *feel* their unworthiness and sin, preachers taught, and this emphasis on the individual's inner choice has remained a part of evangelical theology until today.

The Great Awakening was a dramatic religious movement that contained many elements that today would probably be called "charismatic." People who were spiritually and emotionally moved by a sermon would often faint, scream, sing, jump in the air, groan, or respond with some other physical manifestation. Some preachers began to emphasize these outward demonstrations, insisting that they were necessary to true holiness. Other religious leaders took a more rational approach and condemned this sort of experience. They felt that preachers were merely manipulating people's emotions, creating a religion based on emotional delusion rather than doctrinal authority.

In response to these two conflicting points of view, Jonathan Edwards wrote *Religious Affections.* In this book, he argues that our faith must come from our hearts, not just our intellects. He sees the heart as the seat of our likes and dislikes, our emotions, our inclinations—and he firmly believed that God touches us here. However, he also firmly believed that God made us one being—body, mind, and emotions—and that our spiritual condition includes all three.

Religious Affections examines religious experience with a painstaking thoroughness, and it emphasizes that the quantity of emotion does not prove that it is spiritual. In the same way, physical manifestations may accompany the workings of God's Spirit, but they do not prove His presence. With careful logic, Edwards's book demonstrates that those emotions that come from God have the power to transform us, both internally and externally. It concludes that a self-centered religion makes a big commotion, but a true spiritual experience quietly touches the heart with a vision of God's holiness, and thereby transforms the way we live.

Edwards was deeply intellectual, with a powerful, analytical mind that he devoted to theology. As modern readers, we may feel somewhat intimidated by the depth of his thought. He spells out each aspect of our spiritual lives with such minute attention that we may be left with the discouraging impression that the Christian religion is just too *hard*. That was far from Edwards's intention, however. He makes clear that our salvation depends on absolutely no effort of our own. Grace is completely unconditional, unsurpassingly sweet, totally free. The essence of true religious experience, according to Edwards, is to be so overwhelmed with God's love, beauty, and glory, that we are freed from self-centeredness. Our own lives then become "little suns" that shine with Christ's light, illuminating our world with a practical, active love. "Heaven," wrote Edwards, "is a world of love."

Edwards's Life

Jonathan Edwards was born in 1703. Twenty years later, he met his wife, Sarah Pierrepont, the daughter of a famous minister. Sarah was only thirteen at the time, and she was intimidated by Jonathan's quiet intensity. Four years later, however, they were married, and their marriage was fruitful and happy.

Jonathan became pastor of the Northampton congregation, the same church that his grandfather had led, and the Edwardses were busy with the demands of the active parish and their growing family. Every day, though, Jonathan would ride alone into the woods as part of his private time with God. As he walked and meditated, he would write notes to himself on scraps of paper and pin them to his coat. When he returned to his house, Sarah would meet him and carefully unpin the notes for him.

Their marriage was one of harmony and mutual respect.

They had eleven children, and in a time of high infant mortality, amazingly, all eleven lived. Jonathan was a devoted father, who always took one child with him when he had to travel out of town for speaking engagements. He also gave his full attention to his children for an hour every day before dinner, talking with them about their studies and the happenings of the day.

After twenty-three years at Northampton, Edwards was dismissed from the church in 1750. Fifty years earlier, his grandfather had opened the Lord's Supper to anyone who wanted to take it, but Jonathan had felt convicted that this privilege needed to be revoked. The people of the parish were so angry that they asked him to leave.

The months that followed were economically hard for the Edwardses, but eventually the family moved to Stockbridge, Massachusetts, a town that was then on the edge of the frontier. There Edwards led a congregation that was mostly Indians. His years with them were peaceful, and he spent much time in study and writing.

Edwards was deeply interested in the scientific world as well as in theology. He enjoyed Sir Isaac Newton's works, and he firmly believed that good theology and good science supported and complemented each other, since both sought the truth. In all of Edwards's writing, he tried to be as objective and empirical as any scientist, a goal that he clearly achieved in *Religious Affections*.

Each evening, Jonathan would read what he had written that day to Sarah, his "dear companion." Presumably, they discussed his ideas, and she clearly influenced his thought by contributing her own more emotional and less analytical outlook on life. Edwards understood that the heart is not inferior to the intellect.

The years went by peacefully and happily, and their children grew up. One of their daughters moved to New Jersey, where her new husband was the president of the new university at Princeton. Suddenly, in 1757, the Edwardses' son-in-law died, and the university trustees invited Edwards to succeed him as president. When the invitation reached him, the controlled and intellectual Edwards astonished everyone by bursting into tears.

Edwards traveled immediately to Princeton to be with his widowed daughter, while Sarah stayed behind to pack up their lives in Stockbridge. Before she could join him, a smallpox epidemic struck New Jersey. Edwards, a firm believer in scientific advancement, chose to try out the new and controversial vaccine.

The exact quantities of virus to include in the vaccine had not yet been accurately determined, and Jonathan Edwards died as a result. Two of his daughters were with him, but not his wife. However, his last words were for Sarah: "Give my kindest love to my dear wife, and tell her that the uncommon union which has so long subsisted between us has been of such a nature as I trust is spiritual and therefore will continue forever."

Although Edwards's life was cut off early, he nevertheless left a permanent mark on America. His theology continues to influence spiritual thinkers, and it is still relevant to our world today. But Edwards did not only change the world forever with his great works of intellect. He also touched the world forever simply because he was a loving father.

A twentieth-century reporter once tracked down 1,400 of Jonathan and Sarah's descendants. He found that they included 13 college presidents, 100 lawyers, 66 doctors, 65 university professors, 2 university deans, and 80 holders of public office, including 3 senators and 3 state governors. One hundred thirty-five of them had published books, and all of them were considered "great readers" and "highly intelligent." Many, many of them were missionaries. The reporter concluded, "The family has cost the country nothing in pauperism, in crime, in hospital or asylum service: on the contrary, it represents the highest usefulness."

Jonathan Edwards was a brilliant scholar who has left us a great work of religious analysis. His work is not merely important historically, for it is still as relevant as ever in today's religious world. He may have used fiery images at times, but he always countered them with the deep assurance of God's abiding love. This same love comes through clearly in both his life and his writing.

Although he may be more famous for "Sinners in the Hands of an Angry God," Edwards also wrote a sermon titled "Safety, Fulness, and Sweet Refreshment, to Be Found in Christ." In this sermon, he says, "They who come to Christ, do not only come to a resting-place after they have been wandering in the wilderness, but they come to a banqueting-house where they may rest, and where they may feast. They may cease from their former troubles and toils, and they may enter upon a course of delights and spiritual joys. Christ not only delivers from fears of hell and wrath, but He gives hopes of heaven and the enjoyment of God's love."

It is this same positive theology that shines through *Religious Affections.* Although this contemporary version has condensed Edwards's writing into a package that is more manageable to the modern reader, each of the points in Edwards's careful analysis has been included. As modern thinkers in a world of conflicting Christian viewpoints, we can benefit from his rational, well-balanced thought—and as Christians in an eternal kingdom we can be nourished by his vision of God's utter loveliness and glory.

ELLYN SANNA, EDITOR

AUTHOR'S PREFACE

Undoubtedly, the most important concern of every individual is this: *What distinguishes those who are in favor with God, entitled to His eternal rewards?* Or, which comes to the same thing, *What is the nature of true faith?* And *how do we know when we have the virtue and holiness that is acceptable in God's sight?* But even though these are important questions, and we have clear and abundant light in God's Word to provide us with their answers, yet there is no other point where professing Christians differ more from one another. We would be counting forever if we tried to add up all the different opinions on this point. They divide the Christian world, making obvious the truth of our Savior's declaration, "Strait is the gate, and narrow is the way, which leadeth unto life, and few there be that find it" (Matt. 7:14).

For a long time the consideration of these things has kept me busy, as I studied this matter with utmost diligence and care. The subject has absorbed me ever since I first began my theological studies. How successful I've been must be left to the reader's judgment.

I am aware how difficult it is to think impartially about the subject of this book. Many will probably be disappointed to find that I condemn so much that has to do with religious affection; others may be indignant and disgusted that I justify and approve so much. And it may be some will accuse me of being inconsistent when I approve some things and condemn others. That so much good and so much bad should be mixed together in the church of God is indeed very mysterious, just as it is a mystery that has puzzled and amazed many Christians that the saving grace of God and the new and divine nature should dwell with so much corruption, hypocrisy, and iniquity in the heart of the same Christian. No matter how mysterious, however, these are realities. And neither of them is a new or rare thing. False religion often thrives at the same time as great revivals of true faith, and hypocrites spring up among true saints. This was true in the great reformation and revival in Josiah's time (Jer. 3:10; 4:3–4). The same was true in the great outpouring of the Spirit on the Jews in the days of John the Baptist (John 5:35: "Ye were willing for a season to rejoice in his light"). And many were full of admiration for Christ, flying high with joy, but few were true disciples, who endured to the end. Many were like the stony ground or thorny ground, and comparatively few were like the good ground. Of the whole heap that was gathered, a large part was chaff that the wind drives away later.

Therefore, we need to do our best to clearly discern, without any doubt, just what makes true faith. Until we do, we can expect religious revivals to last only a short while; until we do, all our discussion, whether in dialogues or in print, will do little good, since we have so little idea what we are aiming toward.

My plan is to contribute my bit of insight. In my other books, I have tried to show the *distinguishing marks that belong to a work of God's Spirit;* but my aim now is to show the nature and signs of the *grace-filled operations* of God's Spirit, what distinguishes them from all other human influences that have no power to redeem. If I succeed at all, I hope my efforts will promote humanity's relationship with God—but whether or not I succeed in shedding some light on this subject, I hope God's mercy will grant that readers will believe in my sincerity. I hope also for the honesty and prayers of the true followers of God's meek and loving Lamb.

PART I

THE NATURE OF "AFFECTIONS," AND THEIR IMPORTANCE TO RELIGION

Whom having not seen, ye love;
in whom, though now ye see him not,
yet believing, ye rejoice with joy unspeakable
and full of glory.
1 PETER 1:8

With these words the apostle demonstrates the state of mind of the Christians to whom he wrote. In the two preceding verses, he speaks of their trials: *the trial of their faith*, their *being in heaviness through manifold temptations*. These trials benefit true faith in three ways.

First, above all else, trials like this have a tendency to distinguish between true faith and false, causing the difference between them to be evident. That is why in the verse immediately preceding the text, and in innumerable other places, they are called *trials*—because they try the faith of people who profess to be Christians, just as apparent gold is tried in the fire to see whether it is true gold or not. When faith is tried this way and proved to be true, it is "found unto praise and honour and glory" (1 Pet. 1:7).

Second, these trials are of further benefit to true faith, not only because they reveal its truth, but also because they make its genuine beauty and sweetness remarkably clear. True virtue never looks so lovely as when it is most oppressed, and the divine excellence of real Christianity is never demonstrated as clearly as when it faces trials; that is when true faith appears more precious than gold, "found unto praise and honour and glory."

Last, trials benefit true faith by purifying and strengthening it. They not only show its reality, but they also tend to refine it, delivering it from anything that might get in its way, so that all that's left is what's real. Trials tend to make the loveliness of true faith appear at its best advantage, while also tending to increase its beauty by planting it firmly, making it more lively and vigorous, purifying it from anything that dulls its shiny glory. When gold is tried in the fire, its impurities are purged, and it comes out more solid and beautiful, and in the same way when true faith is tried in the fire, it becomes more precious, and thus, again, it is "found unto praise and honour and glory."

The apostle seems to refer to each of these benefits that trials give true faith. And the apostle also mentions two ways that suffering strengthens true faith.

1. The Love of Christ

"Whom having not seen, ye love." The world wondered what strange principles influenced the saints to expose themselves to such great suffering, to forsake the visible world, and to renounce all the sweet, pleasant things offered by the senses. They seemed to the world around them as though they were beside themselves, as though they hated themselves; nothing in the world's view would justify that kind of suffering, and the world knew of nothing that could carry them through such trials. But although they had no visible comfort, nothing that the world saw, nor that the Christians themselves ever saw with their physical eyes, yet they had a supernatural foundation of love: They loved Jesus Christ, for they saw Him spiritually, even though the world could not see Him and they themselves had never seen Him with physical eyes.

2. Joy in Christ

Though their external suffering was severe, yet the spiritual joy inside them was greater than their suffering, and this joy supported them and enabled them to suffer cheerfully.

The apostle remarks on two aspects of this joy. First, its source: Christ, though unseen, is the foundation of it through faith; which is the evidence of things not seen: "In whom, though now ye see him not, yet believing, ye rejoice." Second, the nature of this joy: "unspeakable and full of glory." It is very different from worldly joys and physical delights; its nature is vastly more pure, sublime, and heavenly, since it is something supernatural, truly divine, and indescribably excellent. There are no words for its exquisite sweetness. And not only is the quality of this joy inexpressible, but its quantity also, for God was pleased to give them this holy joy with a liberal hand, in large measure, in the midst of their trials.

The saints' joy was full of glory. In their rejoicing, their minds were filled, as it were, with a glorious brightness, and their natures were exalted and perfected. This rejoicing was worthy and noble, and it did not corrupt and reduce the mind's strength, as many earthly joys do, but instead it beautified and dignified it. It was a foretaste of the joy that will be poured out in heaven, and it filled their minds with the light of God's glory, so that they themselves shone.

Therefore, based on these verses, I propose that:

True faith mostly depends on having the emotions of God, loving the things He loves.

We see that the apostle singles out the spiritual emotions of love and joy; these are the activities of faith on which he remarks, for these demonstrated that the saints' faith was true and pure, full of God's glory. I intend to:

1. Show what is meant by affections.
2. Point out some things that demonstrate that a great part of true faith lies in the emotions.

You may ask what I mean by affections. I answer: The affections are nothing more than the vigorous and perceptible inclinations of the soul's will. They are the passions that motivate the will, the springs of motion and action, our deepest feelings.

God has given the soul two faculties: one that is capable of perception and speculation, by which it discerns and views and judges things; this is called the understanding. The other faculty allows the soul to not only look at things as an indifferent and unaffected spectator, but to also have an emotional reaction, either liking or disliking, pleased or displeased, approving or rejecting. This faculty is called by various names, sometimes the *character,* sometimes the *will* or the *mind,* and often the *heart.*

When this faculty is exercised, sometimes the soul is fairly indifferent, not inclined much in either direction. Other times, the reactions of this faculty may lift us higher and higher, until we feel our soul move vigorously and perceptibly. The Creator has made us so that soul and body are one being, not separate entities, so when this happens, not only are our souls affected but our bodies too. We experience some physical sensation, especially in our heart; we may begin to cry, and that is why the exercise of this mental faculty, perhaps by all nations and ages, is called the *heart*. And the strongest and most perceptible activities of this faculty are what we call the emotions. The will and the emotions are not two faculties; the emotions are not separate from the will, nor are they different from the mere actions of the will and the soul's inclinations, except that what we call the emotions are usually stronger and more perceptible to us.

I have to admit that language is somewhat imperfect here. The meaning of words is loose and uncertain, not precisely defined by custom. In some sense, the soul's emotions are no different from the will and inclination. But yet many times the will's actions are not usually referred to as *emotions;* in everything we do, whenever we act voluntarily, we use our will, but all these actions of our will, in our everyday behavior, are not normally called emotions. Yet what we usually call emotions are not essentially different from these ordinary acts of our will except in degree. In every act of the will, the soul either likes or dislikes, it is either inclined or disinclined to what is in view; these are not essentially different from the emotions of love and hatred. When the soul is inclined toward something it doesn't actually possess, that is the same as the emotion of desire. And when the soul approves of something present, it experiences pleasure; if that pleasure is strong enough, it is the same as the feeling of joy or delight. And if the will disapproves of what is present, and if that displeasure is strong enough, it is the same as the feeling of grief or sorrow.

Because of the union between our soul and body, our will cannot be moved strongly without some effect on the body. And, on the other hand, since our body and soul are one, our physical condition affects our emotions. But yet it is not the body, but the mind only, that is the seat of the emotions. The human body is no more capable of experiencing love or hatred, joy or sorrow, fear or hope, than the body of a tree—or than the same human body is capable of thinking and understanding. The soul only has ideas, and so the soul only is pleased with its ideas. The soul only thinks, and so the soul only loves or hates, rejoices or grieves at what it thinks. Our bodies' physical responses do not truly belong to the nature of our emotions, though they always accompany them; they are only the effects or by-products of the emotions, entirely different from the emotions themselves, and in no way essential to them. A spirit with no body may be as capable of love and hatred, joy or sorrow, hope or fear, or other feelings, as one that is united to a body.

The emotions and passions are frequently spoken of as the same things, and yet in everyday speech there is some difference. The ordinary meaning of the emotions seems to be more extensive than passion; the emotions are all those mental actions that are strong and vibrant, but passion is more sudden, and its effects on the physical being are more violent; the mind is more overpowered, and self-control is diminished.

The will always either approves and likes, or it disapproves and rejects, and in the same way the emotions either carry us toward the thing we are observing, cleaving to it or seeking it—or they are adverse to it and oppose it. Love, desire, hope, joy, gratitude, complacence are the first sort of emotion, and hatred, fear, anger, grief, and such are the other sort. Sometimes the two are mixed together, as with the emotion of *pity;* we are drawn toward the person who is suffering, while we reject what he suffers. Another example is *zeal;* we admire something, while we vigorously oppose anything we see to be contrary to it.

I could mention other mixtures of emotion, but I want to move along to my second purpose, which is to point out some things that demonstrate that true faith rests largely on our affections (in other words, the deep experiences of our hearts).

Evidence that True Faith Depends a Great Deal on Our "Affections"

1. What we've already said about our affections makes this clear. Who can deny that true faith relies to a great extent on a strong and vibrant will, as well as the heart's deep feelings? The kind of faith acceptable to God does not consist in weak, dull, and lifeless wishes, raising us only a little above a state of indifference: God, in His Word, insists that if we are in earnest, we will be "fervent in spirit," and our hearts will be vigorously involved with our faith: Be "fervent in spirit, serving the Lord" (Rom. 12:11); "And now, Israel, what doth the LORD thy God require of thee, but to fear the LORD thy God, to walk in all his ways, and to love him, and to serve the LORD thy God with all thy heart and with all thy soul?" (Deut. 10:12);

and "Hear, O Israel: The LORD our God is one LORD: And thou shalt love the LORD thy God with all thine heart, and with all thy soul, and with thy all thy might" (Deut. 6:4–5). This sort of fervent, vigorous involvement of the heart in faith is the fruit of a true circumcision of the heart, a true regeneration, that has the promises of life; "And the LORD thy God will circumcise thine heart, and the heart of thy seed, to love the LORD thy God with all thine heart, and with all thy soul, that thou mayest live" (Deut. 30:6).

If we are not serious about our faith, our wills and desires not determined, we are nothing. Our hearts must be invested in our religion if nowhere else, and if they're not, our religion will be a lukewarm, repugnant thing. True faith is always powerful, and its power is first demonstrated within the heart, the site of its source. That is why true religion is called the *power of godliness,* to distinguish it from religion's external appearances of it, that which is merely the *form* of it: "Having a form of godliness, but denying the power thereof" (2 Tim. 3:5). The Spirit of God, in those who have a solid, healthy faith, is a spirit of powerful holy emotions; therefore God is said to have given the Spirit "of power, and of love, and of a sound mind" (2 Tim. 1:7). When these people receive the Spirit of God with His sanctifying and saving influences, they are said to be "baptized with the Holy Ghost, and with fire," because the Spirit of God inspires their hearts, so that they may be said to "burn within" them, as was said of the disciples (Luke 24:32).

The business of religion is sometimes compared to

physical exercises such as running, wrestling, agonizing for a great prize or crown, fighting against strong enemies that threaten our lives, or warring as those who use violence to take a city or kingdom. True grace has various degrees, and some people are only babies in Christ, their inclination toward divine and heavenly things comparatively weak; yet all of us who have the power of godliness in our hearts have our wills and emotions pulled toward God and divine things with such strength and vigor that these holy desires prevail over all natural, earthly affections. "If any man come to me, and hate not his father, and mother, and wife, and children, and brethren, and sisters, yea, and his own life also, he cannot be my disciple" (Luke 14:26).

2. The Creator of human nature not only gave us emotions, but He made them the source of our actions. Just as our emotions are not only a part of our human nature but are a very large part of it, so holy emotions not only belong to true faith but are a very large part of it (for through God's gift of life we are renewed in our whole person, and made whole throughout).

    We would do very little if we were not influenced by some affection, whether love or hatred, desire, hope, fear, or something else. These emotions we see to be the springs that get us going in all the affairs of life; these are what move us forward and carry us along in all our worldly business. The human world is busy and active, and our emotions are the springs of all this motion. Take away all our love and hatred, all our hope and fear, all our anger, zeal, and desire, and the world would become motionless and dead. Emotions motivate the greedy person, emotions inspire the ambitious person's pursuit of worldly glory, and emotions motivate the sensual person's pursuit of pleasure and delight. From age to age, the world continues in continual commotion, pursuing these things—but take away all emotions, and the spring of all this motion would be gone; the motion itself would cease. And just as with worldly things, worldly desires are very much the spring of human motion and action, so in religious matters, the spring of action is very much religious emotion. The person who has doctrinal knowledge and intellectual speculation only, without the heart being engaged, is never truly involved with the business of religion.

3. Obviously, the things of religion take hold of our souls only so much as they affect our hearts. Many people hear the Word of God, but what they hear has no effect on them and neither their natures nor their behavior is changed, because they are not emotionally affected by what they hear. They hear of God's infinite goodness and mercy; they hear of the great works of God's wisdom, power, and goodness; they especially hear of the unspeakable love of God and Christ, and of the great things that Christ has done and suffered; they also hear the commands of God, His gracious counsel and warnings, and the gospel's sweet invitations. They hear all these things, and yet they remain as they were before, with no change in their

feelings, because they are not emotionally affected by what they hear. Until they are affected, they will never be changed.

I assert that no one was ever changed by any religious material she read, heard, or saw, if her emotions were not moved. No one ever wanted to fly for refuge to Christ, while his heart remained unaffected. Nor was there ever a saint awakened out of a cold, lifeless state of declining faith and brought back to God, without having her heart being affected. In short, nothing of any religious substance can take place either in the heart or life of any person if his heart is not deeply affected.

4. The Bible always mixes together faith and emotions, such as fear, hope, love, hatred, desire, joy, sorrow, gratitude, compassion, and zeal.

The Scriptures emphasize that godly fear is important to the spiritual life. It tells us that those who are truly spiritual people tremble at God's Word, their flesh trembles for fear of Him, and that His excellency makes them afraid.

Hope in the Lord is also frequently mentioned when the Bible describes the character of the saints: "Happy is he that hath the God of Jacob for his help, whose hope is in the LORD his God" (Ps. 146:5); "Blessed is the man that trusteth in the LORD, and whose hope the LORD is" (Jer. 17:7); "Be of good courage, and he shall strengthen your heart, all ye that hope in the LORD" (Ps. 31:24). Spiritual fear and hope are often joined together: "Behold, the eye of the LORD is upon them that fear him, upon them that hope in his mercy" (Ps. 33:18); "The LORD taketh pleasure in them that fear him, in those that hope in his mercy" (Ps. 147:11). Hope is so important to true religion, that the apostle says, "We are saved by hope" (Rom. 8:24).

Scripture stresses that love is essential to real spirituality—love for God and the Lord Jesus Christ, love for the people of God, and love for all humanity. Both the Old Testament and the New have innumerable verses that speak of love.

The opposite emotion, *hatred*, is also spoken of in Scripture; when sin is hatred's object, then hatred too is important to true spirituality: "The fear of the LORD is to hate evil" (Prov. 8:13); "Ye that love the LORD, hate evil" (Ps. 97:10); "I will walk within my house with a perfect heart. I will set no wicked thing before mine eyes: I hate the work of them that turn aside" (Ps. 101:2–3); "Do not I hate them, O LORD, that hate thee?" (Ps. 139:21).

Holy desire—longing, hungering, and thirsting after God and holiness—is often mentioned in Scripture as important to true spirituality: "The desire of our soul is to thy name, and to the remembrance of thee" (Isa. 26:8); "One thing have I desired of the LORD, that will I seek after; that I may dwell in the house of the LORD all the days of my life, to behold the beauty of the LORD, and to enquire in his temple" (Ps. 27:4); "As the hart panteth after the water brooks, so panteth my soul after thee, O God. My soul thirsteth for God, for the living God: when shall

I come and appear before God?" (Ps. 42:1–2); "My soul thirsteth for thee, my flesh longeth for thee in a dry and thirsty land, where no water is; to see thy power and thy glory, so as I have seen thee in the sanctuary" (Ps. 63:1–2); "How amiable are thy tabernacles, O LORD of hosts! My soul longeth, yea, even fainteth for the courts of the LORD: my heart and my flesh crieth out for the living God" (Ps. 84:1–2). Christ also mentions this holy desire and soul thirst in His sermon on the mount: "Blessed are they which do hunger and thirst after righteousness: for they shall be filled" (Matt. 5:6). Our thirsty souls will lead us to the blessings of eternal life: "I will give unto him that is athirst of the fountain of the water of life freely" (Rev. 21:6).

Scripture speaks also of holy joy: "Delight thyself also in the LORD; and he shall give thee the desires of thine heart" (Ps. 37:4); "Rejoice, and be exceeding glad" (Matt. 5:12); "I have rejoiced in the way of thy testimonies, as much as in all riches" (Ps. 119:14).

Spiritual sorrow, mourning, and brokenness of heart are also part of real religion. The Bible tells us: "Blessed are they that mourn: for they shall be comforted" (Matt. 5:4); "The LORD is nigh unto them that are of a broken heart; and saveth such as be of a contrite spirit" (Ps. 34:18); "The LORD hath anointed me. . .to bind up the brokenhearted, . . .to comfort all that mourn" (Isa. 61:1–2).

Another deep feeling that the Bible tells us we will experience if we are truly spiritual is *gratitude,* especially thankfulness and praise to God. This is so obvious in the Book of Psalms, as well as other parts of Scripture, that I don't need to mention particular verses.

Scripture also frequently speaks of compassion or mercy; this deep heart experience is essential to a true walk with God. The Bible tells us that a merciful person and a good person are equivalent terms: "The righteous perisheth, and no man layeth it to heart: and merciful men are taken away" (Isa. 57:1); "the righteous sheweth mercy, and giveth" (Ps. 37:21); "He that honoureth [the Lord] hath mercy on the poor" (Prov. 14:31). Christ Himself was fond of quoting Hosea 6:6: "For I desired mercy, and not sacrifice" (see Matt. 9:13; 12:7).

Zeal is yet another deep emotion that is essential to real faith. It is one of the results for which Christ hoped when He gave Himself for us: "Who gave himself for us, that he might redeem us from all iniquity, and purify unto himself a peculiar people, zealous of good works" (Titus 2:14). Zeal is what the lukewarm Laodiceans lacked (Rev. 3:15–16, 19).

These are only a few verses, out of a multitude, that show us that deep-seated feelings are essential to true spirituality. Those people who are uncomfortable accepting that emotions have anything to do with our faith need to realize that if they can't accept a spirituality of the heart, they might as well throw away the Bible. They'll have to use some other standard to judge the nature of religion.

5. The Bible stresses that true religion can be summarized by the word *love*. Love is our primary

"affection," the fountain of all our other heart experiences. Our Savior made this clear when He answered the lawyer who asked Him which was the great commandment of the law: "Jesus said unto him, 'Thou shalt love the Lord thy God with all thy heart, and with all thy soul, and with all thy mind. This is the first and great commandment. And the second is like unto it, Thou shalt love thy neighbor as thyself. On these two commandments hang all the law and the prophets' " (Matt. 22:37–40). These two commandments summarize all the religion taught in the law and the prophets. The apostle Paul says the same thing: "He that loveth another hath fulfilled the law" (Rom. 13:8); "Love is the fulfilling of the law" (Rom. 13:10); "Now the end of the commandment is charity out of a pure heart" (1 Tim. 1:5). Paul also speaks of love as the greatest thing in religion; it is the vital essence, the soul of real spirituality, and without it all knowledge and other gifts are empty and worthless. It is the fountain from which all good things flow (1 Cor. 13).

The word that is translated *charity* in the original means *love*. Now, certainly this sort of love includes the sort of generic kindness and warmth we feel toward God and humanity, and yet clearly the Bible means much more than this. When our souls lean toward God with such strength that we feel it all through our hearts, then this affection becomes affectionate love. Christ speaks of a deep and powerful love as being the sum of all religion, when He speaks of loving God with all our hearts, with all our souls, and with all our minds, and our neighbor as ourselves.

We cannot assume then that this love, what the Bible refers to as the sum of all religion, is merely the act. Behaviors alone are not enough if they are not supported by both the habits of our hearts and our understanding. On the other hand, the Bible makes clear that the essence of all true religion consists of a whole and complete love. We must not only experience divine emotions, but we must open our hearts to them and to the Light from which they spring, until our hearts form habits that will express themselves in action. This is the whole of religion.

6. The faith of the most prominent saints in the Bible included their emotions (holy affections). I'm going to look particularly at three important saints who expressed the sentiments of their own hearts, as well as the way they related to God, in the writings they left us that are now a part of the Bible.

First of all, David, that "man after God's own heart," gives us a clear image of his faith in the Book of Psalms. Those holy songs of his are nothing else but the expression of his deep feelings, such as humble and fervent love for God; admiration of His glorious perfection and wonderful works; earnest longing for God; delight and joy in God; a sweet and melting gratitude to God for His great goodness; his grief for his own and others' sins; and his fervent zeal. These expressions of holy emotion are not only important to our discussion because David is such a valiant biblical hero; the psalms were also inspired by the Holy

Spirit, written for the use of the church of God in its public worship, not only in that age but in all ages to come. These psalms express the faith of all saints, in all ages, as well as the faith of the individual psalmist. Besides this, David, in the Book of Psalms, speaks not as a private person but as the Psalmist of Israel, the subordinate head of the church of God, their leader in their worship and praises; in many of the psalms he speaks in the name of Christ, taking on His voice in these expressions of holy emotion.

Another saint I want to talk about is the apostle Paul, who was, in many respects, Christ's chosen vessel for carrying His name to the Gentiles and establishing the Christian church in the world. From what we can gather from Scripture, he appears to have been a person that was full of deep feelings. When we read his epistles, we can clearly see how essential a holy heart was to the faith he described. Apparently, he burned with love for God; this love made him wholly real, even as it consumed him. He considered everything in his life to be as worthless as manure compared to the total completion of knowing Christ. His epistles are also full of expressions of affection for the people of Christ. He speaks of his dear love for them (2. Cor. 12:19; Phil. 4:1; 2 Tim. 1:2) and of his anguished concern for others: "For out of much affliction and anguish of heart I wrote unto you with many tears; not that ye should be grieved, but that ye might know the love which I have more abundantly unto you" (2 Cor. 2:4). He often speaks of his "affectionate and longing desires" (see 1 Thess. 2:8; Rom.

1:11; Phil. 1:8; 4:1; 2 Tim. 1:4) and also the feeling of *joy* (2 Cor. 1:12; 7:7, 9, 16; Phil. 1:4; 2:17; 3:3; Col. 1:24; 1 Thess. 3:9). He expresses the affection of *hope* (Phil. 1:20); he likewise expresses *godly jealousy* (2 Cor. 11:2–3). We see clearly how emotional his faith was when he speaks of being so full of tears (2 Cor. 2:4; Acts 20:19, 31).

Now if you can read these scriptural accounts of this great apostle and yet not see how much Paul's religion consisted of emotions, you must be able to shut your eyes against the light that's shining full in your face.

The other example I'll mention is the apostle John, the beloved disciple, who was the nearest and dearest to his Master of any of the twelve. His writings clearly show that he was a person remarkably full of affection. He addressed his readers with tender and fervent love, as though he were made up totally of sweet and holy feeling. To prove this point scripturally, we would have to transcribe his whole writings.

7. Jesus Himself, the perfect example of the truly spiritual life, expressed His goodness through healthy emotions. His holy love was stronger than death, so strong that it overcame His fear and grief before His death. We read of His great zeal, fulfilling the sixty-ninth Psalm: "The zeal of thine house hath eaten me up" (John 2:17). We read of His grief for the sins of men: "He. . .looked round about on them with anger, being grieved for the hardness of their hearts" (Mark 3:5). He even broke down in tears at the sight

of the city of Jerusalem: "When he was come near, he beheld the city, and wept over it, saying, 'If thou hadst known, even thou, at least in this thy day, the things which belong unto thy peace! but now they are hid from thine eyes' " (Luke 19:41–42). In Luke 13:34, He said, "O Jerusalem, Jerusalem, which killest the prophets, and stonest them that are sent unto thee; how often would I have gathered thy children together, as a hen doth gather her brood under her wings, and ye would not!" We often read of His being "moved with compassion" (Matt. 9:36; 14:14; Mark 6:34). When Mary and Martha were mourning their brother, their tears soon drew tears from His eyes; He was affected by their grief, and cried with them, even though He knew their sorrow would soon be turned into joy when He raised their brother from the dead (see John 11). When He said good-bye to His eleven disciples the evening before He was crucified (the 13th, 14th, 15th, and 16th chapters of John) and concluded with that affectionate intercessory prayer for them and His whole church (chap. 17), His words were more deeply loving than anything else that was ever penned or spoken by any human being.

8. In heaven our spirits will still experience deep feelings. According to Scripture, our heavenly religion will be one of holy love and joy. It would be silly to think that just because we no longer have earthly bodies in heaven, we will no longer have emotions. I'm not talking here about physiological reactions but

about the deep feelings of the soul, mostly *love,* and *joy*. Of course we have not yet experienced these feelings without a body to experience them, too, but our love and joy on earth is the dawn of heaven's light and blessedness. They are the same in nature, though their circumstances are different. This is clear in many Scripture verses (Prov. 4:18; John 4:14; 6:40, 47, 50–51, 54, 58; 1 John 3:15; 1 Cor. 13:8–12). However the saints in heaven perceive their feelings, we know that their love and joy makes them burn like flame. We can say that these types of love and joy are not emotions, but then we are making emotions into a useless word. How could we look at the glory of our Redeemer and not feel something?

Therefore, heaven's spiritual life is emotional—and therefore, undoubtedly, true faith is emotional also. The way to learn the true nature of anything is to go where that thing is found in its purity and perfection. If we want to know the nature of true gold, we must study it, not in the ore, but when it is refined. If we want to learn about real religion, we must go where the life of the spirit is most real, where there is nothing else besides this life, where nothing detracts from it or obscures it. All who are truly spiritual are not of this world. They are strangers here and belong in heaven; heaven is their native country, and the nature they receive from this heavenly birth is a heavenly nature. Their grace is the dawn of glory, and God fits them for heaven by shaping them so they will fit.

9. We can see that our emotions are important to our

faith because our God-ordained responsibilities affect us emotionally.

For instance, prayer; obviously, prayer's purpose is not to inform God of His own majesty, holiness, goodness, and all-sufficiency. God also knows our own emptiness, dependence, and unworthiness, as well as our wants and desires. Instead, prayers affect our own hearts, preparing us to receive the blessings we ask. Our gestures and external behavior during worship, our expressions of humility and reverence, are valuable only because they affect our own hearts or the hearts of others.

The same is true of singing praises to God. Why should we express ourselves to God in verse rather than in prose, and do it with music? Because song and verse tend to move us emotionally.

The same is true of the sacraments God has given us. God understood our makeup, and He made sure that the gospel did not only come to us intellectually, through His Word; He also showed us the gospel through our five senses in the sacrament, so that we might be more deeply moved by them.

God wants to impress His truth on human hearts through the preaching of His Word. God's aim will not be accomplished if we merely read commentaries and expositions on Scripture; these books may give us a doctrinal or intellectual understanding of the Word of God, but they will not make as great an impression on our hearts and emotions. The Bible says that the preaching of God's Word will bring our emotions to life, especially love and joy: "[Christ] gave some, apostles; and some, prophets; and some, evangelists; and some, pastor and teachers; . . .for the edifying of the body of Christ. . .in love" (Eph. 4:11, 12, 16). Ministers are called "helpers of [their] joy" (2 Cor. 1:24).

10. True spirituality, or heart-wholeness, relies upon the heart's deep feelings; on the other hand, Scripture connects sin with hardness of heart: "After thy hardness and impenitent heart treasurest up unto thyself wrath against the day of wrath and relevation of the righteous judgment of God" (Rom. 2:5). The reason given why the house of Israel would not obey God was that they were hardhearted: "But the house of Israel will not harken unto thee; for they will not hearken unto me: for all the house of Israel are impudent and hardhearted" (Ezek. 3:7). "To day if ye will hear his voice, harden not your heart" (Ps. 95:7–8); "But when divers were hardened, and believed not, but spake evil of that way before the multitude" (Acts 19:9). Hebrews seems to speak of "an evil heart. . . [that departs] from the living God" and a "hard heart" as the same thing (see 3:8, 12). When God delivers a person from the power of sin, the Bible speaks of God's taking away the heart of stone, and giving a heart of flesh (Ezek. 11:19, 36:26).

A hard heart clearly means one that is not moved by emotions. Instead, it is like a stone, insensible, dull, unmoved. A hard-hearted person is not easily impressed. It is called a *stony heart,* opposed to a heart of flesh that has feeling, that can be touched and moved.

The Bible makes clear that a hard heart is empty of healthy emotion. Speaking of the ostrich who lacks natural affection for her young, Job says, "She is hardened against her young ones, as though they were not hers" (39:16). In the same way a person having a heart unaffected in time of danger is described as hardening his heart: "Happy is the man that feareth alway: but he that hardeneth his heart shall fall into mischief" (Prov. 28:14).

Clearly, the Bible connects the heart's sin and corruption with a lack of healthy emotions. I'm not saying, though, that all emotions are healthy. Obviously, a person could be hard-hearted and still be full of hatred, anger, and other selfish emotions. Still, when the Bible speaks of a "hard heart" or a "tender heart," it is indicating that we must be open emotionally if we are to receive God's goodness.

I don't mean, however, that the more emotional you are, the more spiritual you'll be. Even true saints experience emotions that are not spiritual; their emotions are often mixed, some from grace, much from nature. I don't believe our emotions depend on our bodies; nevertheless, our physical constitutions can't help but affect our emotional states. The degree of our spirituality should be judged more by the strength of our emotional habit, rather than by the temporary emotions that come and go moment by moment. The strength of the heart's habit is not always in proportion to our outward behavior; mentally, our busy thoughts may not express our true hearts either. And yet no one can be truly spiritual without healthy emotional habits. Intellectual understanding is a waste of time if it does not produce holy affection in the heart: no habit or principle of the heart is good if it does not grow from these deep spiritual experiences.

I want to move on now to some inferences.

1. People who discard all religious emotions are in error.

Some people who were emotional about their faith have proved to lack a genuine commitment to God—but that does not mean that their emotions were the source of all their error. To make that assumption is to run from one extreme to another. A little while ago we were at one extreme: All religious emotion was considered to be evidence of true grace; no one asked the nature and source of those emotions. If people spoke with great emotion about the things of God, others assumed they were deeply spiritual, filled with the Spirit of God. This was the extreme that was prevailing three or four years ago. Lately, though, instead of admiring all religious feeling without distinction, we are much more apt to reject and discard all feeling without distinction. We see here how clever Satan is. First, knowing how inexperienced most people are when it comes to intense spiritual emotions, he sowed tares among the wheat, and mingled false feelings with the works of God's Spirit; he knew that this would delude many people, hurting religion's reputation as well. But now, as the results of these false affections begin to be seen, the devil works from another direction, convincing people that all religious feeling should be avoided. This way he hopes to bring all religion to a mere lifeless formality, shutting out the power of godliness. If he were to succeed, all true Christianity would be thrown out of our hearts. True spirituality must be something more than pure emotion—and yet we cannot be truly spiritual if our hearts are untouched. The person who has no religious feeling is in a state of spiritual death; she lacks the powerful, life-giving influence of the Spirit of God upon her heart. Just as there is no true religion where there is nothing but emotion, so there is no true religion where there is no religious emotion at all. On the one hand, we must have intellectual light as well as a burning heart, for where there is heat without light, there can be nothing divine or heavenly; on the other hand, where there is a kind light without any heat, a head full of ideas and theories and a cold and unaffected heart, there can be nothing divine in that light. The only reason why people are not emotionally affected by the glorious and wonderful things they hear from the Word of God is undoubtedly because they are blind; otherwise, their hearts would be impressed, greatly moved by these things.

When we are prejudiced against all religious emotions, we allow our hearts to be hardened, and we stunt the life and power of religion, condemning ourselves to dullness and apathy.

There are false emotions and there are true. Because a person is very emotional does not prove that he has any true religion—but if he has no emotion, it proves he has no true religion. The right way is not to reject all feeling, nor to approve all, but to distinguish between emotions, approving some and rejecting others, separating the wheat from the chaff, the gold from the dross, the precious from the worthless.

2. *If true spirituality lies in the heart, then we can infer that we should look for those things that tend to move our hearts—books, ways of preaching the Word, ways of worshipping God in prayer and singing praises.*

Things that appeal to us emotionally are usually popular with most people. We may have become too dependent on being stimulated emotionally—but now we have gone too far in the other direction. We don't want to be merely emotionally excited, without any real transformation of our souls—but neither do we want our faith to be merely a dry, intellectual exercise.

3. *We need to understand why our hearts are not more affected by spiritual matters.*

God has given to humanity emotions for the same reason He gave us all our other faculties: that they might serve our chief end, the great business for which God has created us, that is, the business of growing spiritually in relationship to God. And yet usually our emotions are more engaged in other matters than religion! Our external delights, our ambition and reputation, and our human relationships— for all of these things our desires are eager, our appetites strong, our love warm and affectionate, our zeal ardent. Our hearts are tender and sensitive when it comes to these things, easily moved, deeply impressed, much concerned, and greatly engaged. We are depressed at our losses and excited and joyful about our worldly successes and prosperity. But when it comes to spiritual matters, how dull we feel! How heavy and hard our hearts! We can sit and hear of the infinite height, and depth, and length, and breadth of the love of God in Christ Jesus, of His giving His infinitely dear Son—and yet be cold and unmoved! But these spiritual matters are essential to our eternal being—so why should our emotions be divorced from them? Why would God create our emotions for earthly concerns, and expect them to be dormant when it comes to spiritual matters?

If we are going to be emotional about anything, shouldn't it be our spiritual lives? Is anything more inspiring, more exciting, more lovable and desirable in heaven or earth than the gospel of Jesus Christ? Not only is it worthy of our emotion, but it is shown to us in a way that should affect us emotionally. In the same way, the glory and beauty of Jehovah is worthy in itself to be the object of our admiration and love, but it is demonstrated to us in a way that should shake our hearts, for it shines with the luster of an incarnate, infinitely loving, gentle, compassionate, dying Redeemer. All the virtues of the Lamb of God, His humility, patience, gentleness, submission, obedience, love, and compassion, are exhibited in the gospel so that our emotions should be deeply moved. Christ should move us more deeply than any other thing, for He is the source of our hearts' life, and our hearts' feelings were designed to perceive Him. How can we not be moved when we consider His last sufferings, the unutterable and unparalleled suffering He endured because of His tenderness and love for us?

We must also be moved by the hateful nature of our sins when we see the dreadful effects of them on our Redeemer, who undertook to answer for us and suffered on our behalf.

The gospel story is designed to affect us emotionally—and our emotions are designed to be affected by its beauty and glory. It touches our hearts at their tenderest parts, shaking us deeply to the core. We should be utterly humbled that we are not more emotionally affected than we are.

PART II

HOW TO TELL
WHETHER OR NOT
RELIGIOUS AFFECTIONS COME
FROM GOD'S GRACE

If you read these words and say to yourself, "I am one of those people whose heart is involved with their faith. When I think about my faith, my emotions are often greatly moved," then be glad that you do have an emotional response to your faith. As I said before, we ought not to reject and condemn all emotions, as though true faith had nothing to do with our hearts. On the other hand, however, we ought not to give a blanket approval to all emotional responses to religion, nor assume that being emotional about one's faith is evidence of true grace and the saving influences of God's Spirit. Instead, we must distinguish between religious reactions, between one sort and another.

To do so, I have two objects:

1. I want to mention some things that tell us nothing one way or the other, so that we may be on our guard against judging emotions falsely.
2. I want to point out the ways that spiritual emotions, ones that are full of God's grace, are different from those that are not so, and how we can tell the difference.

First, I will talk about some things that tell us nothing about whether our emotions are full of grace or not.

I. It doesn't mean anything one way or the other if religious emotions are very intense.

Some people are ready to condemn all intense responses to religion; if people appear to have their religious emotions raised to an extraordinary pitch, then others are prejudiced against them, assuming without further inquiry that they are delusional. But as we have already said, true faith does depend on a faith of the heart, and it follows then that if we have an intense faith, we will also have intense feelings about our faith; if faith rises high in our hearts, then divine and holy emotions will also rise high there.

Love is an emotion, but will any Christian say that people ought not to intensely love God and Jesus Christ? Or will anyone say we ought not to have an intense hatred for sin, or a deep sorrow for it? Or would someone say that we ought not to feel a deep gratitude to God for the mercies He has given us and the great things He has done for our salvation? Or will anyone say that we should not have intense desires for God and holiness? Can any of us really say that we have very little emotional response to our faith and yet say, "I have no reason to be ashamed that I'm not more affected by spiritual things; I'm not the least bit sorry that I don't feel more love for God, more sorrow for sin, more gratitude for the mercies I have received"? Who of us will thank God for His wonderful love—and then pray that we won't be emotionally affected by it to any degree, because intense emotions are improper and unbecoming to a Christians, since enthusiasm ruins true faith?

No, the Bible plainly speaks of deep and intense emotions when it speaks of "rejoicing with joy unspeakable, and full of glory" (see 1 Pet. 1:8): The most superlative expressions for emotions are used here. And Scripture often commands us to put our whole hearts into our faith, as in the first and great commandment of the law, where there is an accumulation of emotional expressions, as though words needed to be piled upon words to express the intensity with which we ought to love God: "Thou shalt love the Lord thy God with all thy heart, and with all thy soul, and with all thy mind, and with all thy strength" (Mark 12:30). In the same way, we are called on to feel deep joy: "Rejoice," says Christ to His disciples, "and be exceeding glad" (Matt. 5:12). And in Psalm 68:3, "Let the righteous be glad; let them rejoice before God: yea, let them exceedingly rejoice." In the same Book of Psalms, the author often calls us to shout with joy; and in Luke 6:23, the text speaks of leaping for joy. The same is true when the Bible speaks of the deep gratitude we should feel for God's mercies; we are to praise God with all our hearts, with hearts lifted up in the ways of the Lord, with our souls magnifying the Lord, singing His praises, talking of His wondrous works, declaring His doings, and so on. When we turn to the Scripture, we also find that the heroes of the faith often confess their deep emotions.

The psalmist speaks of his love, "O how love I thy law!" (Ps. 119:97), and he expresses his intense hatred of sin, "Do not I hate them, O LORD, that hate thee? and am not I grieved with those that rise up against thee? I hate them with perfect hatred" (Ps. 139:21–22). He also describes the depth of his sorrow for sin; his sins "go over his head" like a heavy burden too heavy for him, and he "roars all the day," until his moisture is "turned into the drought of summer," and his "bones are broken with sorrow." He uses the strongest expressions he can think of to describe his emotional state, such as his "soul's thirsting as a dry and thirsty land where no water is," his "flesh and heart crying out," his "soul's breaking for the longing it hath," and so on. Furthermore, he speaks of his profound grief for the sins of others: "Rivers of water run down mine eyes, because they keep not thy law" (Ps. 119:136), and then again in verse 53, "Horror hath taken hold upon me because of the wicked that forsake thy law." He describes the heights of joy, also: "The king shall joy in thy strength, O LORD; and in thy salvation how greatly shall he rejoice" (Ps. 21:1); "Because thy loving kindness is better than life, my lips shall praise thee. Thus will I bless thee while I live: I will lift up my hands in thy name. My soul shall be satisfied as with marrow and fatness; and my mouth shall praise thee with joyful lips: When I remember thee upon my bed, and meditate on thee in the night watches. Because thou hast been my help, therefore in the shadow of thy wings will I rejoice" (Ps. 63:3–7).

The apostle Paul also expresses deep emotions. He describes his feelings of pity and concern for others' good, going so far as to call these feelings "anguish of heart," "great, fervent, and abundant love," and "exceeding joy." He speaks of his soul's joys and triumphs, as well as his tears and sorrows. In the same way, John the Baptist expressed great joy in John 3:29, and the women who anointed the body of

Jesus reacted to the resurrection "with fear and great joy" (Matt. 28:8).

The Bible foretells the joys that await the church: "They shall walk, O LORD, in the light of thy countenance. In thy name shall they rejoice all the day: and in thy righteousness shall they be exalted" (Ps. 89:15–16); "Rejoice greatly, O daughter of Zion; shout, O daughter of Jerusalem: behold, thy King cometh" (Zech. 9:9). We read the same prophecy in many other places in the Bible. Overwhelming joy is obviously the genuine fruit of the good news of Christ; that is why the angel calls this gospel, "good tidings of great joy, which shall be to all people" (Luke 2:10).

The saints and angels in heaven, who possess the life of the spirit in its most complete form, are not detached and unemotional when they contemplate God and His perfect works. No, their love is like a pure heavenly flame, and so great is their joy and gratitude, that the Bible speaks of their praise "as the voice of many waters, and as the voice of a great thunder" (Revelations 14:2). The only reason why their response is so much deeper than ours on earth is that they see things the way they truly are, with no barriers to their vision; their emotions, also, are not out of kilter, as ours so often are, but are aligned with the true nature of reality. Therefore, the deeper our faith goes within our hearts, the closer we will be to the angels and saints in heaven, and the closer we will be to reality's truth.

Obviously, then, we should not condemn people for having an emotional response to their faith, or assume that their faith is not real. We are wrong to condemn people for being too enthusiastic, dismissing their faith as mere hysterical emotion, simply because their emotions run high.

On the other hand, though, simply because our faith is emotional does not prove it is deeply spiritual and full of grace. The Bible, our infallible guide for judging things of this nature, makes clear that some intense religious emotions may be neither spiritual nor healthy. The apostle Paul speaks of the Galations' emotions as being extremely elevated, and yet he obviously fears that these emotions were empty and nonproductive: "Where is then the blessedness ye spake of? for I bear you record, that, if it had been possible, ye would have plucked out your own eyes, and have given them to me" (Gal. 4:15), and in the eleventh verse, he tells them, he was afraid that he had worked among them "in vain." In the same way, the children of Israel were deeply moved by God's mercy to them at the Red Sea, but they soon forgot all He had done. And again they were profoundly stirred at Mount Sinai when they saw God's amazing manifestations there, and they vowed with great feeling, "All that the LORD hath said will we do, and be obedient" (Exod. 24:7)—but how soon they forgot these feelings. They quickly turned away from God toward other gods, rejoicing and shouting around their golden calf! Think about the crowd on Palm Sunday who were so excited about Christ's entry into Jerusalem. They cut branches off palm trees and threw them in His way; they even pulled off their clothes and spread those before Him, crying out, "Hosanna to the son of David: Blessed is he that cometh in the name of the Lord; Hosanna in the highest." The Pharisees said to themselves, "Behold, the world is gone after him" (John 12:19), but in reality Christ had only a few true disciples at that time. The crowd's emotions came to an abrupt end! None of their joy and adoration remained when Jesus stood bound, with a mock robe and a crown of thorns. Instead, now the crowd made fun of Him, spit on Him, scourged, condemned, and executed Him. Oh, their emotional response to Jesus was still noisy and powerful, but now, instead of crying, "Hosanna, hosanna!" they yelled, "Crucify, crucify!"

Most theological scholars would agree that a religion may raise a strong emotional response without being true faith in Jesus Christ.

II. Just because we have a physical reaction to our emotions, does not mean that our emotions indicate the nature of our faith.

All emotions have some effect on our bodies. As I observed before, that is our nature. Our souls and bodies are united, and our hearts cannot be greatly moved without our bodies being affected. In fact, I would be surprised if any embodied soul is capable of feeling anything without the body being in some way changed also. And since all emotions have some effect on the body, we can safely assume that the stronger the emotion, the greater will be our physical reaction to that emotion. But the physical reaction tells us nothing as to whether our emotions are truly spiritual or not.

Intense physical reactions prove nothing about how spiritual we are, for we know that we experience the same reactions from strong emotions about temporal things, things that have nothing to do with religion.

The psalmist, speaking of his intense spiritual feelings,

makes clear that he is affected in both his flesh (or body) as well as in his soul. He distinguishes the one from the other: "My soul longeth, yea, even fainteth for the courts of the LORD: my heart and my flesh crieth out for the living God" (Ps. 84:2). Again, in Psalm 63:1 he gives us another clear distinction between the reactions of the heart and the flesh: "My soul thirsteth for thee, my flesh longeth for thee in a dry and thirsty land, where no water is." The prophet Habakkuk speaks of his body being overborne by a sense of the majesty of God: "When I heard, my belly trembled; my lips quivered at the voice: rotteness entered into my bones, and I trembled in myself" (Hab. 3:16). And the psalmist speaks of his flesh trembling (Ps. 119:120).

The Bible makes clear to us that the manifestation of God's glory that is sometimes given in this world has a tendency to overwhelm the body. We have examples in the prophet Daniel and the apostle John. When Daniel gives an account of an external representation of God's glory, he says, "And there remained no strength in me: for my comeliness was turned in me into corruption, and I retained no strength" (Dan. 10:8). And the apostle John, relating a similar manifestation, says, "And when I saw him, I fell at his feet as dead" (Rev. 1:17).

To protest that these were only external manifestations or symbols of the glory of Christ would be a waste of time. True, these were outward representations of Christ's glory, which the saints beheld with their physical eyes; but the reason for these external symbols or representations was to give these prophets an idea of the thing represented: the actual divine majesty of Christ, His spiritual glory. God used these outward signs to convey to His saints an intense and living understanding of the real glory and majesty of God's nature, and thus these signs or symbols had a great effect upon them; their souls were swallowed up, and their bodies were overwhelmed.

Before I move on from this point, I want to observe that clearly Scripture often makes use of physical responses to spiritual events, such as trembling, groaning, being sick, crying out, panting, and fainting. Now some may say that these are only figurative expressions, used to represent the intensity of the emotion. If that is so, I still cannot believe that God would use these reactions to describe spiritual feelings if such reactions were only produced by false emotions, delusions of the devil. I cannot believe God would make use of things that are totally alien to spiritual feelings as beautiful images to convey the intensity of healthy, spiritual emotions, if these things were actually the fingerprints of Satan, reeking of the bottomless pit.

III. Because our emotional reactions make us talk about spiritual matters with great fluency and eagerness, is no proof that our emotions are truly spiritual or not.

Many people are prejudiced against others who talk a lot about their faith. They feel that if people are so full of talk, then that is sufficient ground to condemn them as Pharisees and ostentatious hypocrites. On the other hand, others assume that if someone loves to talk about spiritual concerns, then they must be the true children of God, under the saving influences of His Spirit. They say, "Such and such person can talk so freely now, when he used to be slow to speak; he is able now to open his heart and tell his experiences, declaring the praises of God." They assume that this person is truly spiritual, particularly if he not only talks a lot, but talks lovingly and earnestly of spiritual matters.

This sort of judgment, however, is not based on Scripture. The Bible gives us many guidelines for judging both our own faith and others', but nowhere does it say our judgment should be based on words alone. This is merely a religion of the mouth and of the tongue; words are like the leaves of a tree, which a healthy tree ought to have, but yet provide us no evidence as to the goodness of the tree.

People may want to talk about spiritual matters for good reasons and for bad reasons. On the one hand, their hearts may be full of holy emotions, "for out of the abundance of the heart the mouth speaketh" (Matt. 12:34). Whatever emotions we have, if they are very strong and deeply felt, we will love to talk about the thing that inspires these feelings, and not only will we speak a great deal, we will also tend to speak with great passion on this subject. Therefore people who talk passionately and fluently about the things of religion only prove that they have experienced an intense emotional reaction to those things—but as we have already shown, this proves nothing about the presence of grace. When people are excited about something, so long as that excitement lasts, they will talk about it a great deal, just as the Jews in all Judea and Galilee did for awhile about John the Baptist's preaching and baptism. For awhile they rejoiced in his light, and all over the land all sorts of persons were enthusiastic about this great prophet and his ministry. In the same way the crowd often demonstrated excitement and enthusiasm, at least on an external level, for Christ and His preaching and miracles, "being astonished at His doctrine, anon with joy receiving the Word," following Him sometimes night and day, leaving meat, drink, and sleep to hear Him. Once they even followed Him into the wilderness, going without food for three days to hear Him; sometimes they cried out, "Never man spake like this man!" (John 7:46). They were fervent and earnest in what they said—but in the end what did all their words amount to?

A person may talk too much about her own experiences, bringing them up everywhere to anybody; this is an ominous sign about that person's spirituality rather than a good one. A tree that has too many leaves seldom bears much fruit, and a cloud, though it looks heavy with water, if it brings with it too much wind seldom drops much rain to the dry and thirsty earth. "Whoso boasteth himself of a false gift is like clouds and wind without rain" (Prov. 25:14). The apostle Jude speaks also of people who made a great show of their religion, and yet he said, "Clouds they are without water, carried about of winds" (Jude 12). The apostle Peter, speaking on the same subject, says, "These are. . .clouds that are carried with a tempest" (2 Pet. 2:17). False emotions are more apt to express themselves than are true emotions, for false religion loves to put on a show for others' admiration, just as the Pharisees did.

IV. If people experience emotions that they did not excite by their own efforts, that does not prove one way or another that these emotions are the result of grace.

Many people these days condemn all emotions that are excited in such a way that even the people experiencing them cannot explain. Apparently these emotions are not produced by human efforts, but by some extrinsic and supernatural influence upon their minds. Lately the concept of an inward spiritual experience has been ridiculed and condemned. Critics say that the Spirit of God can only cooperate with our own efforts in a silent, secret, and indiscernible way, so that we can perceive no line between the Spirit's influences and the natural operations of our own mental faculties.

Undoubtedly, no one should expect to receive the Spirit's saving influence if they are neglecting to diligently direct their hearts toward grace. Furthermore, we should not expect that God's Spirit will work in our lives without making use of human tools. And without a doubt, the Spirit of God operates in all sorts of ways in all sorts of circumstances; sometimes He works more secretly and gradually, from smaller beginnings, than others.

But if there really is a Power that is entirely different from and beyond our own power, above any natural power, and if this Power is necessary for the production of saving grace in the heart (as most people in this country would agree), then why is it so unreasonable to suppose that this Power could affect people so that they perceive it as being extrinsic to themselves, beyond their own efforts? It *is* outside of our own strength and experience, so why is it so strange a thing that it should seem to be what it actually is? The grace we feel in our hearts is not produced by our own strength, nor is it created by the natural powers of our own faculties, or by any other means or instruments; it is the workmanship of the Spirit of the Almighty. Obviously, then, some people's experience of this supernatural grace will *feel* supernatural. So why do we look at these people as though they were suffering from delusions? These people affirm that what they perceive seems to be from outside themselves, from the mighty power of God's Spirit—and as a result others condemn them, assuming that their experiences are not from God's Spirit, but from their own delusions or from the devil.

Scripture teaches over and over again that grace in the soul is the effect of God's power; this grace is compared to resurrection, where through no strength of its own, a being is raised from the dead, and to creation, where being is brought out of nothing. How can we explain then why the Almighty would so carefully hide His power that the subject of it should be able to discern nothing of it? Judging from the Scriptures, this is not the way God works; on the contrary, God's way in the Bible is to make His hand visible, His power conspicuous, so that humanity can clearly perceive their dependence on Him. This was true of most of the earthly rescues God performed for Israel in the Bible, and these physical rescue operations were symbolic of the spiritual salvation God would bring to His people, rescuing them from their spiritual enemies. In the redemption of Israel from Egyptian bondage, God redeemed them with a strong hand and an outstretched arm; He waited until Israel was weak and helpless so that His power might be that much more conspicuous. The same thing happened in the great redemption by Gideon; God decreased his army to a handful of men without any other arms than trumpets and lamps and earthen pitchers. Again, the same thing happened when God used a young boy to deliver Israel from Goliath. When God called the Gentiles, He changed our world not with earthly power; no, when the world was utterly helpless, He redeemed it with nothing but the mighty power of God. In the New Testament conversion stories, God does not work so silently, secretly, and gradually that He can barely be noticed (the way people nowadays insist He works); no, God changed the New Testament heroes suddenly, with obvious manifestations of supernatural power. The same sort of conversion in our day would be looked at as being delusional and hysterical.

In Ephesians 1:18–19, the apostle speaks of God enlightening the minds of Christians, bringing them to believe in Christ so that they might know the strength of His power in the lives of those who believe. "The eyes of your understanding being enlightened; that ye may know what is the hope of his calling, and what the riches of the glory of his inheritance in the saints, and what is the exceeding greatness of his power to us-ward who believe, according to the working of his mighty power." Now when the apostle speaks this way, he must mean that he wants them to know by experience. But if Christians know this power by experience, then they have to feel it and perceive it to be separate from their own natural mental reactions. If this is so, then how can God operate so secretly and unnoticeably that they notice nothing beside their own efforts? They may base their faith in God on the Scripture, but that is a different thing from knowing from experience.

Therefore, it is both unreasonable and unscriptural to say that emotions lack the grace of God's Spirit simply because the people who experience them do not produce them by their own efforts.

On the other hand, just because the person cannot account for the emotions she experiences is no proof that they come from God. Some people make this argument to support their spiritual experiences, saying, "I am sure I did not make this reaction happen on my own; it came out of the blue, when I was thinking about something completely different, and I have no idea how to reproduce this reaction again." As a result, they assume that their experience must have been caused by the Holy Spirit's mighty influence, and they are certain that their emotions will thus bring healing to their souls—but their assumptions are both groundless and ignorant. What they experienced may in fact have come from outside themselves, from the work of an invisible agent, some spirit besides their own—but it does not follow that it was from the Spirit of God. Other spirits can influence the human mind besides the Holy Spirit. The Bible tells us not to believe every spirit, but to "try the spirits whether they are of God" (1 John 4:1). Many false spirits are busy in the human world, and they often transform themselves into angels of light; in many amazing ways, with great subtlety and power, they mimic the Spirit's oper-ations. Many of Satan's works are clearly distinguishable from ordinary human thoughts—those dreadful and horrid suggestions with which he follows many people, the fruitless anxiety and terrors which he creates. The power of Satan may be as apparent in false comforts and joys, as it is in terrors and horrid suggestions. Satan can produce raptures in the human mind.

Also, some people whose bodies and brains are un-healthy and unbalanced may have strange anxieties and imaginations; they may experience strong emotions that seem to rise unaccountably within them, without them voluntarily producing these emotions themselves. These same people are liable to have such impressions about earthly matters as well as spiritual ones. They are like sleepers who experience dreams they do not create voluntarily; these people may experience the same sort of involuntary reactions when they are awake.

V. *Because our feelings come to us accompanied by Bible verses proves nothing one way or another about whether they are truly holy and spiritual.*

Some people seem to think that if a thought or emotion came to them suddenly, accompanied by a Scripture verse, then that is good evidence that their emotions are truly spiritual, especially if the emotions they feel are hope or joy, or any feeling that is pleasing and delightful. These people will mention this experience as proof that all is right with their world, because their emotional experience came to them along with something from God's Word. They will say, "Such and such verses came to my mind, containing such sweet promises. They came suddenly, as if they were spoken to me; I had no hand in bringing these verses to my mind; I was not thinking of anything leading to them. No, they came all at once, so that I was surprised. I had not thought of them for a long time before that; I did not even know at first that they were Scripture. I did not remember that I had ever read them." They may add, "One Scripture came flowing in after another, verses from all over the Bible, all of them so sweet and joyful, speaking so directly to my situation, that I was filled to the brim with joy. My tears flowed, and all my doubts disappeared." As a result, they believe they have indisputable proof that their emotions come from God, and they are sure that they are in perfect relationship with Him. In reality, though, they have no grounds for this assumption. Where did they get this rule for judging our spiritual condition? Can it be found in the Bible?

The reason for their deception seems to be that since Scripture is the Word of God, and nothing in it is false, therefore any emotional experiences that contain Scripture must be valid. But remember, Scripture can be abused. Our emotional responses should be in line with what the Bible teaches—but when Bible verses spring to our mind, out of context, the emotions we experience as a result mean very little.

Why couldn't the devil bring Scripture verses to our minds, and use them out of context to deceive people? Why should we assume that only God could bring to Scriptures to our minds? If Satan has power to bring any words at all to a person's minds, he may have power to bring to mind Bible words. Human beings need no greater strength to read the words of Scripture than they need to read an idle story or song. It must be the same with Satan's power. Or do you suppose that Scripture verses are so sacred that the devil dares not abuse them or touch them? If you think this, then you are mistaken. If Satan could grab hold of Christ Himself and carry Him here and there, from the wilderness to a high mountain and from there to a pinnacle of the temple, why should he be afraid to touch the Scripture and abuse it for his own purpose? When he tempted Christ, he offered first one Scripture and then another to deceive and tempt Him. If Satan was allowed to make Christ Himself think of certain Scripture verses in ways that were tempting and out of context, then why should we assume that Satan would not be permitted to use Bible verses to deceive and tempt human beings? If he can bring one comforting text to mind, then he can bring a thousand, choosing those Scriptures that will tend to serve his purpose best, heaping up Scripture promises to confirm the false joy and confidence of a poor deluded sinner.

We know that the devil's instruments, corrupt teachers of heresy, can and do twist the Scripture to their own and others' damnation (2 Pet. 3:16). When they do this, they are Satan's instruments and servants, operating under his influence. Doubtless he does the same work under his own powers. His servants are only following their master's techniques.

What is more, just as the devil can abuse Scripture to deceive and destroy people, so our own hearts are capable of deceiving us as well. The human heart is deceitful like the devil, and it can use the same means to tell ourselves lies.

Clearly, then, people may experience intense hope and joy when Scriptures pop into their minds, as though they were supernaturally spoken to them—and yet this is no proof that these are divine emotions. They may be nothing more than the effects of Satan's delusions.

VI. Just because our emotions appear to be full of love, is no proof one way or the other that these emotions are healthy and spiritual.

Some people argue that Satan cannot love, this emotion being totally contrary to the devil, whose nature consists of enmity and malice. And certainly nothing is more heavenly and divine than a spirit of true Christian love for God and others; love is better than knowledge or prophecy or miracles or speaking with the tongues of men and angels. It is the chief of the Spirit's graces, the life, the essence, and the sum of all true religion; through love we are made ready for heaven, and love is totally contrary to hell and the devil. Given that all this is true, however, does not prove that love has no counterfeits. In fact, the more excellent anything is, the more often do people try to reproduce counterfeit versions of it. Silver and gold have more counterfeits than do iron and copper; the world makes many false diamonds and rubies, but who would bother to counterfeit common stones? Of course the finer the quality of a substance, the more difficult it is to mimic, but human beings exert all their art and cleverness to reproduce an exact imitation of the substances' outward appearances. So it is with Christian virtues and graces; the subtlety of Satan, as well as human deceit, will strive to counterfeit those virtues that are the most precious. As a result, probably no other graces have as many counterfeits as do love and humility, since these are the virtues that most demonstrate a real Christian's true beauty.

The Scripture makes clear that a person may appear to have a deeply spiritual love, and yet have no saving grace. Christ speaks of many professing Christians who have such love, whose love will not endure, falling short of salvation; "And because iniquity shall abound, the love of many shall wax cold. But he that shall endure unto the end, the same shall be saved" (Matt. 24:12–13). These words clearly demonstrate that only those whose love endures to the end shall be saved.

Persons may seem to love God and Christ, they may even appear to have deep and intense feelings of this nature, and yet they have no grace. The apostle Paul seems to imply that many people in his day had a counterfeit love for Christ; "Grace be with all them that love our Lord Jesus Christ in sincerity" (Eph. 6:24). This last word, in the original Greek, means "incorruption," showing us that Paul knew that many people had a kind of love for Christ, and yet their love was not pure or spiritual.

In the same way, Christian love for the people of God may be counterfeited. Scripture clearly tells us that we may experience strong feelings of this kind without any saving grace, as when the Galations were ready to pluck out their eyes and give them to the apostle Paul. Paul's response to this exuberant demonstration of affection was to express his fear that their emotions amounted to nothing much at all, and that he had worked among them in vain (Gal. 4:11, 15).

VII. Because a person experiences many different kinds of religious emotions does not prove one way or the other that these feelings are produced by grace.

False religion tends to be unhealthy and absurd, lacking the wholeness and symmetry of true faith, and yet false religion may still produce all sorts of false emotions that look like true ones.

We have already mentioned that love for God and

one another can be counterfeited; we also see in the Bible accounts of other false emotions. The accounts of Pharaoh, Saul, Ahab, and the children of Israel in the wilderness show us examples of false sorrow (Exod. 9:27; 1 Sam. 24:16–17; 26:21; 1 Kings 21:27; Num. 14:39; 40). The Samaritans, who, "feared the LORD, and served their own gods" (2 Kings 17:33) at the same time show us that the fear of God is not always genuine; and in Psalm 66:3, we read of those enemies of God, who, "through the greatness of [God's] power, . . .submit themselves unto [him]," or, as it is in the original Hebrew, "lie unto him." In other words, they give God a counterfeit reverence and submission. The children of Israel, who sang God's praise at the Red Sea (Ps. 106:12), and Naaman the Syrian, after the miraculous cure of his leprosy (2 Kings 5:15), show us that gratitude may also be false. The same thing is true of spiritual joy, as in the listeners who were like stony ground (Matt. 13:20), and again as with many of the people in John the Baptist's audience (John 5:35). Zeal too can lack spiritual truth, as with Jehu (2 Kings 10:16), with Paul before his conversion (Gal. 1:14; Phil. 3:6), and with the unbelieving Jews (Acts 22:3; Rom. 10:2). People who lack God's grace may still experience intense spiritual desires, also, as Balaam did (Num. 23:9–10). Or, like the Pharisees, they may possess a strong hope for eternal life.

If, then, human beings in their natural state can demonstrate what looks like all sorts of religious feelings, there is nothing to say that they cannot experience a whole bunch of these feelings at once. In fact, this often happens. A person who has a strong emotional response to religion tends to have many different kinds of emotional responses all at the same time. We see that this is true of the multitude who followed Christ into Jerusalem, after the great miracle of raising Lazarus; apparently they were filled with admiration, a deeply emotional love, and a strong reverence, all at the same time, as they threw their clothes on the ground for Christ to walk on; they also seemed to feel great gratitude to Him for His good works, for they praised Him loudly for His salvation. They showed heartfelt desire for the coming of God's kingdom, which they supposed Jesus was about to set up, and they had great hopes for it, expecting that it would soon appear. As a result they were filled with joy, and their voices were so animated that the whole city rang with their noise. They appeared to possess great zeal for Christ's kingdom.

Obviously, when our passions run high, they produce all sorts of emotional reactions along with the original "love" that got us going. As I mentioned before, love is the primary feeling, and from it flow all our other responses.

Imagine that a person, through the delusions of his own mind or through Satan's lies, hears a voice say to him, "Son, be of good cheer, thy sins be forgiven thee," or, "Fear not, it is your Father's good pleasure to give you the kingdom." He assumes that it is God speaking to him, even though he has had no previous contact with Christ. If such a thing were to happen, this person would naturally experience a whole flood of emotional responses to this "message." He will experience overflowing joy and be filled with fervent affection for the imaginary God or Redeemer who he supposes has rescued him from the jaws of some dreadful destruction. Obviously, this person will be filled with admiration and gratitude for God; he will be full of talk about what he has experienced, so that for awhile he can barely speak of anything else. He will seem to magnify the God who has done so much for him, calling upon his friends to rejoice with him. Next, he will enjoy being with people who believe in his experience, acknowledging it as real and paying special attention to him because of it—and he will begin to zealously oppose anyone who doubts his experience. Eventually, an entire group might rise around him, and he would lead their fight against all those who refused to conform to their ideas. I could go on and describe many other events that could easily follow these circumstances. If you think I am exaggerating, then you have little knowledge of human nature.

Just as all pure emotions flow from divine love, so a counterfeit love naturally produces other false emotions. In both cases, love is the fountain, and the other emotions are the streams. The various faculties and feelings of human nature are like the channels from a single fountain; if the source of fountain is clear and pure, then clean, sweet water will flow out into all the channels—but if the water at the fountain's source is polluted and poisonous, then unhealthy streams will also flow out into all the channels. Human nature can also be compared to a tree with many branches coming from one root; if the sap in the root is healthy, good sap will flow out through the branches, and the fruit that the tree produces will be wholesome and nutritious—but if the root's sap contains poison, the same poison will be in all its branches, and the fruit the tree produces will be deadly. In both cases, the trees may look alike; the difference is found only when one eats the fruit. That is the way it often is with saints and hypocrites. True and false experiences can look very similar, but their results are very different.

*VIII. The joy and comfort we feel after a religious expe-
rience tell us nothing either way about the reality
of that experience.*

Many people are prejudiced against dramatic emotional
experiences. On the one hand, some spiritual leaders have
insisted that all religious awakenings must begin with fear
and awful anxiety, followed by a sense of total sinfulness
and helplessness, and then end with a specific sort of light
and comfort. Others, however, distrust any such experience; they say that if we spell out stages and steps within
religious experiences, then we are reducing spirituality to
human terms. These spiritual scholars are particularly
critical if an intense experience of joy follows an equally
intense experience of distress and terror.

Scripture gives us no grounds for this sort of skepticism.
Clearly, before God delivers people from a state of sin, He
often gives them first a great sense of the evil from which
He is about to deliver them; this way they understand
exactly what their deliverance means, and they understand
the depth of their own salvation. When people experience
a terrifying sense of their own need and lack, it only makes
sense that they will then feel a great happiness when they
experience all that Christ offers them.

God often leads us into the wilderness before He comforts us. That way we first see our own helplessness and absolute dependence on His power and grace—and then He
works our deliverance, as so often happened in the Bible.
Before God delivered the children of Israel out of Egypt,

they first experienced terrible circumstances, so that they cried "unto God by reason of the bondage" (Exod. 2:23). When they came to the Red Sea, they were completely surrounded by difficulty. They could not turn to the right hand or the left, for the Red Sea was in front of them and the Egyptian army was behind; they could do nothing to help themselves. If God did not help them, they would be swallowed up and destroyed—and then God rescued them and turned their cries into songs. In the same way, before they could enjoy the milk and honey of Canaan, God "led [them]. . .in the wilderness, . . .that he might humble [them], and that he might prove [them], to do [them] good at [their] latter end" (Deut. 8:2, 16).

The woman who had the issue of blood twelve years teaches us the same lesson. She was not delivered until she had first "spent all her living upon physicians, neither could be healed of any." When she was helpless, with no more money to spend, then she came to the Great Physician, without any resources of her own, and was healed by Him (Luke 8:43–44). Before Christ would answer the request of the woman of Canaan, He seemed to utterly deny her, humbling her completely—and then He showed her mercy and received her as though she were His own dear child (Matt. 15:22–28).

The apostle Paul before a remarkable deliverance was "pressed out of measure, above strength, insomuch that [he] despaired even of life: But [he] had the sentence of death in [himself], that [he] should not trust in [himself], but in God which raiseth the dead" (2 Cor. 1:8–9). When the disciples were caught in a storm at sea, the ship was covered with the waves, ready to sink—and only then did they cry to Jesus, "Lord, save us: we perish." As soon as they did, He rebuked the winds and seas (Matt. 8:24–26). When Joseph is reunited with his brothers who sold him into slavery, he manipulates the situation until they are upset and overwhelmed with guilt; only when they are at last ready to surrender themselves to him, does he reveal himself to them, as their brother and their savior.

When we look at all these ways that God showed Himself to the Bible's heroes, we find that almost always His revelation of Himself is first terrible—and then loving and full of comfort. That's the way it was with Moses at Mount Sinai: First, God appeared so terrifying to him, so full of dreadful majesty, that Moses said, "I exceedingly fear and quake"—but then God made all His goodness pass before Moses, so that this time Moses said, "The Lord God, merciful and gracious." Remember Elijah? First, he experienced a stormy wind, earthquake, and devouring fire—and then a still, small, sweet voice (1 Kings 19). Daniel is another one; when he first saw Christ's face it was like lightning, terrifying him so much that he fainted away—but then he was strengthened and refreshed with comforting words like these: "O Daniel, a man greatly beloved" (Dan. 10).

Many passages of Scripture tell us that God first shows people their own terrifying need before He shows them His grace and bounty. The servant that owed his master ten thousand talents is first held to his debt, while the king sentences him to be sold, along with his wife and children; but when the servant is completely humbled, then the master forgives him completely, erasing his debt. The prodigal son spends all he has and finds himself so humbled that he's ready to eat pig food—and then he is welcomed home by his father, and his homecoming is celebrated and feasted (Luke 15).

The old wounds that refuse to mend must be probed to their depths before they can heal. The Bible compares sin to a soul wound; we cannot hope to heal this desperate sore without first examining it thoroughly. We are only deceiving ourselves if we think we can slap on a quick bandage and expect our mortal wound to close (Jer. 8:11). Psalm 72:6 compares the work of Christ's grace on our hearts to rain on the new mown grass; in other words, He comforts and refreshes our wounded spirits. Christ is called "an hiding place from the wind, and a covert from the tempest; as rivers of water in a dry place, as the shadow of a great rock in a weary land" (Isa. 32:2). But we can only receive the gospel's bounty when we fully perceive our own lack.

When people have gone through this time of pain and conviction, they are reluctant to believe that any of us deserve spiritual joys. They are suspicious of these pleasant emotions, believing that we cannot be sufficiently aware of our sin if we are experiencing such joy. But that is exactly why Christ's redemption is such good news—because it saves us out of the blackest, darkest pain.

On the other hand, simply because joy and comfort follow terror and intense fear is no proof that that joy is spiritual and true. Terror and spiritual conviction are two different things. Conviction can cause fear, but they are not one and the same thing, and terror can spring from many causes. Satan can terrify people with visions of hell, a dreadful pit ready to swallow them up with devils all around waiting to seize them, but this sort of terror does not lead to repentance and life. Instead, Satan uses these fearful fantasies to lie to people, convincing them that they are beyond God's forgiveness. Some people, also, simply have a fearful temperament; they tend to experience terror whenever their imagination runs away from them. Their fear and their imagination work together—the more they imagine, the more scared they become, and the more scared they are, the more they imagine—until they are so worked up that their fear consumes them.

Other people do experience the Spirit's conviction, and this is the source of their fears—but their own hearts quench the Spirit's work. Not every woman who is in labor gives birth to a wholly formed child, and not every experience of the conviction of sin will lead to the joy of salvation. Satan can—and does—mimic the works of the Spirit.

That is why we cannot say that a spiritual experience is genuine just because great joy follows intense fear. By the same token, if a person's spiritual progress follows a different route we should not assume that it is not a true faith experience. We cannot spell out definite rules and steps that the Holy Spirit must follow, for we have not been given that knowledge. A prescribed set of emotions cannot bring us to salvation; only grace can make us whole.

The Spirit's paths are mysterious and unknowable; like the wind, we can hear the sound it makes, we can see what it does, but we cannot tell from where it came or where it will go next. The Spirit's actions are just as mysterious in the soul's new birth as in a physical birth: "Thou knowest not what is the way of the Spirit, nor how the bones do grow in the womb of her that is with child: even so thou knowest not the works of God who maketh all" (Eccl. 11:5). The Bible seems to compare the Spirit's action in our hearts to Christ's physical conception; just as He was conceived in Mary's womb by the power of the Holy Spirit, so He is born in the lives of all believers by the power of the same Spirit. We cannot understand how the Spirit works; we don't know how bones grow in a woman's womb any more than we can comprehend how the heart can conceive this holy Child.

Isaiah 40:13 says, "Who hath directed the Spirit of the LORD, or being his counsellor hath taught him?" Unfortunately, some people have gone too far toward directing the Spirit of the Lord; they try to mark out His footsteps for Him, limiting Him to certain steps and methods. When they do this, creating a human scheme for God's actions, others tend to shape their own realities according to this scheme. As human beings we can't seem to help doing this. We take a confused mass of experiences, and we try to make sense out of them any way we can. If we have been give a certain paradigm to apply, then without realizing what we are doing, we pick out those experiences that will fit into this already existing structure. We notice those things that fit our paradigm; we are blind to aspects of our experience that are incongruent to this human structure. Our spiritual leaders tend to follow right along, using these same paradigms, shaping our religious experiences to fit their preconceived notions of the Spirit's working.

However, people who have actual experience with souls, if they are not blinded by their own prejudice, must be aware that the Spirit works in so many extremely different ways, that they can never predict His path. We can never confine Him to a set of rules; He will never conform to our human paradigms.

When we probe our own spiritual condition, or if we try to help others evaluate their spiritual life, we should concentrate instead on the effects of the Spirit's action in our hearts. How His Spirit accomplished these effects is His own business. After all, doesn't the Bible expressly tell us to judge our spiritual health by the fruits of the Spirit? Nowhere does it ask us to investigate the Spirit's methods for producing fruit.

Many people try to prove the reality of conversion by describing a series of steps that make sense to them. The clearest proof, however, has nothing to do with the *method,* but only with the *result.*

IX. *You cannot equate the time and effort people spend on religion with the depth and sincerity of their spiritual feeling.*

Lately people argue against religious feeling by saying that it causes you to spend too much time reading, singing, hearing sermons, and other religious activities. This makes no sense; Scripture makes clear that true grace causes people to delight in these sort of religious activities. Think about Anna the prophetess; "She. . .departed not from the temple, but served God with fastings and prayers night and day" (Luke 2:37). Grace had the same effect on the early Christians in Jerusalem: "And they, continuing daily with one accord in the temple, and breaking bread from house to house, did eat their meat with gladness and singleness of heart, praising God" (Acts 2:46–47). Grace made David delight in prayer: "Evening, and morning, and at noon will I pray" (Ps. 55:17). Grace makes the saints delight in singing praises to God: "Sing praises unto his name; for it is pleasant" (Ps. 135:3); "Praise ye the LORD: for it is good to sing praises unto our God; for it is pleasant; and praise is comely" (Ps. 147:1). It also causes them to delight in hearing the Word of God preached; it makes the gospel a joyful sound to them (Ps. 89:15), and makes the feet of those who spread the good news to be beautiful: "How beautiful upon the mountains are the feet of him that bringeth good tidings!" (Isa. 52:7). This is the nature of true grace.

On the other hand, just because people are active in their religion does not necessarily prove the depth of their faith. Remember the Israelites, whose services were abominable to God; they attended the "new moons and sabbaths, the calling of assemblies, . . .and spread forth [their] hands, . . .[and made] many prayers" (Isa. 1:13, 15). Think about the Pharisees, who "made long prayers, and fasted twice a week." Some people may simply enjoy empty religious practices, and hypocrites can pray loudly and earnestly. These sort of people may enjoy listening to God's Word, but it makes no change in their lives: "And they come unto thee as the people cometh, and they sit before thee as my people, and they hear thy words, but they will not do them: for with their mouth they shew much love, but their heart goeth after their covetousness. And, lo, thou art unto them as a very lovely song of one that hath a pleasant voice, and can play well on an instrument: for they hear thy words, but they do them not" (Ezek. 33:31–32).

X. Verbal expressions of praise do not prove anything as to the depth of a person's spiritual feeling.

What we've already said implies the truth of this. The external practice of religion proves nothing. However, since so many people judge others by their words, I thought I should elaborate on this point particularly.

None of us would ever say that someone who talks about God a great deal is a bad person. And yet someone who has no real relationship with Christ may still experience intense religious emotions; undoubtedly, this person will tend to talk at length. Scripture tells us clearly that talk alone is not enough.

In the same way, verbal confession of God's mercy and our own sins proves nothing. Saul said, "I have played the fool, and have erred exceedingly"; he appeared to express great affection and admiration for David—and yet in reality he was still full of pride and hatred (1 Sam. 24:16–19, 26:21). Once again, our words cannot prove the inner state of our hearts.

XI. Self-confidence proves nothing one way or the other about a person's heart.

Some people argue that you must be deluded if you have no doubts whatsoever about your salvation. They feel that no one in this life can have that sort of absolute confidence in God's favor, except in very extraordinary circumstances (for instance, martyrs immediately before their deaths).

This way of thinking, however, is not supported by

Scripture. Biblical heroes had an obvious confidence, for God plainly and positively assured Noah, Abraham, Isaac, Jacob, Moses, Daniel, and others of His special favor. Job often speaks of his sincerity with total confidence; "I know that my redeemer liveth, . . .whom I shall see for myself, . . .and not another" (Job 19:25, 27). Throughout the Book of Psalms David speaks without the slightest hesitancy of God being *his* God, glorying in Him as his Portion and Heritage, his Rock and Confidence, his Shield, Salvation, and High Tower. Christ Himself clearly and definitely expressed His special and everlasting love for His disciples. Clearly, Christ wants us to be sure of our salvation.

The apostle Paul, in all of his epistles, speaks of that same assurance. He refers with certainty to his special relationship with Christ, his Lord and Master and Redeemer: "Christ liveth in me; and the life which I now live in the flesh I live by the faith of the Son of God, who loved me, and gave himself for me" (Gal. 2:20); "For to me to live is Christ, and to die is gain" (Phil. 1:21); "I know whom I have believed, and am persuaded that he is able to keep that which I have committed unto him against that day" (2 Tim. 1:12); "I have fought a good fight, I have finished my course, I have kept the faith: Henceforth there is laid up for me a crown of righteousness, which the Lord, the righteous judge, shall give me at that day" (2 Tim. 4:7–8).

Without a doubt, God wants us to be certain of His love and favor. Again and again in the Bible, He spells out promises and covenants that will assure us that we are eternally safe; "Wherein God, willing more abundantly to shew unto the heirs of promise the immutability of his counsel, confirmed it by an oath: That by two immutable things, in which it was impossible for God to lie, we might have a strong consolation, who have fled for refuge to lay hold upon the hope set before us" (Heb. 6:17–18).

Furthermore, this assurance is not intended merely for extreme, extraordinary cases; *all* Christians are meant to be firm in their knowledge of God's love. In fact, the Bible instructs us to practice our faith with confidence; "I therefore so run, not as uncertainly" (1 Cor. 9:26). The Bible even gives us the criteria for our confidence: "And hereby we do know that we know him, if we keep his commandments" (1 John 2:3); "We know that we have passed from death unto life, because we love the brethren" (1 John 3:14).

Therefore, we would be unreasonable to think people are hypocrites, filled with delusional emotions, simply because they are totally confident of their salvation.

On the other hand, self-confidence doesn't mean people are saints, either. No matter how strong and absolute their certainty, it proves nothing. The person may proclaim over and over, "I know God loves me. I know I am going to heaven. I am certain that God is smiling on my life." This sort of overbearing and boasting confidence doesn't wear the same face as a true Christian does; in fact, this arrogant confidence smacks of the Pharisees' confidence, who never doubted that they were saints, better in God's eyes than ordinary people. When Christ hinted to them that in reality they were blind, lacking any grace at all, they despised the suggestion (John 9:40). Meanwhile, the publican, sensing his own unworthiness, stood away from them, barely daring to lift his eyes to heaven as he confessed his sins. If the Pharisees had been more like him, then their confidence would have been based on a humble trust and hope in Christ, rather than in themselves.

Consider for a moment how full of blindness, self-flattery, pride, and delusion our hearts are without God's light. No wonder then that some people have a high opinion of themselves; when their consciences are blind, their convictions killed, their emotions excited, then their self-confidence soars, prompted by their own imaginations as well as Satan's lies.

Once people become settled in this sort of delusion, they do not experience the same sort of doubts that a true saint does. They lack any sense of caution; they feel no sense of the vast importance of Christ as their only foundation; they do not worry at all about being deceived. When we are in a living relationship with God, we become sensitive of how great and awesome, how complete and omniscient our God is, but false confidence kills this sort of humility. It numbs the mind and dulls our perceptions. The hypocrite has no knowledge of her own blindness, nor does she sense the deceitfulness of her own heart; instead, she grows more and more conceited, relying ever more on her own strength. The true saint, however, has a realistic understanding of human nature. Furthermore, the devil does not attack the hypocrite's confidence as he does the confidence of a true saint. A hypocrite may keep his self-confidence as long as he lives, for all the devil cares—but all true Christians will find their faith assaulted by Satan. Christ Himself was attacked with doubts by the devil, when Satan asked him to prove He was the Son of God, and the servant is not above the Master, nor the disciple above his Lord. The hypocrite, though, has no vision of her own flaws and failures, while a true Christian has a heightened sensitivity to the sin in her own heart. This awareness of sin increases our appreciation for Christ's overwhelming grace, but the person who deludes even himself looks in the mirror and sees himself as clean and bright.

There are two sorts of hypocrites: One is deceived by their external morality and the other is deceived by false doctrine. The second kind of hypocrite is the hardest to show the truth. They often have experienced visions and delusional emotions that confirm their false ideas, and they only become more and more certain of their delusion as they go deeper and deeper into it. They hate to encounter any argument against their theories, and they appear oblivious to common sense. I have known, for instance, several people who were convinced that God had promised them something, something earthly and physical rather than spiritual, something for which they had long yearned. Events did not confirm these promises, but these people continued to believe that God would yet bring about what they desired. No matter what happened or what was said to them, these people remained ridiculously confident that God had given them a promise. I don't see why the same sort of thing couldn't happen where a person was falsely convinced of his salvation.

This sort of confidence is like the delusion of disturbed people who believe they are kings, despite all evidence to the contrary. True Christians are in touch with reality. Our confidence is built on a living relationship with grace. As we fall out of this relationship, we will experience doubt, for we sense we are no longer in touch with the source of our life. Hypocrites, however, maintain their confidence even in the midst of the most obvious sickness and sin. This is a sure sign of their delusion.

The Bible does say that we walk by faith and not by sight, but we need to be careful how we interpret Scriptures like this. Our faith depends always on Christ; He alone can lead us through darkness and doubt and death. By His grace alone can we walk confidently into the light. Faith that lacks this sort of spiritual light is not the faith of the children of the light and the day, but the presumption of the children of darkness.

It is true that God's people should trust Him even in the darkness, even when it seems as though He has forsaken them and does not hear their prayers. When we cannot see God, we still must trust Him; when we can see no way for God to keep His promises to us, still we must hope against hope. Job and David, Jeremiah and Daniel, Shadrach, Meshach, and Abednego, and the apostle Paul all gave glory to God by trusting Him in the midst of darkness. But that is very different from trusting God when we have no living relationship with Him!

Sometimes, we may have spiritual light in one part of our souls but not another. We may trust God in some areas, even while we lack confidence in others. Even Christ, when He was on the cross, experienced this. He knew He was still God's Son, and yet He no longer had the same sense of God's presence with Him. This is a very different thing from the sort of hopeful delusion that persists in the deepest spiritual darkness!

Faith alone is not enough. If it were, then the Pharisees should have been in fine shape, for they had faith in abundance. Life-giving faith, however, leads us forward on our journey toward God. It is very different from the sort of confidence that insists no journey is even necessary. The kind of faith I'm talking about here does not look beyond ourselves for its foundation. Instead, it is an egocentric circle, like saying, "I have faith because I believe I have faith," or "I believe because I believe that I believe."

When people lack confidence in their salvation, usually they lack a clear sense of God's infinite riches and Christ's total sufficiency. They doubt that God can eternally save them, because from a human perspective it seems so unlikely. This sort of doubt grows when we depend more on our own intelligence than on God's almighty power and wisdom. We have the responsibility to stay close to God, relying only on Him, and we are to blame if we find ourselves far from His saving presence—but once we are in this condition, we cannot help the doubts that assail us while we are there. A healthy spiritual confidence cannot live in these circumstances, any more than you can keep light in a room once you've blown out the candle, or sunshine in the air when the sun has set. The spiritual experiences you had long ago will never be enough to keep your faith living and real, when their memories are darkened by the circumstances of your present life. Instead, your faith will grow weak and sickly, like a child who has been beaten. Actually, however, this sort of doubt is for your good; it is a message from God letting you know that you need to correct the state of your life. When love grows in your heart again, fear will disappear. This is the way God created us. Fear serves its purpose when we are at a low spiritual level, but once we climb higher, we are no longer inspired by fear, for love impels us now.

Fear and love are the two deep feelings that drive our lives. As one grows, the other diminishes. When we fall into selfishness, when our love falls asleep, we are exposed to spiritual danger; that is why God has wisely created us so that these two opposite feelings, love and fear, rise and fall in our hearts, like the two opposite scales of a balance: when one rises the other sinks. Light and darkness naturally follow one another; when light comes, darkness disappears, and when light fails, darkness rushes in. It's the same way in the human heart: If love falls asleep, selfishness rushes in; the light and joy of hope go out, and fears and doubts darken our lives. On the other hand, if God's love flourishes, the brightness of hope drives away the blackness of selfishness and fear. Love is the spirit of adoption; it affirms the childlike inner person who is intimately connected to God. If we lose touch with this part of ourselves, we experience anxiety and a spirit of bondage; we become slaves to our selfish drives. But when love, the spirit of adoption, grows in our hearts, it drives away all fear. As the apostle John said, "There is no fear in love, but perfect love casteth out fear" (1 John 4:18). These two opposite drives—selfishness and holy love—bring us hope and fear by turns, in proportion to their control within our hearts

Love is the only way that God's Spirit casts out our fear, and fear can only exist in our hearts when love is asleep. When this happens, all the self-examination in the world will do us no good. We can analyze our past experiences, trying to regain our peace and confidence, but it will be a waste of time. God will not allow us to regain our assurance without love being born anew in our hearts.

That is why spiritual advisers should never council

people to be confident in their hope even when their hearts feel dead, thinking that they are advising them to "live by faith and not by sight." This sort of council encourages hypocrites never to get in touch with reality. Wickedness rages in their hearts, but they continue to hope against hope, confidently trusting in God no matter how dark things look.

These people have no evidence of grace in their lives. Instead of concentrating on God's glory and Christ's excellency, they only look at themselves, entertaining themselves with thoughts of their own attainments and ideas. This sort of religion consists of living on human experiences rather than Christ. Hypocrisy like this looks uglier to God than the gross immoralities of those who make no pretense at religion.

But to get back on topic, I want to mention one more thing about the nature of "religious affections."

XII. Truly spiritual people may be pleased and inspired by others' outward demonstrations of religious feeling, but this proves nothing one way or another about how deep and real those emotional demonstrations are.

No matter how spiritual we are, we do not have the discernment to tell who is in right relationship with God and who isn't. We can discern our own internal spiritual reality, but we cannot judge the external demonstrations of others, for the only thing of others we can see is merely appearances; we cannot see their hearts. The Bible plainly tells us that our ability to judge others is fallible: "The LORD seeth not as man seeth; for man looketh on the outward appearance, but the LORD looketh on the heart" (1 Sam. 16:7); "He shall not judge after the sight of his eyes, neither reprove after the hearing of his ears" (Isa. 11:3). People who pride themselves on being able to judge the souls of others usually suffer from one of these three problems: They are inexperienced; they have poor judgment; or they are so conceited and self-confident that they are unaware of their own ignorance. When it comes to discerning another's spirituality, people who are wise and experienced proceed with great caution.

When people claim to love God, then as Christians it is our duty to welcome them with love, accepting them as brothers and sisters in Jesus Christ. But yet even the best Christians can be deceived by appearances. In the end, though, these people who claim so glowingly to be Christians usually fall away and come to nothing. After all that we've said already, this only makes sense. Counterfeit love and joy, as well as other spiritual emotions are all too common. They may be accompanied by a good-natured personality and great doctrinal knowledge; these people may have a natural ability to communicate with others and be well-educated and likable. They may look exactly like one of God's true saints. Only the omniscient God, the great Searcher of hearts, can separate between sheep and goats. If we pretend that we can, we are only being conceited and arrogant.

We can't help but be taken in by others' deceit. Even David was deceived this way: "It was not an enemy that reproached me; then I could have borne it. . .but it was thou, a man mine equal, my guide, and mine acquaintance. We took sweet counsel together, and walked unto the house of God in company" (Ps. 55:12–14). When God's Spirit is outpoured, just like in the spring, many blossoms appear on the trees. They all look lovely and promising, and yet many of them never come to anything. They look just as beautiful as the others and they smell just as sweet, but after a little while they wither and drop off the tree to rot on the ground. Our human senses are incapable of perceiving which blossoms have that secret identity that will one day produce fruit, that inner reality and strength that will allow them to be creative and growing all through the hot summer sun that will dry up the others. Mature fruit, not the beautiful colors and smell of the blossoms, is what counts. The same is true of new converts who claim to have given their hearts to Christ.

How strange we are! We can't accept the guidelines Christ gave us, but instead we invent ones of our own that seem so much better to us. I can't think of anything Christ made more plain than this particular rule He gave us for judging others' sincerity, that is, that we should judge the tree by its fruit. People seem to think this rule will not do, and they search for others that they imagine will be more definite and certain. Unfortunately, whenever we set our own wisdom over Christ's, the consequences are not good. Those who are most certain that they know the most about other's spirituality are probably hypocrites themselves.

In the parable of the wheat and tares, Christ said, "When the blade was sprung up, and brought forth fruit, then appeared the tares also" (Matt. 13:26). If we cannot discern between a blade of grass and a blade of wheat, then how do we expect to be able to tell the difference between real and counterfeit grace? Yet another metaphor that teaches us the same thing is the way the priests in Bible times could not easily judge whether a person had leprosy or not. No matter how closely they examined each spot on the person's body, all they could do was quarantine the person and wait to see what "fruit" the spots brought forth.

While I'm on this subject, I want to mention one more strange idea I've encountered. Some people believe that they can tell others are deeply spiritual simply because these people are so easy to love. They argue that they wouldn't love these people so much if God's Spirit had not inspired them to do so, and they then reason that the Spirit would not have inspired them to feel such love if these people were not truly His children. However, God may have other reasons for our love. Why should we suppose that we are inspired to love merely to reveal the true nature of others' spirituality? Instead, God may have practical uses for this love; it may change the hearts of others or it may change our own heart—but nowhere does the Bible say that we love only those who are in right relationship with God. Again, the only basis Scripture gives us for judging another's heart, is by the fruits produced in that person's life.

According to Scripture, the state of another's soul before God cannot be known by us; "To him that overcometh will I give to eat of the hidden manna, and will give him a white stone, and in the stone a new name written, which no man knoweth saving he that receiveth it" (Rev. 2:17); "He is a Jew, which is one inwardly; and circumcision is that of the heart, in the spirit, and not in the letter; whose praise is not of men, but of God" (Rom. 2:29); "Therefore judge nothing before the time, until the Lord come, who both will bring to light the hidden things of darkness, and will make manifest the counsels of the heart: and then shall every man have praise of God" (1 Cor. 4:5); "But with me it is a very small thing that I should be judged of you, or of man's judgment: yea, I judge not mine own self. For I know nothing by myself; yet am I not hereby justified: but he that judgeth me is the Lord" (1 Cor. 4:3–4).

How arrogant we are if we assume we can know anything for certain about others' godliness. Even the apostle Peter made no claim to discern the true heart of the evangelist Silvanus, saying only that he *supposed* that Silvanus was a faithful brother (1 Pet. 5:12)—despite the fact that Silvanus was apparently a close friend of the apostles! (See 2 Cor. 1:19; 1 Thess. 1:1; 2 Thess. 1:1.)

PART III

THE TRUE CHARACTERISTICS OF "HOLY AFFECTIONS"

I now come to the second part of my plan for this book: I want to point out the ways that true heart experiences differ from counterfeit ones. But first, let me make three points.

1. I am not attempting to say that if you read this part of my book, you will be able to discern the truth about others' hearts. If I were to make that claim, then I would be guilty of the same arrogance that I have been condemning. Only God can see into the human heart, and He has reserved this prerogative to Himself. However, Christ did give us guidelines to follow for our own protection, so we would not be deceived by false teachers. These guidelines can be helpful as well to anyone who is a spiritual director or counselor. But they are guidelines only, not proof, and we should not make something from them that Christ never intended.

2. We should not expect to determine from these guidelines just how far from God a person can go and still be in a state of grace. In fact, as I already mentioned, the fear we experience as we drift out of God's presence is actually healthy. The further

we are from Him, the more anxiety we will feel, and this impels us to examine ourselves and draw closer to Him again.

When things are very small we cannot see them clearly. Not only are our eyes unable to discern their forms, but their true natures are not yet revealed, just as different sorts of animal embryos all look very similar. As an animal grows, however, its true identity is revealed. To use another metaphor, we look at the spiritual world as though we were peering through clouds of smoke; the differences between objects may be real and obvious, and yet we cannot see them because of all the smoke that clouds our eyes. When the sky is clear, to use yet another figure of speech, we can easily tell a star from a comet, but when the sky is cloudy and overcast, we are unable to see what is what. In the same way, we may be God's children and yet be unable to see the truth; guilt lies on our conscience, bringing fear, and our vision of our eternal hope is clouded. The sin in our lives obscures our vision of God's grace. Or you might say that sin is like being color blind: It makes reality look different. Or you could compare sin to some illness that makes everything taste bitter, so that we can't distinguish wholesome food from bad. When we are deep in sin, our spiritual senses are affected in the same way; we are unable to discern spiritual reality.

That is why anything I am about to say will do you little good if you are not right with God. It would be like giving someone a set of rules for how she can distinguish visible objects in the dark; each rule may be accurate, and we might explain each rule perfectly, and yet the person will still be unable to *see* anything. How can she? She is in the dark. That is why it's a waste of time for you to analyze your hearts using the signs of grace that you've heard about from the pulpit or in books. You have other work you should be doing. Until you find the enemy that's hiding in your heart and destroy it, you will be in trouble.

God made us so that the only way we can be confident of our salvation is by dying to ourselves, killing our selfish, self-centered natures. Self-examination can be an important part of this process, and we should not neglect to examine our own hearts—and yet this sort of introspection alone will never give us the assurance we need. Self-examination is all well and good, but the time comes for action. The apostle Paul sought assurance this way by "forgetting those things which are behind, and reaching forth unto those things which are before, [pressing] toward the mark for the prize of the high calling of God in Christ Jesus; . . .if by any means [he] might attain unto the resurrection of the dead" (Phil. 3:13–14, 11); "I therefore so run, not as uncertainly" (1 Cor. 9:26). His assurance of winning the prize came more from running than from considering, and the swiftness of his pace did more for his confidence than any self-examination, no matter how intense.

That is why rules for distinguishing true grace from counterfeit may be useful in some ways, and yet I am far from pretending that we should rely on such rules for our own assurance of salvation.

3. I do not have much hope that anything I say here will convince hypocrites of their folly. Past experience tells me that once people are settled in their

conceit and false confidence, they become blinded and hardened. Beneath their guise of humility, they have such a sense of self-righteousness that nothing I could say would shake them. Changing the hearts of these people seems impossible—and yet God is able to convince even them; His grace cannot be limited. Therefore, something I say here may be used by the Holy Spirit to convict even those hardened in their hypocrisy. Besides, the rules I am about to set forth may be of use to those who are true saints, helping their religion to become more pure, like gold tried in the fire.

Having said all that, I will now point out twelve way that true "religious affections" are different from false ones.

I. *Heart experiences that are truly spiritual have a spiritual source.*

First, let me explain what I mean by "spiritual." The New Testament refers to true saints, those people who have been made whole by the Spirit of God, as spiritual persons. This spirituality is what makes them different from people who live their lives only on the physical, earthly level. Thus the spiritual person and the natural person are set in opposition to one another: "The natural man receiveth not the things of the Spirit of God: for they are foolishness unto him: neither can he know them, because they are spiritually discerned. But he that is spiritual judgeth all things" (1 Cor. 2:14–15). The apostle

Jude, speaking of certain ungodly men who had crept in among the saints (Jude 4), explains that "These. . .[are] sensual, having not the Spirit" (Jude 19). Jude is explaining why these men behaved themselves in such a wicked way: because they were "sensual." In the original, the word translated "sensual" is *psychikoi,* the same word that is translated "natural" in the verses from the second chapter of First Corinthians. Clearly, someone who lives a life controlled by the body's senses and impulses is not consecrated to God—and from the other side, someone who is spiritual, *is* consecrated.

Scripture refers to these people as "spiritual," but it also speaks of certain qualities and characteristics that are also "spiritual." We read of a "spiritual mind" (see Rom. 8:6), of "spiritual understanding" (Col. 1:9), and of "spiritual blessings" (Eph. 1:3).

This does not mean that the Bible is speaking in these references of the human spirit, the intangible part of a person as opposed to the physical part; it is not saying that this sort of mind or understanding or blessings pertain only to that nonphysical aspect of a human being. We can see this is true because Scripture refers to some "carnal" or "natural" human qualities that are seated just as firmly in the human soul as those qualities that the Bible calls spiritual. Pride is one example of this, as is self-righteousness or trusting in our own wisdom; the Bible makes clear that these are "fleshly" rather than spiritual qualities (Col. 2:18). By the same token, things are not called spiritual in the Bible because they have to do with things that are intangible. Many philosophers can fluently discuss these sort of disembodied concepts, and yet the apostles spoke of these philosophers as "natural men," totally ignorant of spiritual things (1 Cor. 2).

No, the New Testament speaks of things as "spiritual" only because they have some relationship to the Holy Ghost, the Spirit of God. Spirit, as the word is used for the third Person in the Trinity, is the noun form and the adjective is spiritual. That is why Christians are called spiritual people—because they are born of the Spirit, because they have the indwelling and healing influence of God's Spirit within them. Inanimate qualities are called spiritual only because they are related to the Spirit of God: "Which things also we speak, not in the words which man's wisdom teacheth, but which the Holy Ghost teacheth; comparing spiritual things with spiritual. But the natural man receiveth not the things of the Spirit of God" (1 Cor. 2:13–14). Here Paul himself expressly states that by spiritual things he means the things of the Spirit of God, the things which the Holy Ghost teaches. Again, Romans 8:6 says that "to be carnally minded is death; but to be spiritually minded is life and peace." The apostle goes on to explain what he means by being carnally and spiritually minded in the ninth verse that follows; for him being spiritually minded means having the indwelling and holy influences of the Spirit of God in the heart: "But ye are not in the flesh, but in the Spirit, if so be that the Spirit of God dwell in you. Now if any man have not the Spirit of Christ, he is none of his." The New Testament is full of examples like this.

Clearly, however, a person may exhibit the extraordinary gifts of the Spirit, and yet still be "natural"; this sort of person is not called "spiritual" in the New Testament. The gifts of the Spirit are not enough; we must have the virtues of the Spirit if we are to be spiritual, as is clear in Galatians 6:1: "Brethren, if a man be overtaken in a fault, ye which are spiritual, restore such an one in the spirit of meekness." Meekness is one of the virtues Paul refers to as the fruits of the Spirit. These "spiritual" qualities are only evident in the lives of those who are living in grace.

The Bible makes clear that "natural" people can be influenced by God's Spirit (Num. 24:2; 1 Sam. 10:10; 16:14; 1 Cor. 13:1–3; Heb. 6:4–6, etc.), and yet they are not, in a scriptural sense, spiritual people. The difference lies in these two things.

1. The Spirit of God builds His permanent home in the hearts of true saints, influencing their hearts and inspiring them to live and act in new ways. The Bible describes the Holy Spirit not only as moving and influencing the saints externally, but as dwelling within them. They are His temple, His home, His eternal dwelling place (1 Cor. 3:16; 2 Cor. 6:16; John 14:16–17). He becomes so united to the person's inner faculties that He is now the source of their very being, a living fountain of new life.

That is why the saints are said to live by Christ living in them (Gal. 2:20). Christ's Spirit not only is in them, but they live now because of His life. His Spirit is so united to them that it is the source of their life. They not only drink living water, but this living water becomes a well or fountain of water in the soul, "springing up into everlasting life" (John 4:14). John explains that this living water is the Spirit of God (John 7:38–39). To use another metaphor, the light of the Sun of righteousness not only shines upon them; it becomes a part of them, so that they shine also. We do not merely reflect God's light; we are little images of the Sun. Using yet another image, we could say that the sap of the true vine not only flows into us the way a straw might suck up a tree's sap, but it is flows into us the way sap flows from the tree to one of its living branches, where it becomes a source of life. We are spiritual because we are united with the Spirit; He indwells us and we share His nature.

On the other hand, though, God's Spirit can influence "natural" people in many ways, even though He is not one with them in the same way. Light may fall upon something that has no light of its own, and that object may appear to shine, but it has no true light-producing ability. In the same way, the Spirit of God can act on a person's life without becoming one with that person.

2. The principle reason why the saints and their virtues are called spiritual is that the Spirit of God, once He is vital source of life in their souls, shares His own nature with them. Holiness (or completeness, wholeness, wellness, integrity) is the nature of God's Spirit; therefore the Bible refers to Him as the Holy Spirit. Holiness, the beauty and sweetness of God's nature, is as essential to the Holy Spirit as heat is to the nature of fire, or as sweetness is to perfume. When the Spirit of God dwells in our hearts, He is like a seed of life within us or a fountain of water; He nourishes our hearts with God's beauty and Christ's joy, so that we have true fellowship with the Father and with His Son Jesus Christ.

We possess in our hearts the divine nature; as Christ says, "That which is born of the Spirit is spirit" (John 3:6). In other words, the grace that is born in our hearts shares the same nature with the Spirit, and that is why it can be appropriately called a spiritual nature. On the other hand, that which is born in us from our "flesh," the part of us that is twisted and alien to God, will also be a twisted and alien nature.

God never joins Himself intimately with those who do not welcome Him; He does not impose His nature on those who are following the "natural" aspects of their hearts. When He influences this sort of person, it is from the outside only, although His own nature is unchanged. Thus, for instance, the Spirit of God moved upon the face of the waters, and there was nothing contrary to His nature in that action—yet He did not become one with the water; it remained separate. In the same way, He may act on the human mind in many ways, while not uniting with it any more than when He acts on inanimate things.

When God's Spirit lives in us, then, the feelings we experience share in His nature. The spiritual sensations are vastly different from the normal experiences of "natural" humanity. Through our own efforts, we cannot create these effects, nor can any devil produce them in us. We have each become "partakers of the divine nature" (2 Pet. 1:4). We are the saints of which the Bible speaks when it says that "God dwelleth in [them], and [they] in God" (1 John 4:15), and "Christ [is] in [them]" (Rom. 8:10), being "the temple of the living God" (2 Cor. 6:16). "Christ liveth in [them]"

(Gal. 2:20), being made "partakers of [God's] holiness" (Heb. 12:10), "that the love wherewith [God the Father] hast loved [Christ] may be in them" (John 17:26), having His "joy fulfilled in themselves" (John 17:13), being made to "drink of the river of [God's] pleasures [and]. . .in [God's] light shall [they] see light" (Ps. 36:8–9), having fellowship "with the Father and with his Son Jesus Christ" (1 John 1:3).

This does not mean that the saints are partakers of God's essence; they do not become like little gods nor are they little "christs." This is heresy. To use a Scripture phrase, however, they are made partakers of God's fullness (Eph. 3:17–19; John 1:16). God's fullness is His spiritual beauty and happiness; that is what nourishes His creation, according to the measure and capacity of each creature. The particular kind of grace that lives in the hearts of the saints is doubtless the most specific and concrete demonstration of God's nature in all of His creation. That is what I mean when I say that truly spiritual experiences of the heart have a spiritual source.

The apostle James tells us that "natural" people do not have the Spirit; and Christ teaches the necessity of a new birth, or of being born of the Spirit (John 3:6). Paul said that all who have the Spirit of God dwelling in them are His (Rom. 8:9–11). Having the Spirit of God is spoken of as a sure sign that people have an eternal inheritance, for the Spirit is spoken of as the foretaste of eternity (2 Cor. 1:5, 22; Eph. 1:14). Having anything of the Spirit is mentioned as evidence of being in Christ: "Hereby know we that we dwell in him, and he in us, because he hath given us of his Spirit" (1 John 4:13). A "natural" person has no experience of any of these spiritual things: "The natural man receiveth not the things of the Spirit of God: for they are foolishness unto him: neither can he know them, because they are spiritually discerned" (1 Cor. 2:14), "Even the Spirit of truth; whom the world cannot receive, because it seeth him not, neither knoweth him" (John 14:17). "Natural" people are described in Scripture as having no spiritual light, no spiritual life, and no spiritual being; their conversion is often compared to opening the eyes of the blind, raising the dead, a work of creation (one where creatures are made entirely new), and becoming newborn children.

All that we've said makes evident that things of the Spirit are entirely different than the things we experience humanly. No matter how we manipulate our human natures, with our own powers we can never change them into spiritual substance. The self-centered "natural" person is completely different from the "spiritual"; no matter how we worked to raise our selfish natures, we cannot change them, because their very substance is opposed to the spiritual. This opposition is not a question of degree, so that human nature is merely a lower version of the spiritual version; on the contrary, human nature is a completely different kind of thing than the Spirit. That is why we refer to spiritual things as being supernatural, and that is what I mean when I say that spiritual heart experiences are caused by supernatural influences.

It follows, then, that the feelings we experience through the healing influence of the Spirit are entirely different from anything we experienced before we were consecrated to God. Without a doubt, if God by His mighty power produces something new in our hearts, then we perceive or feel something altogether new as well; we experience some new mental sensation or perception, something which could never be produced no matter how we tinkered with the emotions we felt before this. This new perception or spiritual sensation is so different from any previous mental sensation, that it is as though we discovered a new sense, something as different from our other senses as tasting is different from seeing, or hearing from touching. If we merely thought about honey or looked at honey, we would have a very different idea about the nature of honey than if we tasted honey. In the same way, a "natural" person could never imagine the spiritual perceptions experienced by spiritual people. That is why the Bible often compares the regenerating work of God's Spirit to the giving of a new sense: making blind eyes see and unstopping the ears of the deaf. This new spiritual perception and the new feelings that go along with it spring from a new foundation for the very being of our souls. The root of our being is entirely new now, so that we experience a new reality.

With people who are not spiritual, however, God uses the same faculties and senses that human beings had all along; He does not create an actual new physical sense, but He makes use of the ones we already have. That is what He did with Balaam: He improved Balaam's physical vision so that he could perceive spiritual reality. God's Spirit can do the same thing with a person's imagination, so that either in a dream or awake, she forms the shape of things to come, things that at a later date she will experience with her physical senses. God's Spirit can also help a person's natural ingenuity, as He assisted Bezaleel and Aholiab with building the tabernacle. In the same way, He may assist a person's natural political abilities, or He may improve a person's courage or intelligence. But when the Spirit of God influences on the hearts of His saints, He infuses new, supernatural faculties, faculties that are far beyond anything a person experiences in their natural condition. The "natural" person can no more conceive of these spiritual experiences than a blind person could imagine a rainbow or a deaf person comprehend a melody.

But in order to understand this correctly, I must point out two things.

1. On the one hand, the spiritual emotions are not entirely different from what we experienced before we received Christ. Our love for God may feel very like a person's natural love for family or friends. And yet, on the other hand, even those things that seem similar are not truly alike. Spiritual emotions have a different quality and depth that the "natural" person has never experienced. It is like two people who desire a certain kind of fruit. They both are delighted by the fruit when they possess it, but one person has no sense of taste, and he only loves the fruit because of its beautiful color and shape, while the other person loves the fruit's sweet taste as well as its lovely appearance; this person's perception of the fruit is fuller and more complete.

2. A "natural" person may experience some degree of spiritual perception, as Balaam did. And yet this is different from the inner experience of the Spirit. A person may be dressed up as a king and brought to

court, but he will not be any different in his heart than before, even though he will undoubtedly have many new experiences while he is in court. External perceptions are not the same as having the very roots of our hearts made new.

All in all, I think we can safely say that only God's Spirit can create entirely new experiences in our hearts. I have put so much emphasis on this because it helps us to discern Satan's delusions and it also answers some of our doctrinal questions about God's Spirit and the nature of true grace. Now, therefore, I want to apply these things to the purpose of this discussion.

People can have imaginary ideas about God and Christ, or heaven, or anything that has to do with religion, and yet these people do not possess any true grace; they totally lack all spiritual qualities.

Let me make clear what I mean by imaginary ideas. The imagination is the mental power that allows the human mind to make an interior picture of external objects when they are not actually present nor actually perceived by the senses. The word "imagination" comes from *image,* because this faculty allows us to create mental images of external things that are not present in reality. By "external things" I mean all those things that we perceive with our five external senses: seeing, hearing, smelling, tasting, and feeling.

Now many people who have lively imaginations think that they are experiencing spiritual discoveries. For instance, they may have a vivid mental picture of a human shape with a beautiful face, and they call this spiritually seeing Christ. Or they may have a strong mental impression of a great outward light, and they assume that they are perceiving God's glory. Some people have had ideas about Christ's hanging on the cross, imagining the way His blood ran down from His wounds and they call this a spiritual vision of the crucified Christ and the way of salvation through His blood. Other people may "see" Him with His arms open, ready to embrace them, and they call this a revelation of the sufficiency of Christ's grace and love. Still others have experienced intense images of heaven—Christ on His throne there and the shining ranks of saints and angels —they say that heaven was opened up to them. They may have a particularly vivid picture of a beautiful person smiling at them, and they assume this is a spiritual revelation of Christ's. None of these people are using their physical eyes for any of these visions, and so they all assume that their experiences are spiritual. They may also imagine that they hear certain words being spoken to them, sometimes the words of Scripture and sometimes other words, and they believe that they are hearing Christ's voice. They refer to these experiences in various ways: as the inward call of Christ, hearing the voice of Christ spiritually in their hearts, having the witness of the Spirit, and the inward testimony of His love, etc.

People make this mistake because they hear the Bible and religious leaders speak of spiritual experiences with metaphors that refer to the external world. Spiritual things are invisible; we can't point them out with our fingers, and so we are forced to use figures of speech when we talk about the spiritual world, borrowing words from the external world we perceive with our sense. For instance, we may speak of light or the call of Christ; Scripture itself is full of these sort of metaphors. Our human imaginations can't

help but respond to these words with mental pictures—
and unthinking people assume then that they have experienced some sort of spiritual revelation. As a result, their
emotions are deeply stirred.

Obviously, though, these mental pictures are neither
spiritual nor divine, not in the sense that we have been discussing. Our imagination is only yet another of our human,
natural faculties, and to confuse it with spiritual perception
is to degrade our sense of what is truly supernatural. We
need no influence of the Spirit to excite our imaginations;
in fact, they tend to be most excited when we are physically
sick or mentally unbalanced.

A real spiritual revelation is quite different. But Satan
is able to use our imaginations to delude us. The Bible
speaks of false prophets who were influenced by lying spirits (Deut. 13:1; 1 Kings 22:22; Ezek. 13:7). Satan was even
able to work in the mind of the Man Christ Jesus, when he
showed Him all the kingdoms of the world, when those
kingdoms could not have been really in sight.

That is why no mental image we experience of any
external shape or thing can be evidence of divine power. We
use the same mental faculty to imagine a wood chip or a
block of stone as we do to imagine a beautiful human body
wearing a sweet smile, with arms open and blood running
from the hands, feet, and side. We can paint on our brains'
mental canvases the shape of a royal man or a magnificent
city paved with gold just as easily as we can paint a straw or
a stick. That is why I will say it one more time: Our imaginations' revelations are not spiritual, supernatural, or divine,
not in the sense that we have already discussed.

The emotions that spring from these mental experiences may be deep and intense, but they are clearly built on a foundation that is not spiritual. Therefore, we cannot say that these are "religious affections"; they are not those feelings of our heart that spring from a supernatural source.

Again, from what we've just said about the imagination, we can see that when words of Scripture come to our minds, it does not mean that God's Spirit is speaking to us. I've talked about this already earlier, but I want to repeat here that the human imagination is perfectly capable of bringing to mind either a visual or auditory image of certain passages of Scripture. When this happens, we should not assume that we are experiencing divine revelation. And it follows that the emotions we experience as a result are neither spiritual nor evidence of grace.

Having said that, I want to observe that God *can* inspire spiritual feelings in us through His Word. When this is a genuine experience, the *content* of those Scriptures is the thing that excites our emotions, rather than the extraordinary and sudden manner that the words came to our minds. We respond emotionally to the instruction we receive from these passages and the glimpse they give us of the glorious things of God that are beyond our human vision. When we are misled, however, we assume that because Scripture popped suddenly into our heads, that means that God is approving our human circumstances, or that He is promising some wonderful thing to us—and this selfish delight in external events is what affects us emotionally. We have no new spiritual understanding of the divine things contained in Scripture; no new spiritual sense of the Bible's truth acts as the foundation for our emotional response. Instead, our emotions are built entirely on the sand, for they lack a firm foundation in reality.

True faith is not built on a shaky foundation like this. If we want to confirm our salvation in God, we do not need to experience any new revelation unique to ourselves only; the Bible is full of promises that assure us that we are all invited to partake of the Good News. Real faith takes God at His word and does not insist that God speak some new personal message.

And yet some people actually imagine that the revelation in God's Word is not enough to meet our needs. They think that God from time to time carries on an actual conversation with them, chatting with them, satisfying their doubts, testifying to His love for them, promising them support and blessings. As a result, their emotions soar; they are full of bubbling joy that is mixed with self-confidence and a high opinion of themselves. The foundation for these feelings, however, does not lie within the Bible itself, but instead rests on the sudden creations of their imaginations. These people are clearly deluded. God's Word is for all of us and each of us; He does not need to give particular messages to particular people.

By this time, some of you are probably saying, "What! Is there no such thing as a particular spiritual application of the Scripture's promises by the Spirit of God?" I answer that there is doubtless such a thing as a spiritual and saving application of Scripture's promises, but at the same time, I have to specify that the nature of this application is often misunderstood, confusing a great many people and allowing them to be trapped by Satan. The spiritual application of a Scripture promise does not consist in its being suddenly suggested to our thoughts by some extrinsic agent, whether it be our own imaginations or Satan himself. The sense we have that words are being spoken directly to our hearts does not mean that they come from God; this sort of thinking is a very shallow notion of a spiritual application of Scriptures, for an experience like this could be caused by the devil's power. Nothing about this experience proves that it is a genuine and living communication from God.

No, a truly spiritual application of God's Word is much higher and deeper; it is as far beyond the devil's power as it would be for him to apply the Word of God to a dead corpse and raise it to life. A spiritual application of God's Word means that we apply it to our hearts, allowing it to shed spiritual light on our understanding, so that we may be more totally surrendered to God. A spiritual application of Scripture means that we are more receptive to the gospel's invitation, more sensitive to Christ's nature. False application of the Bible allows us to settle more deeply into our own selfish ways as we focus on the "promises" we believe we have received, but true application of Scripture encourages us to embrace the Promiser rather than the thing promised. When we focus selfishly on the promise, this is a blind application that belongs to the spirit of darkness rather than the light.

When people are deceived by this sort of false application of the Bible, the emotions they feel are not really inspired by the Word of God; the Scripture is not their source. The Bible nowhere suggests that God imparts a unique message to a particular person, some newly coined word from His mouth that was omitted from the Bible.

At this point in our discussion it seems plain that the revelation of secret facts through sudden mental suggestion is neither spiritual nor divine. By secret facts I mean things that have happened or are happening or will happen that are secret in the sense that we could not know about them through any evidence given us by our five senses. For instance, suppose that I received a revelation that next year our country would be invaded by France; or through no information that I now possess, I suddenly became aware that today in Europe a great battle was fought. This is a revelation of secret facts by a sudden mental suggestion, and it does not matter if the facts revealed pertain to the future, for current events or even past events can be just as hidden from my senses and intelligence. If I become suddenly aware that a revolution will occur today in the Ottoman Empire, it is the very same sort of revelation as if I suddenly knew that this revolution would take place a year from now; though one is present and the other future, both are equally hidden from me by any other means than a sudden and direct revelation. The Bible tells us that this sort of revelation does occur (see 1 Sam. 10:2–3)—but clearly the revelation of secret facts by direct mental suggestions does not prove that God's Spirit lives within us. Nothing in these sort of revelations inspires us to draw closer to God; they do not reveal the truth of the greatest and most important facts that have ever been or are or ever shall be.

Unspiritual human beings are capable of receiving this sort of extraordinary revelation, as we see in the story of Balaam. Apparently, then, this sort of extraordinary knowledge is not spiritual, not in the sense that we have already spelled out, for the ideas themselves contain nothing that is holy and divine. As a result, this secret knowledge has no power to heal our minds or save our hearts; God may choose to put this sort of special perception directly into a person's mind, and yet He does nothing to change that person's na-ture. The person is still natural, selfish, unspiritual, despite the extraordinary revelation he has experienced. Some revelations of this nature may be attended by Scripture verses, but they nevertheless remain unspiritual in their nature. Scripture alone, as we have already said, does not prove that a particular heart experience is spiritual—and Scripture added to extraordinary revelation still lacks divine grace. When you add two things together, if neither of them is spiritual in nature, then their sum will never be spiritual either.

Furthermore, the emotions we experience as a result of this sort of revelation are not spiritual. How could they be, when their source lacks spirituality? Of course, we may experience God's grace in our hearts at any time, but this is just coincidence if it occurs immediately after such an extraordinary revelation. The source is not the experience itself, but God, for truly spiritual feelings come only from the supernatural working of the divine. However, people who experience this unusual type of knowledge are frequently emotional about their revelations; in fact, their emotions may be intense and overwhelming, and consequently, they assume they have had a deeply spiritual experience. This is an out-and-out delusion—and this delusion only serves to further feed their deep emotions.

At this point, I should probably point out that clearly, many people feel they have the "witness of the Spirit" that they are the children of God—and yet this "witness" actually lacks anything that is spiritual or divine; as a result, the feelings they build on this "witness" are empty delusions.

All sorts of ideas may pop into our heads; some of them may be true and some of them may not be, but none of them prove that we are spiritual people. We could receive a direct mental suggestion that we might one day be converted and go to heaven, and this foreknowledge could actually be accurate, but this sort of secret message is no more spiritual than the ones I have already mentioned. The content of this sort of perception does not change the fact that this is not a spiritual experience. For all that it may be an extraordinary experience, it is still a natural one and not spiritual. God's grace is not communicated to our hearts.

As one theologian has said, "God's Spirit does not testify to individuals that they are spiritual. Some people think that He does, basing their opinion on Romans 8:16: 'The Spirit itself beareth witness with our spirit, that we are the children of God.' They think that the Spirit reveals itself by a direct inner testimony, but that is not what Paul was talking about in this verse. The Spirit of God stirs our hearts; from Him, God's love streams into our hearts, and some mistake this for a "testimony." But Paul meant that the Spirit opens our eyes so that we can see what is revealed in the Word; He reveals Christ to us; but He does not show us new truths that were never written in God's Word. The Word contains all the revelation we will ever need; we have no need for new revelations."

When we suppose that the Spirit's witness is a commonplace thing, something that any human being can experience, no matter their standing with God, then we are trivializing the amazing and vital way that God shares Himself with us. The "witness of the Spirit" that is referred to in Romans 8 is called the "seal of the Spirit" in other parts of the New Testament (see 2 Cor. 1:22; Eph. 1:13; 4:30), alluding to the seal of princes. This princely seal was a token of the prince's special favor; he used it ceremonially each time he gave one of his subjects some special honor or privilege. When the Spirit of the Prince of Princes places His seal on one of His favorites, this is an event that is far from commonplace. Nothing that God's Spirit does more clearly demonstrates the divine nature; no experience is like it, for this witness is matchless and distinct, like nothing else in the world.

Nothing is more royal than the royal seal, nothing more sacred, for this seal belongs intimately to the prince. It not only conveys his authority, but it also symbolizes his unique identity. The seal's mark proclaims what things are royal property. Therefore, when the King of heaven and earth stamps His seal on our hearts, He changes the very nature of our identities. The water from God's infinite fountain of divine beauty and glory flows directly into our hearts, merging with our being. This is far more than merely communicating some secret fact by revelation or suggestion; even the devil's children can experience that sort of revelation. No, the Spirit's seal transforms our hearts, and "natural" humanity cannot even begin to comprehend what this means. "To him that overcometh will I give to eat of the hidden manna, and will give him a white stone, and in the stone a new name written, which no man knoweth saving he that receiveth it" (Rev. 2:17). I suspect that this passage refers to the same mark of the Spirit, the same blessed token of special favor, that in other places in Scripture is called the seal of the Spirit.

The confusion about this comes from the fact that

people have misunderstood the meaning of the word "witness." They assume that it is a sort of internal verbal suggestion, rather than an ongoing work of the Spirit within our hearts. They think that God speaks to us mentally, conveying by some sort of secret voice the message that we are His children. In the New Testament, however, the term "witness" often has a deeper meaning than merely a declaration or an assertion that a thing is true. We think of "witness" in these terms, but the New Testament sees it to mean the actual proof of something, the living demonstration of the truth, rather than a mere statement of the truth.

That is why in Hebrews 2:4 God is said to bear witness, "with signs and wonders, and with divers miracles, and gifts of the Holy Ghost." These miracles are called God's witness, not because they are mere statements, but because they provide active living evidence and proof. We see the same sort of meaning in Acts 14:3: "Long time therefore abode they speaking boldly in the Lord, which gave testimony unto the word of his grace, and granted signs and wonders to be done by their hands." And John 5:36: "But I have greater witness than that of John: for the works which the Father hath given me to finish, the same works that I do, bear witness of me, that the Father hath sent me." Again, in John 10:25: "The works that I do in my Father's name, they bear witness of me." In the same way, the water and the blood are said to bear witness (1 John 5:8); they do not speak or assert anything, but they are actual proof, living evidence. God's works of providence, demonstrated by rain and fruitful seasons, are also spoken of as witnesses of God's being and goodness; in other words, they are vital proof of these things. And when the Scripture speaks of the seal of the Spirit, the divine mark that is stamped upon the soul, this is the living evidence by which God's children can be recognized.

This seal is God's unique mark that sets apart those things which belong to Him, as in Revelation 7:3: "Hurt not the earth, neither the sea, nor the trees, till we have sealed the servants of our God in their foreheads"; "Set a mark upon the foreheads of the men that sigh and that cry for all the abominations that be done in the midst thereof" (Ezek. 9:4). When God presses His seal on the human heart with His Spirit, it leaves an image there, just as the seal presses a certain shape into the soft wax. This holy stamp, this impressed image, gives us proof of the Holy Spirit's reality in our lives, for the image stamped on our hearts is God's own image. We bear Christ's identity intimately within our hearts through the Spirit of adoption.

In the old days, seals were engraved with two things: the image and the name of the person whose seal it was. For instance, Caesar Augustus's image was carved onto a precious stone, and during Christ's and the apostles' time, this seal symbolized the authority of the Roman Empire. We are God's precious stones, His jewels, and He has authority over the empire of the universe. We carry His image on our hearts, stamped there by His signet ring, the Holy Spirit. So when Christ says to His bride in the Song of Solomon 8:6: "Set me as a seal upon thine heart, as a seal upon thine arm," He is saying, "Let My name and image be impressed upon you, physically and emotionally a part of your very identity." When this happens, our consciences—what the Bible calls our spirits—have no doubt that the Holy Spirit lives within us.

This meaning of the word "witness" is far deeper than

any specific revelation or insight. Our hearts are supernaturally changed, and no human faculty could ever produce this same effect. We receive the beautiful nature of God into our very being. The devil could never imitate this.

The Scripture gives us further evidence that the seal of the Spirit is not merely revelation of any fact, but the action of grace itself within the soul. Another term for the seal of the Spirit is the "earnest of the Spirit." Clearly, these two terms are synonymous; "Who hath also sealed us, and given the earnest of the Spirit in our hearts" (2 Cor. 1:22); "In whom also after that ye believed, ye were sealed with that Holy Spirit of promise, Which is the earnest of our inheritance until the redemption of the purchased possession, unto the praise of his glory" (Eph. 1:13–14). Now, the earnest is the same as a down payment, the partial payment of money that is given as a token of the whole that will eventually be paid; it is a small piece of the entire thing, and the earnest's nature is no different from the whole.

So what is the earnest—the down payment—of eternal glory? Clearly it cannot be something so trivial that its equivalent can be produced by human faculties. No, eternity's down payment is grace itself, the sort of grace that is living and obvious. The Bible tells us that this earnest is not prophecy, nor tongues, nor knowledge, but that far more excellent thing—unfailing, unconditional love. This is the foretaste of the light, sweetness, and blessedness of heaven, a world of love. Grace is the seed of glory, the dawning of glory in the heart, and therefore grace is the earnest of our future inheritance in heaven. Or we could say that spiritual life is the down payment, because grace and unconditional love and spiritual life are all one and the same.

The inheritance that Christ has purchased for His chosen people is the Spirit of God Himself. It is not in some extraordinary gifts, such as prophecy or tongues or anything else, but His living indwelling within our hearts as He shares with us His own identity. This is the sum total of the inheritance that Christ bought for us.

Within redemption's economy, the Father provides the Savior as the purchaser; the Son makes the purchase, but He is also the price; and the Holy Spirit is the thing purchased, the inheritance bought for us by the Son. This is hinted at in Galations 3:13–14, and that is why the Spirit is often spoken of as the sum of all the blessings promised in the gospel (Luke 24:49; Acts 1:4; 2:38–39; Gal. 3:14; Eph. 1:13). This inheritance was the marvelous legacy Christ left His disciples and church in His last will and testament (John 14, 15, 16), and this is the sum of the blessings of eternal life that will one day be given in heaven. (Compare John 7:37–39 and John 4:14 with Rev. 21:6; 22:1, 17.)

Through the Spirit's vital indwelling the saints have all their light, life, holiness, beauty, and joy in heaven—and through the vital indwelling of the same Spirit the saints have all light, life, holiness, beauty, and comfort on earth, only to a lesser extent. This living inhabitant within our hearts is "the earnest of our inheritance until the redemption of the purchased possession" (Eph. 1:14). In conclusion, then, this earnest of the Spirit, the firstfruits of the Spirit, and the seal of the Spirit are all the same thing: the vital, consecrating, grace-filled influence of the Spirit within our hearts—and they are not any direct revelation of facts by the Spirit.

Actually, when Paul speaks of the Spirit's bearing witness

with our spirit that we are the children of God (Rom. 8:16), he explains himself quite clearly, if we only pay attention to what he is saying. We have to look at his words in context, for they are connected with the two preceding verses. The three verses together are this: "For as many as are led by the Spirit of God, they are the sons of God. For ye have not received the spirit of bondage again to fear; but ye have received the spirit of adoption, whereby we cry, Abba, Father. The Spirit itself beareth witness with our spirit, that we are the children of God." Now we can plainly see that when Paul speaks of the Spirit giving us witness or evidence that we are God's children, he is referring to His dwelling in us and leading us, with a spirit of adoption; the Holy Spirit brings to life the spirit of a child within our hearts, disposing us to behave toward God the way we would with a beloved parent. This is the witness or evidence that Paul is talking about. This childlike spirit, this spirit of adoption, what is that but the spirit of love?

Paul speaks of two kinds of spirits: the spirit of a slave, or the spirit of bondage, that is fear; and the spirit of a child, or the spirit of adoption, and that is love. He says we have not received the spirit of bondage, or of slaves, which is a spirit of fear; but we have received the more innocent, simple spirit of children, a spirit of love, and this naturally disposes us to go to God; we behave toward God as children. *This* is the evidence or witness that the Spirit of God gives us that we are His children. Obviously, this is Paul's meaning here, and doubtless he is speaking of the very same way of erasing doubt and fear that the apostle John speaks of (1 John 4:18)—by love or the innocent, childlike spirit within us.

The spirit of bondage controls us through fear, for the slave fears being beaten—but love cries, Abba, Father; it inclines our hearts toward God, so that we feel intimately and simply connected to Him, like children to their parents, and we behave with God as loving children. This gives us clear proof of our union with God as His children, and as a result, our fear is thrown out of our hearts. Consequently, Paul seems to imply that the witness of the Spirit is far from being any mental whisper or direct revelation; instead, it is the healing effect of God's grace on our hearts, giving us the temperament of children. We are filled with sweet childlike love for God, and this casts out fear; it erases the spirit of a slave.

These same ideas are plain in the context of Scripture, for Paul speaks over and over of the Spirit living in the hearts of the saints, so that they have a living source of grace within them, and he sets this in opposition to the "flesh" or death. Look at the verse that comes immediately before the ones we have been discussing. "For if ye live after the flesh, ye shall die: but if ye through the Spirit do mortify the deeds of the body, ye shall live" (Rom. 8:13).

Without a doubt, Paul understood that the spirit of grace is the same as a spirit of love—the innocent spirit of a living child within us. But only perfect love, unconditional love, could make us into fearless children, delivering us from the spirit of bondage. The love we feel, an active, childlike, humble love, proves our relationship to God as His child, and this proof nourishes our hearts. This sort of proof does not demand that we put our faith in some brief statement of private revelation, without any supporting evidence in reality, for our faith rests on the clearest evidence of all. We have no need for continued signs, nor do we need to spend our time examining our lives for evidence of the supernatural. Our revelation of our union with God does come to us through a channel, but that channel is love, and so we have a direct vision of our relationship with God, because the love we feel is so strong and living that we cannot doubt its reality. This is what assures us that we are God's children. How can we doubt our childlike union with Him when in our hearts we are simply children, delighting in our parents' love? That is why we can fearlessly and naturally cry out to God, "Daddy."

When Paul says, "the Spirit itself beareth witness with our spirit," by our spirit he means our conscious awareness of ourselves, our conscience. Proverbs 20:27 says, "The spirit of man is the candle of the LORD, searching all the inward parts of the belly." 2 Corinthians 1:12 tells of this same witness: "For our rejoicing is this, the testimony of our conscience." And 1 John 3:19–21: "And hereby we know that we are of the truth, and shall assure our hearts before him. For if our heart condemn us, God is greater than our heart, and knoweth all things. Beloved, if our heart condemn us not, then have we confidence toward God." When the apostle Paul speaks of the Spirit of God bearing witness to our spirit, don't misunderstand him; he is not saying that our spirit and God's are two separate, collateral, independent witnesses. No, through one we receive the witness of the other: The Spirit of God proves Himself by infusing God's love into our being, radiating this love into our hearts, revealing the inner child that lives there—and our spirit or conscience receives this love and perceiving it, provides us with the joyful proof of God's favor.

Many errors have grown in the church because of false ideas about the witness of the Spirit, thinking that it is a kind of inward voice, suggestion, or declaration from God to us that we are beloved of Him, pardoned, chosen, and the like. Many empty emotions have risen around these ideas, and they tend to very deep and excited feelings—and yet it is all a delusion. That is why I have spent so much time on this point, for I would hate to have multitudes of people miss the real eternal delight of God's love in our hearts. But let me move on now to the second characteristic of spiritual feelings.

II. The basis for all spiritual emotions is God's nature rather than our own; spiritual feeling focuses on God and is not concerned with the self.

Earlier I said that love is the source of all other feeling, and particularly that Christian love is the fountain from which all grace-filled emotions flow. When we love the glory of God, Jesus Christ, the Word of God, the works of God, and the ways of God, we do so simply because of what they are—not because of any benefit they bring us.

Some people will disagree; they say that all love comes from self-love, and human nature is incapable of feeling any love, whether for God or others, that is not based on self-interest. With all humility, I can only suppose that these people have not given the matter sufficient thought. They argue that if we love God, desiring His glory and enjoying Him, then we do so because these things make us happy. God's glory and the enjoyment of His perfect nature are pleasing; they fill us with delight and joy. Therefore, these people say, self-love, the desire for our own happiness, motivates us when we desire that God should be glorified, or when we long to behold and enjoy His amazing nature. But we need to go further and ask how human beings can get to the point where they enjoy God in this way. Without a doubt, these things will eventually make us happier than anything else ever has, and we will long for them the way we long for our own pleasure. But the question is, how do we get there? Isn't this the answer: Love brought us there? We must first love God and have our hearts united with Him, before we will think of God's good as our own. Only love will make us desire God's glory as much as we desire our own happiness, and only love will make us enjoy God more than anything else.

The argument against this goes like this: Because our hearts are united with God in love, and, as a result, we desire God's glory the same way we desire our own well-being, then we are therefore motivated by self-interest. But this is circular reasoning. It would make as much sense to argue that because a parent gave birth to a child, therefore the child must have given birth to the parent. Once we love God and have been united with Him, we will see Him as the best thing in our lives; we will desire God's good as our own, and as a result, even our self-interest will only cause us to want God's glory all the more. But that does not mean that our self-love came first, before our love for God, or that our love for God is the fruit of our selfish natures.

Something else, something entirely different from self-love, has happened to our hearts when we fall in love with God. Our outlook on life, the things we enjoy, our perception of beauty and pleasure, have all been transformed; our natures now reflect God's. This transformation is what draws us closer to God, prior to any considerations for our own interests or happiness. After this, however, we cannot help but seek our happiness in God.

Human love, however, is often based on self-love. We look at others and see that they can be of use to us in some way, and that is the foundation for our love; self-interest precedes any delight in the beloved for its own sake. A judge may love and favor a person who bribed her—or a man may favor another because that person has some relation to himself, as a man loves his child. Both of these loves have their roots in self-love. On the other hand, if we are drawn to another simply because of the loveliness we see in their being, the source of our love is very different, for it is dependent on no benefit to ourselves.

If we love God or Jesus Christ simply because of what He can do for us, if that is the source of our affection, than we do not experience a truly grace-filled and spiritual love. As we have already demonstrated, self-love is a natural emotion that appears as often in the hearts of devils as it does in the hearts of angels. How can anything that has selfish roots turn into something supernatural and divine? Christ speaks plainly about this kind of love; "If ye love them which love you, what thank have ye? for sinners also love those that love them" (Luke 6:32). In the story of Job, the devil accuses Job of having a mercenary love for God; Job loves God, the devil claims, because God has blessed him, and so God allows Satan to remove Job's blessing one by one to test whether Job's love is truly spiritual or not. And Job's love for God turns out to be truly spiritual, unfazed by the loss of God's blessings.

The logical inference, then, is that the only good foundation for our love for God is His supreme loveliness and worthiness. God's nature or divinity is infinitely marvelous; He possesses infinite beauty, brightness, and glory. How can our love for Him be built on anything but His utter loveliness? How can we truly love beauty and brightness if we do not love it merely for the sake of beauty and brightness? How can we value something that is infinitely worthy and precious if we do not appreciate worthiness and preciousness? The infinite excellence of the divine nature, in and of itself, is the true basis for all that is good in God in any respect—so how can we truly love God without loving Him for that excellence? If we love God because of the good He can do us, then we are beginning at the wrong end, and our vision of God is limited. We are only catching a glimpse of God's outermost limits, dipping into the very edge of the stream of divine goodness where it reaches our own interests. We lack any concept of the infinite glory of God's nature, which is the original good, the foundation of all good, the first fountain of all loveliness of any sort, and the deepest root of all true love.

And yet self-love may inspire us to feel deeply about God and Christ, while we remain blind to the beauty and glory of the divine nature. Gratitude is merely a natural feeling, just as anger is, and gratitude can rise from self-love in very much the same way that anger does. When we are angry, it is because someone or something has frustrated our interest; on the other hand, when we feel gratitude, it is because someone has gratified us in some way, feeding the demands of our self-love. We may experience a kind of gratitude without any true love, just as we may be angry without feeling any real hatred, just as parents may be angry with the same children they deeply love. In the sixth chapter of Luke, Christ speaks about the selfish sort or gratitude: "Sinners also love those that love them." This kind of gratitude is actually little better than bribery, and even an animal may feel it, as when a dog loves a master who is kind to it. Anyone may feel grateful; sometimes we even feel grateful to our enemies, as Saul did when David spared his life—and yet Saul continued to be David's enemy. So if human nature experiences this sort of emotion in relation to other human beings, logically, we may also feel gratitude toward God for the same sort of reasons; we can be selfish with Him as easily as we can with each other. The Scripture gives us plenty of examples: the children of Israel who sang God's praises at the Red Sea but soon forgot God's works; Naaman the Syrian, who was deeply moved by the miraculous cure of his leprosy, so much so that he would have liked to worship God—if only that worship hadn't interfered with his earthly interests; and Nebuchadnezzar, who was also deeply grateful when God restored to him his reason and his kingdom.

Since gratitude is such a natural feeling that all humans experience, ingratitude is that much more ugly and hideous, for it shows that evil has suppressed humanity's natural goodness. However, simply because a lack of gratitude indicates deep wickedness, does not mean that all gratitude and natural fondness prove our goodness.

In many ways, self-love can inspire us to feel a sort of love for God. However, often we will find that what we love is an imaginary God. We may not realize our own sinful condition, or how far away from God our selfishness puts us. In our minds, we form a God that suits us, one who favors us and always agrees with us. We may feel very fond of this God—but we have created a God that pleases us, and we love this image, rather than the real and living God that rules the universe.

Again, as we mentioned earlier, some people may have a deep affection for God that is rooted in their fears about hell and damnation. They feel that God is whispering directly into their minds some message that reassures them of their eternal safety, and as a result, they feel affection for God and Jesus Christ. After this, based on this foundation, many things about God may appear lovely to them, and Christ may seem wonderful. If they were asked whether God appears lovely and pleasing to them simply for Himself, they would probably quickly answer, "Yes." Actually, though, if we were to study their hearts closely, we would find that their good opinion of God was purchased and paid for by what they believe He has done for them. The only reason they love God is because the idea they have of Him relieves their unbearable anxiety about hell. Once they have been completely reassured on this score, they can easily believe that they are captivated by love for the Lord of the universe. They stroke themselves with the thought that Christ loved them so much that He valued them far more than most of their neighbors, so much that He died for them and will make them reign in eternal glory with Him in heaven. In reality, however, their love had its roots in their selfish fear; this is what made Christ look so lovely to them, and their pride only feeds this self-centered affection.

When this is the case, their selfishness makes Christ

look that much more lovely. After all, self-centered people love anything that gratifies their ambition. And as these people begin, so they continue. They may become emotionally moved from time to time, but their excitement is based on this same self-centered foundation. They imagine that they have communion with God, as though such a union could be conducted through impulses and whispers and external events that they interpret to suit their delusion. They experience these sort of things often, and they take them to be manifestations of God's great love for them; they assume that they are favored over the rest of humanity, and this delusion further feeds their emotions.

But the expressions of true and healthy love come from a different source. When we have a spiritual love for God, we do not first see what He can do for us and then see that He is lovely; instead, we first see that God is lovely, and then we see how much He loves us. Our hearts are entirely won by the sight of Christ's glorious excellence. Our love's root is in God Himself, and self-love has a hand in our love only secondarily. In contrast, false love begins with the self, and any appreciation of God's nature is secondary, dependent on the satisfaction of self-interest. When we truly love God, however, this love is the deepest foundation of our lives; all of our other concerns are built on it, and self-love acts only as a servant to our heart's most basic love. Selfish people, on the other hand, always have themselves at the deepest level of their being, and they try to build on God as the superstructure that rests on this foundation. Even their acknowledgment of God's glory depends on their private interest.

Self-love may influence people corporately as well as

privately. Just because people are concerned for their community does not mean they are motivated by anything other than self-interest. For instance, during war, self-love may make people rejoice at our nation's success and feel sorrow for its losses. This sort of selfishness may be extended even further, beyond our nation to the entire earth or to humanity as a whole. When this happens, we look at our world as the center of creation. If we knew about inhabitants of other planets, we would not care about anything that might happen to them, but we would rejoice at any benefit to our own planet, no matter what the cost to other creatures. This sort of thinking might make people be impressed that God has blessed us more than He has the fallen angels. That Christ would go to such lengths to save humanity can fill people with the same natural sort of gratitude we discussed earlier in relation to personal benefits.

Do not think, though, that I am saying that any gratitude toward God must always be motivated by self-interest. There is such a thing as spiritual gratitude, which is a holy and divine emotion. Grace-filled gratitude is different from natural human gratitude in these ways:

1. True gratitude or thankfulness to God for His kindness to us is built on a foundation that has already been laid down—love for God for what He is in Himself. In contrast, natural human gratitude has no such preexistent foundation. When our hearts are stirred by grace, so that we are filled with grateful love for God for all the kindness He has shown us, we will always have a stock of love stored up already in our hearts. This stockpile of love was

built in the first place on the grounds of God's own excellency—and from this already-existing love, our hearts' emotions pour out toward God. When we have seen the glory of God, and our hearts have been overcome by it, totally captivated with love for God, then our hearts will become tender, sensitive to God, easily moved at each new blessing.

When a person dislikes someone, she may still feel gratitude if that person is kind to her, just as Saul was grateful to David, but this is not the same kind of thing as when we are grateful to a dear friend, someone who already possesses our heart. This kind of loving gratitude springs from the love we already feel, for our hearts are particularly sensitive when it comes to our most loved friends. Self-love is not excluded from this grace-filled gratitude; the saints do love God for His kindness to them, as in Psalm 116:1: "I love the LORD, because he hath heard my voice and my supplications." But something else is included in this self-love; another love prepares the way and lays the foundation for this grateful affection.

2. When we feel grace-filled gratitude, we are moved by God's goodness, not only as it concerns ourselves or as it affects our own interests, but simply because it reveals to us more of the glory and beauty of God's nature. The wonderful and unparalleled grace of God that is demonstrated in the work of redemption, that shines forth from the face of Jesus Christ, is infinitely glorious in itself, and even the angels think so, regardless of the fact

that it does not concern them. God's work through Christ is the most perfect and complete revelation of the beauty of God's nature. It would be glorious even if it were not directed toward us, and true saints gratefully delight in it in this unselfish way. The fact that it *is* directed toward humanity only serves to engage the saints' minds, increasing their attention and feeling. Subservient to higher impulses, self-love works now as a helper, leading the mind to complete attention and heightening the heart's joy and love. God's kindness to us becomes a mirror where we can look to see an image of God's beauty and goodness. The mirror is directly in front of us, for God's kindness is ever present in our lives, and we delight to look into it.

At this point, some readers may be ready to object against everything I have said, pointing to 1 John 4:19: "We love him, because he first loved us." They think this verse implies that God's love for us is the reason for our love for Him.

In answer to this, I would say that John is pointing out that God loved us while we had no love for Him; John is demonstrating the nature of God's grace and love. This will be clear to anyone who compares this verse and the two following with the ninth, tenth, and eleventh verses. God loved us when we had no love for Him, and the apostle John is proving this fact by saying that God's love for His people is the basis of their love for Him in three ways:

First, the saints' love for God is the fruit of God's love for them, the gift of that love. God gave them a spirit of love for Him, because He loved them from eternity. In this respect, God's love for His people is the deepest foundation of their love for Him, just as it is the foundation of their regeneration and the whole of their redemption.

Second, the revelation of God's love through Jesus Christ is the clearest demonstration God has made to both angels and humanity of the glory of His perfection, and therefore it is the only objective ground for the love of both for God. This is consistent with what I have said before.

Third, God's love for a particular person, revealed to him at his conversion, is a great demonstration of God's perfection and glory, and this will give rise to a spiritual love that will in turn inspire holy gratitude. This contradicts nothing that I have said before. The saints in these respects *do* love God because He first loved them, and this is totally consistent with the sense of John's message in context. First John 4:19 is not a good argument against my premise: Spiritual and grace-filled love springs from wonder at divine things merely for themselves, and not because they benefit the self in some way.

And just as the saints' love for God is the foundation for all the other loves in their lives, so their joy and spiritual delight and pleasure is also based on the joy and delight they find in God, enjoying Him for Himself only, rather than because He benefits them in some way. In fact, this is the main difference between the joy of the hypocrite and the joy of the true saint: The former rejoices in herself; self is the primary source of all her joy, while the latter rejoices in God. A false person is only pleased by his own interests, and he only enjoys those things that will help him attain his ambitions. True saints, however, are fundamentally delighted with the sweet contemplation of God's glorious and pleasing nature. This is the source of all their other delights, the cream of all their pleasures, the joy of their joy. This joy causes them to find a deeper and sweeter joy in all those things that once would have pleased their self-interests only; these joys do not disappear once we are focused on God, but instead their pleasures are heightened. But false people approach pleasure from the other direction: as it affects themselves first, and only then as it may be related to God.

True saints center their attention on Christ, and His beauty transcends all others; His delight is the source of all other delight; He in Himself is the best among ten thousand and altogether lovely. These saints delight in the way of salvation through Christ, because it demonstrates God's perfection and wonder; they enjoy holiness, wholeness, while they take no pleasure in sin; God's love is a sweet taste in their mouths, regardless of whether their own interests are met or not. They rejoice over all that Christ has done for them, but that is not the deepest root of their joy. No, they delight merely because God is God, and only then does their delight spill over onto all God's works, including their own salvation.

But what is secondary to true saints is primary to the false saints. True saints build a superstructure of human pleasures upon a foundation of divine love, but hypocrites try to turn the building upside down, making the proper foundation—divine love—the superstructure, and the superstructure—human pleasure—the foundation. When they hear about the wonderful things of the gospel, of God's great love in sending His Son, of Christ's dying love for sinners, and all the great things Christ has promised the saints, they may feel a great deal of pleasure; their emotions may be elevated by all they have heard, but if you were to examine their joy, you would find that they are interested in Christ's works only so far as they relate to themselves. They love to hear about Christ's great love, because it feeds their self-love and even their pride, for they assume that somehow Christ's favor will lift them above those around them. When they are so full of arrogant self-confidence, so pleased to think that God and Christ approve of them, no wonder that they enjoy hearing doctrine like this. In other words, their joy focuses only on themselves and not on God.

The joy of false people is found only in themselves; anything that gives them pleasure allows their attention to always remain firmly on themselves. When they believe they have received revelations or spiritual experiences, their minds are absorbed by them as they admire their own experience. What fascinates them so is not the glory of God or the beauty of Christ, but the beauty of their own experiences. They can never forget about themselves; they keep thinking, "What a good experience is this! What a great revelation this is! What wonderful things I have found!" And so they put their experiences in the place where Christ and His beauty and fullness should be. Instead of nourishing themselves on something beyond their own lives—the innate, sweet refreshment of the gospel—they are absorbed totally by their own lives, and all the nourishment they take in only feeds their own selfishness. If they catch a glimpse of the wonder of the gospel, their vision is distant—or else they see it sideways, with their peripheral vision. They are more pleased by the revelation itself than by that which their experience should have revealed: Christ Himself. Instead of building their lives on reality, these people rise higher and higher in their own minds, creating a structure that is built totally from imagination, self-love, and pride. In the end, they are dwelling in a castle in the air, rather than a true home.

The way these people talk is just as empty as the thoughts that consume their inner lives, for "out of the abundance of their heart their mouth speaketh." Their emotions all center on their own wonderful experiences, and so does their conversation. True saints, when they are greatly moved, their hearts full, are apt to talk a great deal about God and His glory, the beauty and pleasure of Christ, and the gospel's wonder. Hypocrites, on the other hand, when they are feeling emotional, will be more likely to talk about the revelation experience, rather than the thing it revealed. All of their talk centers on themselves; they will mention how blessed they are, how much God loves them, how sure they are of their own salvation, and so on.

True saints find themselves to become almost invisible when they are looking on the loveliness of Christ. If they found themselves getting in the way of their view, they would be frustrated, for looking at themselves would seem like a waste of time compared to the wonder and glory of Christ.

And just as all false love and selfish joy rises from the root of self-love, so do all the other emotions—the hypocrite's sorrow for sin, her humiliation and submission, her religious desires and zeal. Everything is paid for ahead of time by God's gratification of her self-love. When all her selfish cravings are being satisfied, at least in her imagination, no wonder she loves the imaginary God she has created! He suits her so well, that she easily worships Him and submits to Him; she may even be fierce and zealous in His defense.

Fervent spiritual feeling is often built on the supposition of being a prominent saint. If the high opinion that the person has of himself were taken away, if he suddenly realized he was not the great saint he had always supposed, his emotions would immediately drop to the ground. If he only caught a glimpse of his own selfish ugliness, the deformity that hides in the midst of even his best works and noblest emotions, that glimpse would knock his emotions on the head. With this sort of people, their emotions are built totally upon self, and therefore, self-knowledge would destroy them emotionally. But for those who experience truly grace-filled heart experiences, their emotions rest somewhere else. Their deepest root is no longer buried deep within themselves, but rather it draws upon God's life; so if they catch sight of their own flaws and imperfections, the vision will only purify their feelings that much more. They will not be destroyed, however, for their life comes from God and Jesus Christ; if anything Christ will look that much sweeter to them as they become more aware of their dependence on Him.

III. Truly spiritual heart feelings are built on the delight God gives because of His moral excellence.

In other words, the love of divine things because their

moral excellence makes them beautiful and sweet is the source of all holy feeling.

But let me explain what I mean by moral excellence.

I am not speaking here of the ordinary concept of morality, where moral behavior is assumed to consist of an external conformity to society's duties. These duties include such things as honesty, justice, generosity, good nature, and public spirit, but these are all natural human qualities. I am speaking here of internal virtues, like faith, love, humility, and a perspective that is heaven-directed rather than self-directed. So let me repeat, I am not talking about a morality that is merely external.

Theologians often distinguish between moral good and evil and natural good and evil. By moral evil they mean the evil of sin, or that which is contrary to what is right; things ought to be a certain way, according to God's design, but evil twists them away from this. But when theologians speak of natural evil, they do not mean the sort of evil that is opposed to what is good, but that which is contrary to mere nature, without any respect for duty's rules. Suffering is an example of a natural evil, and so are all kinds of pain and torment, disgrace, and the like; these things are contrary to mere nature, hateful to wicked people and devils as well as to good people and angels. In the same way, a birth defect might be called a natural evil, but not a moral evil, for the harm caused by such an event has nothing to do with sin. In the same way, natural good involves no moral choice; it simply occurs in our world according to the natural conditions of things.

Using these definitions, pleasure is a natural good; so is honor, so is strength, so is intellectual knowledge, human learning, and policy. Clearly then, there is a difference between humanity's natural goodness and their moral goodness, just as there is for the angels in heaven. Angels have great intellectual powers, great strength, and authority; that is why they are called thrones, dominions, principalities, and powers. But this is the natural goodness they possess. Their moral goodness, however, rests on their perfect and glorious completion and goodness, their pure and flaming love for God and to the saints and each another. In the same way, theologians make a distinction between the natural and moral goodness of God; when they speak of God's moral perfection, they refer to those attributes that God exercises as a moral agent, those things that demonstrate that the heart and will of God are good, right, and infinitely lovely—His righteousness, His truth, His faithfulness, or, in a word, His holiness. When theologians refer to God's natural perfection, though, they are speaking of His omnipotence, His omniscience, His infinite existence, from everlasting to everlasting, His omnipresence, and His awesome majesty.

The moral excellence of an intelligent free agent is seated in the heart or will. An intelligent being whose will is truly pure and lovely is morally good or excellent. This moral excellence, when it is true and real and not merely external or counterfeit, is holiness. Holiness comprehends all the true moral excellence of intelligent beings: There is no other true virtue besides genuine holiness. Holiness includes all the true human virtues: love for God and others, justice, charity, humility, gentleness. All of them are part of one whole, the completeness God gives us in Him: true holiness. Some may not understand God's holiness in these terms, but this is the common, if not universal, definition of holiness within the Bible. God's holiness includes all His other moral perfections—His righteousness, faithfulness, and goodness. In the same way, for human beings, love, kindness, and mercy are all included in a person's complete holiness. Human holiness is the image of God's holiness; we cannot possibly possess more virtues than what exists in the original. The grace God puts in our hearts cannot be greater than the source of that grace.

Just as God possesses both kinds of goodness, both moral and natural, His holiness and His omnipotence, so humanity possesses God's twofold image—His moral or spiritual image, which is His holiness, God's moral excellence (the image that was lost to humanity at the Fall), and God's natural image, which is reflected in humanity's reason and intellectual abilities, strength, and dominion over the earth.

By now I hope you can understand what I mean when I say that when we love divine things for the beauty of their moral excellence, that is the beginning and source of all holy emotions and love. We have already demonstrated that the primary objective basis for spiritual emotion is the beauty of divine things simply in and of themselves. It follows, then, that we love God simply for His moral excellence, His holiness. This does not mean that we do not love God's natural attributes as well; we delight in every divine quality. The infinite greatness, power, knowledge, and awesome majesty of God all fill us with wonder and joy. But God's holiness is what is essential to our love. This is where true love for God begins; all other spiritual love flows from this source.

Moral excellence or holiness is essential to the true beauty and loveliness of all intelligent beings. That is what makes the angels lovely; without it, despite all their natural perfections, their strength, and their knowledge, they would be as ugly as the devils. Moral excellence alone, in and of itself, is what gives intelligent life its loveliness. Strength and knowledge do not make beings lovely if they lack holiness; if anything, power without love makes a being hateful and hideous, though strength finds its full beauty when it is combined with holiness. That is why the angels are so glorious, for their strength and knowledge have been consecrated by their moral perfection. On the other hand, the devils are more hideous and horrible because their strength and intelligence lacks love.

That is why, if we think of God in these terms, we see that His holiness is what makes Him so utterly lovely. The psalmist speaks of the "beauty of holiness" (Ps. 29:2; 96:9; 110:3), and it is this quality that renders all His other attributes glorious and lovely. God's wisdom is glorious because it is a holy wisdom, not a wicked craftiness. His majesty is lovely, because it too is holy, not merely dreadful and horrible. God's unchanging nature is holy too; otherwise it would be inflexible obstinate wickedness.

Consequently, our vision of God's loveliness must begin here. If we truly love God, we must begin with a delight in His holiness, and not with a delight in any other attribute of His, for no other attribute is truly lovely without His holiness. We cannot even clearly see His other attributes if we have not grasped the real meaning of His holiness; we will not be able to grasp their true quality if we try to see them divorced from holiness. People who are blind to the glory of God's holiness cannot see anything of the true glory of His mercy and grace. They try to break off little pieces of God's nature and apply them to their own lives, seeing where they will best suit their self-interests. In this way, they imagine they love God and His attributes, but their vision is distorted; they have failed to grasp God's holiness, and so they can never truly know Him or love Him.

Just as God's holiness contains all the beauty of the divine nature, so God's holy image in His saints is what makes them beautiful. That is why the angels in heaven are beautiful also; it is what makes them angels and not devils (Dan. 4:13, 17, 23; Matt. 25:31; Mark 8:38; Acts 10:22; Rev. 14:10). Holiness is what makes the Christian religion beautiful, and the Bible's loveliness is contained in its holiness; "Thy word is very pure: therefore thy servant loveth it" (Ps. 119:140); "I esteem all thy precepts concerning all things to be right; and I hate every false way" (Ps. 119:128); "Thy testimonies that thou hast commanded are righteous and very faithful" (Ps. 119:138); "My tongue shall speak of thy word: for all thy commandments are righteousness" (Ps. 119:172); "The law of the LORD is perfect, converting the soul: the testimony of the LORD is sure, making wise the simple. The statutes of the LORD are right, rejoicing the heart: the commandment of the LORD is pure, enlightening the eyes. The fear of the LORD is clean, enduring for ever: the judgments of the LORD are true and righteous altogether. More to be desired are they than gold, yea, than much fine gold: sweeter also than honey and the honeycomb" (Ps. 19:7–10).

The Lord Jesus is filled with a pleasing beauty; He is the

best among ten thousand and altogether lovely, for He is the holy One of God (Acts 3:14), God's holy Child (Acts 4:27), and all that is holy and true (Rev. 3:7). All the spiritual beauty of Christ's human nature—His gentleness, humility, patience, and heavenliness, His love for God and His love for humanity, His willingness to walk with the small and the weak and the poor and His compassion for the miserable — all are summed up in His holiness. And the beauty of His divine nature, that same beauty that shines in His human nature, is also contained in His holiness.

That is why the gospel is so beautiful: It is holy, because it emanates from the holiness of Christ. The gospel's doctrines are filled with spiritual loveliness, because they are holy doctrines, doctrines that reflect the very nature of God. And that is why the way of salvation through Jesus Christ is so beautiful also—because it is so holy. Heaven itself will be glorious because it is a holy city, the holy Jerusalem, the dwelling place of God's holiness and glory (Isa. 52:1). All the beauties of the new Jerusalem, described in the last two chapters of Revelation, are but various representations of this. (See Rev. 21:2, 10–11, 18, 21, 27; 22:1, 3.) The holiness that is to be found in divine things is what feeds truly spiritual emotions and lifts them high.

When I was talking about some of the first ways we could tell if a feeling was spiritual, I observed that those of us who have been brought back to life by Christ have a new supernatural sense, a sort of spiritual taste. It is as different from our other mental perceptions as tasting is different from any of the other five senses, and the things it perceives could never be experienced any other way. Now the beauty of holiness is that which is perceived by this spiritual sense, and this is the thing that natural human beings can never really understand. Our new spiritual sense was designed to perceive this kind of beauty; this is the sweetness for which our spiritual taste was intended. Scripture often speaks of the beauty and sweetness of holiness in terms of tasting and appetite: "I have meat to eat that ye know not of. . . . My meat is to do the will of him that sent me, and to finish his work" (John 4:32, 34); "The law of the LORD is perfect, . . . the statutes of the LORD are right, rejoicing the heart: the commandment of the LORD is pure, . . .the fear of the LORD is clean, . . .the judgments of the LORD are true and righteous altogether. More to be desired are they than gold, yea, than much fine gold: sweeter also than honey and the honeycomb" (Ps. 19:7–10).

A holy love has a holy object. A holy nature must love that which is holy. A sinful nature is contrary to holiness, however, for the two qualities, sinfulness and holiness, lack a common ground on which to stand. The mind that centers only on itself is the enemy of God, and it works against the law of God and the people of God. The nature of holiness is to love holiness, but the nature of selfishness is to hate holiness, for holiness is made of an unconditional love that crosses out the self.

The holy nature of the saints and angels in heaven (where holiness has its full power) is focused on the holiness of divine things. This is the divine beauty that engages the attention, admiration, and praise of the bright and burning seraphim: "One cried unto another, and said, Holy, holy, holy, is the LORD of hosts: the whole earth is full of his glory" (Isa. 6:3); "They rest not day and night, saying, Holy, holy, holy, Lord God Almighty, which was, and is, and is to come" (Rev. 4:8); "Who shall not fear thee, O Lord, and glorify thy name? for thou only art holy" (Rev. 15:4).

The Bible tells us that the saints on earth adore God for this same reason, admiring and praising all God's attributes as deriving from the loveliness of His holiness. Thus when they praise God for His power, His holiness is the beauty that draws their hearts: "O sing unto the LORD a new song; for he hath done marvellous things: his right hand, and his holy arm, hath gotten him the victory" (Ps. 98:1); "The LORD is great in Zion; and he is high above all the people. Let them praise thy great and terrible name; for it is holy" (Ps. 99:2–3); "Exalt ye the LORD our God, and worship at his footstool; for he is holy" (Ps. 99:5); "Thou wast a God that forgavest them, though thou tookest vengeance of their inventions. Exalt the LORD our God, and worship at his holy hill; for the LORD our God is holy" (Ps. 99:8–9). When they praise God for His mercy and faithfulness, again their praise centers on His holiness: "Light is sown for the righteous, and gladness for the upright in heart. Rejoice in the LORD, ye righteous; and give thanks at the remembrance of his holiness" (Ps. 97:11–12); "There is none holy as the LORD: for there is none beside thee: neither is there any rock like our God" (1 Sam. 2:2).

This is one way we can prove the true nature of our emotions, particularly our love and joy. Various kinds of creatures indicate the differences in their natures by demonstrating the various sorts of things to which they are attracted; what one naturally craves another may abhor. The same is true with true saints and natural humanity: Natural humans have no taste for holiness; in fact, they are completely blind to it. But the saints, by the mighty power of God, can perceive holiness all around them, for they have been given a supernatural sense that reveals to them the truth. As a result, the saint places all her happiness here, and she looks to holiness as her only solace and entertainment in this world, and her full satisfaction and blessedness in the world to come. This is the way you examine your love for God, and for Jesus Christ, and for the Word of God, and your joy in them, as well as your love for the people of God. If you look at these things with a set of expectations in your mind, focusing on them only in relation to yourself, then you will not experience any of the holy relish I have been describing.

Even the devils may have a great awareness of God's natural attributes, His mighty power, and awful majesty; and so may natural human beings, but they lack a spiritual knowledge of God, and they are blind to the sweetness of His moral excellence. The Bible speaks often of evil people perceiving God's natural power: "And they shall know that I am the Lord" (Exod. 29:46); "As truly as I live, all the earth shall be filled with the glory of the LORD" (Num. 14:21). But when the saints and angels behold God's glory, the beauty of His holiness, the sight melts and humbles their hearts, weaning them from the world, drawing them to God, and transforming them. The vision of God's awful greatness may overpower human strength, it may be more than any human being can endure, but if God's moral beauty is concealed, the human heart will be just as full of hatred as before. No love burns there, and the will remains inflexible. But if we catch so much as a glimpse of the moral and spiritual glory of God shining into our hearts, we are immediately changed.

The sense that natural people may have of God's awesome greatness may affect them in various ways; on the one hand, it may terrify them, but on the other, it may elevate them in their own eyes. This happens when they suppose that God's power will somehow be put at their disposal, increasing their own importance and strength.

Given that this is true, undoubtedly too much stress has been placed on revelations of God's greatness, majesty, and natural perfection. These revelations have lacked any real vision of the *holy* majesty of God. Both the Bible and experience confirm that when this happens, the results are just the opposite of true spirituality. The people affected are far from possessing Christian love and kindness; in other words, this sort of revelation works exactly opposite from truly spiritual revelation.

Of course, a sense of God's greatness and natural attributes is useful and necessary. But if His power is to be clearly seen, it can only be seen in the context of God's complete nature. Natural human beings may catch a glimpse of this, but grace sharpens our perceptions. It allows us to see God's holiness.

IV. The grace-filled feeling of the heart springs from a spiritually enlightened mind.

Holy feeling is not heat without light; it is not emotion without understanding. True "religious affections" are born from intellectual understanding, some spiritual instruction that the mind receives, the light of some actual knowledge. Children of God are affected by grace when they see and understand a little more about divine things than they did before; they have a clearer concept of God and Christ, and of the glorious things shown in the gospel. In some cases, they may receive new light that they have never possessed before; in other words, they may gain a new understanding that they had previously failed to grasp. In other cases, they may have understood a spiritual concept once but then they lost their clear view of it, and now their former knowledge has been renewed; "Every one that loveth, . . .knoweth God" (1 John 4:7); "I pray, that your love may abound yet more and more in knowledge and in all judgment" (Phil. 1:9); "They have a zeal of God, but not according to knowledge" (Rom. 10:2); "The new man, which is renewed in knowledge" (Col. 3:10); "O send out thy light and thy truth: let them lead me; let them bring me unto thy holy hill" (Ps. 43:3); "It is written in the prophets, And they shall be all taught of God. Every man therefore that hath heard, and hath learned of the Father, cometh unto me" (John 6:45). Knowledge is the key that first opens a hard heart, making room for deeper feeling, and so it also opens the way for us to walk into the kingdom of heaven; "Ye have taken away the key of knowledge" (Luke 11:52).

Many emotional experiences, however, do not come from any intellectual light. These sort of feelings are clearly not spiritual, no matter how deep and fervent they are. In fact, though, even these false emotional experiences are based on some mental activity, for human nature insists that we cannot be moved emotionally by something that our mind has not conceived. False feeling, however, is based on mental concepts that are also false; they lack any true insight into reality. For instance, a person may be suddenly moved by an exciting idea, some shape or beautiful pleasant form or some shining light; these are external images, but the mind can shape them easily. However, these images do not instruct us or make us wiser; they do not show us more of God, or of the Mediator between God and humanity, or the way of salvation through Christ, or anything else that is contained in any of the gospel's doctrines. These ideas about external things give us no deeper acquaintance with God, nor any greater understanding of His Word, of His ways, or His works. Truly spiritual and grace-filled feelings are not inspired by these sort of intellectual concepts; instead, they arise when our understanding is enlightened to grasp spiritual concepts in a new way. Then we will have a new comprehension of God's excellent nature and His wonderful perfection, some new glimpse of Christ in His fullness. The way of salvation through Christ is opened to us in a new manner, and we find we understand spiritual doctrines that once made no sense to us. This sort of intellectual enlightenment is entirely different from the sudden sharp fancies we sometimes experience, visions of shapes and colors, external brightness and glory, or sounds and voices. Spiritual feeling is not inspired by fantasies.

In the same way, Scripture without real understanding cannot move us spiritually. Many people have used the Bible to support their own self-centered emotions, but when Christ made use of Scripture He opened it to His hearers, so that they could truly understand it; "Did not our heart burn within us, while he talked with us by the way, and while he opened to us the scriptures?" (Luke 24:32). All sorts of emotions can be built on false interpretations of Scripture, but if our emotions spring from a mistake or a misunderstanding, than those emotions are empty and pointless. They are based on ignorance rather than enlightenment.

For instance, a person may have all sorts of ideas pop into his head, and these ideas may even contain Scripture; because these thoughts appeared so suddenly, the person assumes the Spirit of God is teaching him. This person is filled with his own importance, and so he is deluded that each thought he thinks is spiritually significant. Another person may mistake a physical sensation for enlightenment. Some sort of natural internal working within her body's parts causes her physical pleasure, and since the body and the soul are united, she thinks she has had a spiritual experience. Our bodies are not generally affected by mental enlightenment, however, and physical pleasure is usually merely the result of good health or a pleasant external sensation. However, through ignorance, this person, surprised by her own high spirits, thinks that surely the Holy Ghost has come into her. As a result, she becomes emotionally moved, feeling first great joy and then many other feelings, until her mind and body are all aflutter.

Our emotions may also be excited by some instruction or mental understanding that merely pertains to natural human learning, and these feelings are not truly spiritual either. Human beings study all sorts of things, and gain enlightenment in many areas, but this is merely a natural human undertaking rather than a spiritual one. Philosophers can be greatly moved by their studies, transported beyond themselves with joy, and scholars of mathematics and science may experience the same reaction. We can even study religion in this same way, merely as an intellectual exercise, but our hearts remain untouched, for all that we may be emotionally moved. I am not saying that God's Spirit is not present in these sort of intellectual endeavors, but He works with human faculties on a natural level rather than a supernatural one. The feeling that comes from these studies are not spiritual.

Only when we are spiritual can we understand spiritual things. Paul speaks of this kind of spiritual discernment and comprehension in 1 Corinthians 2:14: "But the natural man receiveth not the things of the Spirit of God: for they are foolishness unto him: neither can he know them, because they are spiritually discerned." John refers to the same thing in 1 John 3:6: "Whosoever sinneth hath not seen him, neither known him." Again in 3 John 11: "He that doeth evil hath not seen God." The Gospel of John contains references to the same concept: "This is the will of him that sent me, that every one which seeth the Son, and believeth on him, may have everlasting life" (6:40); "The world seeth me no more; but ye see me" (14:19); "This is life eternal, that they might know thee the only true God, and Jesus Christ, whom thou hast sent" (17:3). The rest of the Bible has many verses that speak on the same subject: "No man knoweth the Son, but the Father; neither knoweth any man the Father, save the Son, and he to whomsoever the Son will reveal him" (Matt. 11:27); "He that seeth me seeth him that sent me" (John 12:45); "They that know thy name will put their trust in thee" (Ps. 9:10); "I count all things but loss for the excellency of the knowledge of Christ Jesus my Lord" (Phil. 3:8); "That I may know him" (Phil. 3:10). All over the Bible we find further proof that the understanding of spiritual things is different from natural understanding. "We. . .do not cease to pray for you, and to desire that ye might be filled with the knowledge of his will in all wisdom and spiritual understanding" (Col. 1:9).

From all that we've said so far we should be able to infer the nature of this spiritual understanding. Clearly, this perception is different from any faculty that natural humanity possesses; in other words, it is an entirely new faculty that human beings in their natural state lack. I've given numerous examples of this already. And I have also shown already that this new spiritual sense is given to the saints when Christ brings them back to life—and I have shown that the object of this spiritual faculty, the thing it is designed to perceive, is the excellence of divine things, in and of themselves, regardless of their benefits to the self.

All of this is consistent with what the Bible teaches. For example, Paul makes clear that the marvelous thing that is revealed by spiritual light, the wonder that is understood by spiritual knowledge, is the glory of divine things: "But if our gospel be hid, it is hid to them that are lost: in whom the god of this world hath blinded the minds of them that believe not, lest the light of the glorious gospel of Christ, who is the image of God, should shine unto them" (2 Cor. 4:3–4); "For God, who commanded the light to shine out of darkness, hath shined in our hearts, to give the light of the knowledge of the glory of God in the face of Jesus Christ" (2 Cor. 4:6); "But we all, with open face beholding as in a glass the glory of the Lord, are changed into the same image from glory to glory, even as by the Spirit of the Lord" (2 Cor. 3:18).

Scripture plainly teaches that all true religion can be

summed up as the love of divine things. Therefore, the kind of understanding or knowledge that is an appropriate foundation for true religion must be knowledge of the loveliness of divine things. Without a doubt, the knowledge that is the proper foundation of love is the knowledge of loveliness. In the last section, we already discussed that spiritual loveliness comes from a divine moral perfection—or holiness—and with this in mind, we can see better the nature of spiritual understanding; it can be nothing else except the ability to see God's holiness. Any other kind of knowledge would be accessible to both evil people and devils; only this is unique to children of God.

Having said all this, we come to a definition of spiritual understanding: "a heartfelt sense of the supreme beauty and sweetness of God's holiness, the moral perfection of divine things, and the discernment and knowledge that flows from this vital and living sense." Spiritual understanding is rooted in the heart; it is a heart-sense that perceives spiritual beauty. I say a heart-sense because mere intellectual speculation is different from this kind of understanding. No clear distinction can be drawn between the understanding and the heart, because these two faculties do not act separately here. When the mind perceives something that is sweet and pleasing, than this delightful, lovely thing is also felt on an emotional level.

I want to underline the fact that the mind can have an intellectual understanding that is merely a speculative exercise, mental gymnastics rather than a perception of the heart. When the heart senses what the mind understands, we do not merely look at something from the outside in, but we experience it from deep within our being as well.

For instance, our knowledge of sweetness or nausea, friendliness or hatred, is a very different sort of understanding than our knowledge of the definition of a triangle or a square. The latter is merely intellectual knowledge, but the other is knowledge based upon the senses, rooted in experience. The heart perceives spiritual light, because it feels it; it actually experiences it, even as it is instructed by it intellectually.

Paul also seems to make a distinction between mere intellectual religious knowledge and spiritual knowledge. The former he calls the "form of knowledge and of the truth" (Rom. 2:20), "Which hast the form of knowledge and of the truth in the law." The latter, spiritual understanding, the Bible often refers to as relishing, smelling, or tasting: "Now thanks be unto God, which always causeth us to triumph in Christ, and maketh manifest the savour of his knowledge by us in every place" (2 Cor. 2:14); "Thou savourest not the things that be of God, but those that be of men" (Matt. 16:23); "As newborn babes, desire the sincere milk of the word, that ye may grow thereby: if so be ye have tasted that the Lord is gracious" (1 Pet. 2:2–3); "Because of the savour of thy good ointments thy name is as ointment poured forth, therefore do the virgins love thee" (Song of Sol. 1:3); "But ye have an unction from the Holy One, and ye know all things" (1 John 2:20).

When our souls discover the true beauty and sweetness of holiness, it opens a new world to our view. Suddenly, we can see the glory of all God's perfections; we realize how everything is related to the divine Being, for, as I have observed before, all beauty in the world rises from God's holiness. We see the glory of all God's works, both in creation and in His revelations to humanity. Holiness, complete and utter perfection, is the end of all God's works, but only as we see it in relation to God can we truly grasp this holiness. For instance, through seeing Christ we become aware of how precious His life and blood are; we realize that He is everything needed to heal the world's sin, and that is why His life and blood are so precious. He would not be sufficient for the world's sin were He not obedient to love, nor could He intercede for us in our weakness. But the first step is our vision of holiness, and when we start there, God's moral perfection shines forth in each of salvation's steps from beginning to end.

This process also works in our comprehension of divine matters as much as it does in our direct relationship with God. For instance, our perception of the excellence of God's Word works the same way. If you were to take away all the moral beauty and sweetness in the Word, the Bible would be left as merely dead letters, a dry, lifeless, tasteless thing. We see our duty by this same light, for when we grasp God's holy worthiness, then we naturally respond by wanting to love Him and submit to His will. Submission that was not built on spiritual light would be slavery, a destructive tyranny, but when we comprehend God's holiness, then our spiritual duties become joyful and sweet. And our spiritual understanding enables us also to see the true evil of sin, for if we see the beauty of holiness, it follows that we will also see the ugliness of sin, for sin is the opposite of holiness.

If we can perceive the beauty of holiness, then we are seeing the thing most essential to the world. It is the fullness of all things, the created world's deepest principle;

without it, the world would be empty and meaningless, nothing at all, even worse than nothing. Unless we see this, we see nothing that is worth seeing, for all other excellence or beauty is illusion. Unless we can understand this, all other learning merely wastes the intellect God gave us. This is the beauty of the Godhead, the divinity of Divinity, the good of the infinite Fountain of good; without it, God Himself would be an infinite evil (if that were possible); without it, we ourselves would be better off to have never existed; and without it, all reality would be better to have no being.

If we do not have this spiritual light, then in effect we have no knowledge at all; our knowledge is only a shadow of knowledge, "the form of knowledge," as Paul calls it. That is why Scripture speaks of those who lack this spiritual sense as being totally blind, deaf, and senseless—dead, in fact. That is why Christ brings us back to life, opening our blind eyes as He brings us into a new world. Once this has happened to us, nothing looks the way it did before; "after the flesh, yet now henceforth know we him no more; . . .[and] he is a new creature: old things are passed away; behold, all things are become new" (2 Cor. 5:16–17).

Besides all the things I have already mentioned, from this sense of spiritual beauty springs all true experiential religious knowledge, which is in itself a whole new world of knowledge. If we are blind to the beauty of holiness, we cannot understand anything about God's grace; we are ignorant of His greatest works; nor can we understand the nature of God's saints. In effect, we will be ignorant of the entire spiritual world.

Once God has implanted this new perception in our

hearts, however, our very identities will be changed. Imagine how different life would be for a blind person who could suddenly see! The reason that we do not often realize the remarkable transformation that takes place in the human heart is because in most cases this new spiritual sense is given gradually, a little at a time. Otherwise, our conversion experience would be like a blind person whose eyes were suddenly and completely opened to glaring sunlight. If this person would be transformed by the experience, think how greater is the change wrought by the opening of a sense that is deeper and more essential than any of our physical senses.

This spiritual understanding is the source of all spiritual feelings, and by it they should be proved. Fallen human nature alone can never produce this sort of light and perception, though God may make use of human faculties. For instance, He may use our consciences, our human sense of what is right and wrong, to convict us of sin, but nevertheless, our perception of sin's ugliness will be more shallow, not as complete, as if we had a truly spiritual understanding. In the same way, fallen human nature may perceive the sweetness and beauty of the gospel story; after all, who would not be pleased to hear that God loves human beings or that He has prepared eternity for them? All this love for Christian virtue, however, is based on no higher principle than concern for human welfare. The gospel looks good the same way silver and gold look good to a merchant, or the way black soil looks beautiful to a farmer's eyes.

From what we have said so far, clearly spiritual understanding is not the same thing as doctrinal knowledge, neither is it some new doctrine created fresh in our imagination, nor is it some new interpretation of Scripture.

This would be merely intellectual knowledge, mental activity rather than spiritual. Therefore, spiritual understanding can-not mean that we should open our minds to some mystical interpretation of the Bible, for this is merely a more complete mental comprehension of theology.

For instance, if a religious leader explains what is meant by the stony ground and the seeds springing up suddenly and quickly withering away, he is only explaining the doctrinal content of the allegory. Or if another spiritual leader explains what Jacob's ladder symbolizes and the angels of God ascending and descending on it, or what was meant by Joshua's leading Israel through Jordan, she is only digging out the meaning already hid in these passages. Many people can analyze the Bible this way, and they do not all necessarily have spiritual knowledge. In fact, a person could know how to interpret all the symbols, parables, enigmas, and allegories in the Bible, and still not have one beam of spiritual light. If we do not perceive that all these things demonstrate God's holiness, His unconditional love and goodness, then we will be blind to the glory contained in these stories.

Understanding the world's mysteries will not save our souls. "And though I have the gift of prophecy, and understand all mysteries, and all knowledge; . . .and have not charity, I am nothing" (1 Cor. 13:2). Therefore, people who pride themselves on their religious understanding, resting their confidence on the fact that they are great biblical scholars, are deluding themselves. They may be emotionally excited by their studies, but their feelings are empty. This is not the source of spiritual "affections."

In the same way, I doubt that people are informed of

their duty by having it directly suggested to their minds that they should perform such and such external actions or deeds in order to fulfill God's will. If we believe that God *does* tell us His will in this way, by direct mental directions, then nevertheless, these directions are not the same as spiritual light. This kind of knowledge would only be another kind of doctrinal knowledge. This particular instance of God's will would be a religious doctrine just as much as the more general doctrines about God's nature or work. If we receive a doctrine through some direct mental perception, rather than through the more ordinary means of speech or reading, then this is still very different from the sort of deep awareness of God's holiness and beauty that I have been discussing. Remember Balaam? He obviously lacked spiritual light—but God whispered His will directly into Balaam's mental ear from time to time, telling him the way he should go and what he should do and say. Therefore, being led and directed in this manner is not the same as the holy and spiritual leading of God's Spirit, for this is something that only the saints experience. It is the distinguishing mark of God's children; "For as many as are led by the Spirit of God, they are the sons of God" (Rom. 8:14); "But if ye be led of the Spirit, ye are not under the law" (Gal. 5:18).

Receiving instruction from a text of Scripture, even if it comes suddenly and extraordinarily to our minds, does not mean that we have spiritual light. God *may* direct us this way (though I suspect that often we are deluded, as I have already discussed), but this is still quite different from true spiritual insight. For instance, if a person in New England was considering traveling to some foreign land, where he would be likely to experience much hardship and danger, he might pray that God would show him what he should do. After earnest prayer, the words God spoke to Jacob might leap into his mind, as if they were spoken directly to him: "Fear not to go down into Egypt; . . .for. . . I will go down with thee into Egypt; and I will also surely bring thee up again" (Gen. 46:3–4.) Clearly, within the context of the Bible, these words relate only to Jacob and his behavior, and yet this person assumes that God has a deeper meaning hidden there only for him. Accordingly, he understand the verses in a new sense, deciding that by Egypt he should understand the particular country he has in his mind, and that the action God wants is for him to go there, and that God is assuring him that He will bring him safely back home. This is not a spiritual leading, however, for it demonstrates none of the spiritual insight that we have been discussing.

To spiritually understand Scripture means we correctly understand the Scripture's objective content; it does not mean that we create some new meaning for it. Spiritual enlightenment allows us to see what we would have otherwise been blind to—but in this case, no one could see this obscure new meaning, blind or not, for it was never there before this man's circumstances occurred. The spiritual enlightenment of which the Bible speaks means that our eyes are opened to what has always been there; "Open thou mine eyes, that I may behold wondrous things out of thy law" (Ps. 119:18). This verse implies that the meaning was there all along, but that the psalmist's eyes were shut; the psalmist does not indicate that he hopes to discover some new meaning that never existed prior to his prayer.

When we create a new meaning for the Scripture, it is the same as if we were making a new Scripture; it is adding to the Word, which the Bible warns us not to do. True spiritual enlightenment does not discover private meanings hidden in the Bible; it does, however, perceive the sweet, bright revelation of Christ and the excellence of salvation. Real spiritual enlightenment enables us to understand that Christ is the sum of our hearts' need, and spiritual light shines on the Bible's promises, making them glow with meaning. All this was always in the Bible; there are no new meanings meant for individual persons.

When the Spirit leads us, He does two things: First, He shows us our duty, and second, He helps us to follow His instruction. His instruction, however, is accomplished in a general way rather than a specific one. He helps us to be guided by the spiritual perception that allows us to see what is true moral beauty. As I have already shown, spiritual knowledge is mainly a taste for the beauty of that which is truly good and holy. This sense of the holy discerns be-tween good and evil, between holy and unholy, without being dependent on a mental train of reasoning, just as a person can look at a beautiful physical object and know that it is beautiful without working it out intellectually; she does not need to work out the formulas for proportion and balance and perfection of features, for she has an eye for beauty and can recognize it at a glance. In the same way someone with a musical ear knows when he hears true harmony; he does not need to analyze the piece mathematically. Someone who has a healthy palate knows what is good food as soon as she tastes it, without depending on a nutritionist to tell her. In the same way, then, words and actions have a holy beauty and sweetness that can be perceived by a spiritual heart the same way our human eyes can discern beauty or our ears hear harmony or our mouths taste sweetness; "Doth not the ear try words? and the mouth taste his meat?" (Job 12:11).

When a sweet and holy action is suggested to a saint's thoughts, if he is actively using his spiritual taste, he will at once see the beauty in this action—and so he is inclined to do this thing. On the other hand, if an unloving action occurs to this person, his spiritual eye sees no beauty in it and is not pleased with it; the spiritual heart tastes no sweetness in it, but instead finds it nauseous. A healthy spiritual taste and appetite will naturally lead us to spiritual loving actions, just as a healthy physical taste and appetite will lead us to nutritious food. This is the way we are led by the Spirit, instructed and led by our spiritual, healthy tastes, which are now an essential part of our hearts' being. When we actively live in grace, we can thus easily distinguish between good and evil, knowing at once what is the loving way to act toward God and others. Our spiritual perception spontaneously judges what is right, without laborious intellectual deductions and arguments; all we need is to see beauty and taste goodness.

That is why Christ blamed the Pharisees for being unable in their own hearts to judge what was right, depending instead on external miracles for proof (Luke 12:57). Paul also seems to have been talking about this way of judging spiritual beauty in Romans 12:2: "Be ye transformed by the renewing of your mind, that ye may prove what is that good, and acceptable, and perfect, will of God."

We know what the phrase "good taste" means when

it comes to natural beauty: It means using appropriate words, dressing with style, possessing graceful manners, appreciating artistic beauty. A philosopher wrote this about good taste:

"To have a taste, is to give things their real value, to be touched with the good, to be shocked with the ill; not to be dazzled with false luster, but in spite of all colors, and everything that might deceive or amuse, to judge soundly. Taste and judgment, then, should be the same thing; and yet it is easy to discern a difference. The judgment forms its opinions from reflection: The reason on this occasion fetches a kind of circuit, to arrive at its end; it supposes principles, it draws consequences, and it judges; but not without a thorough knowledge of the case; so that after it has pronounced, it is ready to render a reason of its decrees. Good taste observes none of these formalities; before it has time to consult, it has chosen its side; as soon as the object is presented, the impression is made, the sentiment formed. As the ear is wounded with a harsh sound, as the smell is soothed with an agreeable odor, before reason has meddled with those objects to judge them, so taste opens itself at once, and prevents all reflection. Reason may come afterward to confirm taste, justifying the secret reasons for its conduct; but reason will not know them all, and no matter how it tries, it cannot discover what made taste think as it did. Judgment takes time, but taste, with one glance of

> the eye, reveals to us the nature and relations of
> things in a moment."

This philosopher is speaking of natural taste, a perception that reveals the quality of external reality, but there is also such a thing as a divine taste. It is given by the Spirit of God, and He keeps it alive in the hearts of the saints, so that they are led to discern spiritual reality and the holy beauty of certain actions. The more of God's Spirit that they possess, the more easily, quickly, and accurately will they be guided. That is the way that "the sons of God are led by the Spirit of God" (see Rom. 8:14). This spiritual taste works far more effectively than any human faculty when it comes to judging right and wrong.

Some people are habitually and naturally inclined to follow the path of love. For instance, a good-natured man knows how to be kind to others, and his good nature is what makes his words and actions so kind; a grumpy person could have far better intellectual reasons for behaving kindly, but she would still not treat others as well as this naturally pleasant man. The same sort of thing applies when people are good friends; the long habits of kindness and intimacy will induce them to treat each other far more sweetly and kindly than they would a stranger, even if they had strong rational reasons for treating the stranger well. You might say that friends have a spirit within them that guides their behavior, even when they are normally unkind people. Their mental habits give them a sense of what sort of behavior is appropriate to a friendship; they do not need to spend hours figuring out just how they should act toward each other, for something inside them tells them instantly.

To use another example, if you drop a stone, in an instant it will show you the way to the center of the earth far more directly than the fastest mathematician could determine by her most accurate observations in a whole day. A spiritual sense of taste teaches us in the same way, showing us instantly and directly the way we should behave in the world. As God's children, we do not require tremendous intellects for figuring out how God wants us to behave; the simplest minds are taught by God's Spirit to be humble, gentle, and loving far more effectively than the most intelligent person in the world could learn through reason and study. As we love God, as we feel awe and reverence for Him, as we trust Him as His children, our hearts will be filled with heaven, and we will know how we should behave.

An evil person would find it very hard to truly act like a Christian, for he lacks any real sense of love and holiness. He cannot understand the life and beauty and heavenly sweetness of holy, humble, Christ-like behavior; he can't figure out how to put on the costume—and even if he could, he'd find it didn't fit him.

Scripture gives us abundant proof of this truth: "A wise man's heart is at his right hand; but a fool's heart at his left. Yea also, when he that is a fool walketh by the way, his wisdom faileth him, and he saith to every one that he is a fool" (Eccl. 10:2–3); "The labour of the foolish wearieth every one of them, because he knoweth not how to go to the city" (Eccl. 10:15); "The lips of the righteous know what is acceptable" (Prov. 10:32); "The tongue of the wise useth knowledge aright: but the mouth of fools poureth out foolishness" (Prov. 15:2); "The heart of the wise teacheth his mouth, and addeth learning to his lips" (Prov. 16:23).

As God's children we judge all our actions using this spiritual taste for what is right and loving, but we do not have a rule book to which we can turn. The Bible does not give us express guidelines for each situation we encounter. However, our spiritual perception is subject in general to the rules spelled out in Scripture; we need to make sure that our spiritual sense is working properly by testing it against the Bible. In the same way, a healthy person can judge food simply by its taste, without needing to examine each morsel for nutritional content—but her tastes must be evaluated by basic nutritional rules, to be sure that the food she desires is truly healthy.

But given that we must evaluate our hearts in light of Scripture, our spiritual taste will help us to decipher God's Word more accurately; it will help us decide just what the Bible's rules really mean, for when we are filled with God's Spirit, we no longer judge everything from a selfish perspective. Our perceptions that for so long were skewed and warped by self, now accurately see the Bible's reality and truth. Now we are in harmony with the Word's message, and so its true meaning comes more naturally into our minds. In fact, this harmony tends to bring verses to our minds at appropriate occasions; just as the stomach's momentary condition may make us think of some particular meat or drink that would most satisfy our hunger. This is the way God's Spirit leads His children, teaching them to evaluate their own behavior and apply the rules of God's holy Word. As the psalmist so often prayed, God "teaches them his statutes, and causes them to understand the way of his precepts."

This sort of spiritual leading is very different from the leading that some people call spiritual. Instead of judging our particular behaviors against the Bible's general rules, these people believe that God's Spirit will suggest new rules directly to our consciousness. These people have no new perception of love and holiness; they do not determine what is the will of God by any sense of taste or enjoyment; they do not judge the nature of a particular action. Instead, they simply follow a rule that they believe God has laid down for their ears alone. This sort of "leading" is as much like true spiritual leading as a glowworm is like a star. Human nature will never experience true spiritual guidance until it has been transformed.

What I have said about the nature of spiritual understanding also reveals the difference between true spiritual understanding and all forms of hysterical enthusiasm. By this, I mean all imaginary visions of God and Christ and heaven, all so-called witnesses of the Spirit by direct inner suggestion, and all impressions of future events, and direct applications of Scripture that contain some new esoteric meaning for the Bible's words. These sort of experiences and revelations usually stir up the emotions, making an uproar in both the soul and body. Many false religions started from just these sort of emotional experiences.

Satan likes to mix his seed with the Spirit's good seed, in hopes that confusion will grow and spread. The greatest danger exists at the times of the greatest spiritual awakening, for that is when Satan will try his hardest. Religious showmanship is glittery and attractive, particularly to simple people. That is why spiritual leaders should always be on their guard, for the devil loves to disguise himself as an angel of light, so people will adore him rather than fear him.

All of Satan's delusions seem to be formed in our imaginations, and people are then carried away by their emotional reactions to these fancies. The imagination is where the devil loves to lurk, the home of all sorts of ugly delusions. As I explained before, the imagination is the faculty we use to shape images of things not actually present; it is a physical faculty rather than a spiritual one.

I doubt that the devil can shape our behavior by any other means than our imagination. We do not know how spirits without bodies communicate with each other, but we do know how we who have bodies communicate: We depend upon our bodies for conveying meaning to each other. Consequently, I suspect that the devil cannot affect us except by communication in some way through our physical beings. Scripture makes clear that he cannot read our hearts, so it follows that the only way he can affect our souls is through our imaginations, by exciting them to produce false images of external reality. He may do this at a purely physical level, inducing physical responses in our bodies that produce all sorts of wild fancies. These physical responses, however, do not affect us intellectually so much as perceptually, for our reason is not influenced by external events and physical impressions as greatly as our imagination is. That is why Satan uses the imagination to tempt and delude us.

Perhaps that is why those who are mentally and emotionally unstable are also most apt to be obviously controlled by Satan's suggestions. These people suffer from a physical illness, one that specifically affects their brains, the seat of their imagination, but their physical weakness gives the devil a greater advantage over them, working through their fancies. Satan casts hideous suggestions into their minds, through no fault of their own, inspiring dreadful imaginary ideas.

We do not need to be mentally ill, however, to be tempted through our imagination. Satan can just as easily present us with some lifelike, alluring image that seems to satisfy all our selfish cravings. He can present twisted images of various circumstances, or inspire us to imagine all sorts of strange messages. These are merely ideas about external reality, but they can lead us into evil thoughts.

We must be on our guard against these sort of fancies; if we're not, we will undoubtedly be subject to them. Some people go even further and intentionally lay themselves open to these kinds of delusions, assuming that they are pursuing an angel of light rather than Satan. They experience many beautiful images and whispered revelations, all of which feed their good opinion of themselves. As they sink deeper into delusion, they continue to have these extraordinary experiences; eventually, they can produce them almost at will, particularly on occasions when they will impress others. Satan is always on hand to feed their minds with the images they crave.

Before I finish talking about the imagination, however, let me make plain that I am not saying that anytime we use our imaginations we are being spiritually deluded. True spiritual perception is accompanied by mental fancies, simply because that is the way we are made: We cannot think deeply about anything without some kind of mental image of external reality popping into our heads. These images are always present when we think, though sometimes they are very confused and hardly seem to pertain to the subject of which we are thinking. The more intensely we ponder something, the more active our imagination will be, and some people are simply more imaginative than others. There is nothing wrong with this.

But there is a big difference between an active imagination that is inspired by deep feelings and deep feelings that are inspired by an active imagination. Undoubtedly, an active imagination is often inspired by spiritual, grace-filled feeling. The feeling is not produced by our fancies, nor does it depend on them; on the contrary, our fancies are merely the coincidental product of our feeling. This is the way human nature operates, even among spiritual people. But when our heart-feeling is built on our imagination rather than any spiritual illumination, then no matter how deep and fervent our emotions are, they are empty and worthless.

Having said that, let me move on to another sign of grace-filled feeling.

V. *True grace-filled emotions are accompanied by reasonable evidence and a spiritual conviction that is based on divine reality.*

This seems to be implied by the text that I used as the foundation for this entire discourse: "Whom having not seen, ye love; in whom, though now ye see him not, yet believing, ye rejoice with joy unspeakable and full of glory" (1 Pet. 1:8).

People who are truly filled with grace have a solid, full, thorough, and active conviction of the gospel's truth. What

I mean by this is that they are no longer frozen between two opinions, pulled equally in both directions. They no longer doubt the gospel's doctrines nor think of them as merely matters of opinion that could easily be argued either way. For them, all this is settled now, and thus they can venture all their being on the truth they know to be real. Their conviction is an active conviction; the gospel's spiritual and invisible mysteries have the same power to influence them as anything else that is real and certain, and thus they govern their entire lives. Their belief in Christ's being the Son of God and the Savior of the world, and their confidence in the things He revealed concerning Himself and His Father and the eternal world are wholehearted and sure. Their eyes have been opened, and they *see* (not merely imagine or surmise) that Jesus really is the Christ, the Son of the living God. Consequently, all that Christ revealed during His life is of infinite importance to these people, and it has power over their hearts and actions.

The Bible makes clear that all true Christians have this kind of conviction in regards to the gospel: " 'But whom say ye that I am?' And Simon Peter answered and said, 'Thou art the Christ, the Son of the living God.' And Jesus answered and said unto him, 'Blessed art thou, Simon Barjona: for flesh and blood hath not revealed it unto thee, but my Father which is in heaven' " (Matt. 16:15–17); "Thou hast the words of eternal life. And we believe and are sure that thou art that Christ, the Son of the living God" (John 6:68–69); "I have manifested thy name unto the men which thou gavest me out of the world. . . . Now they have known that all things whatsoever thou hast given me are of thee. For I have given unto them the words which thou gavest me; and they have received them, and have known surely that I came out from thee, and they have believed that thou didst send me" (John 17:6–8); "If thou believest with all thine heart, thou mayest" (Acts 8:37); "We which live are alway delivered unto death for Jesus' sake. . . . Death worketh in us. . . . We having the same spirit of faith, according as it is written, I believed, and therefore have I spoken; we also believe, and therefore speak; knowing that he which raised up the Lord Jesus, shall raise up us also by Jesus, and shall present us with you" (2 Cor. 4:11–14); "For which cause we faint not" (2 Cor. 4:16); "Therefore we are always confident, knowing that, whilst we are at home in the body, we are absent from the Lord: (For we walk by faith, not by sight:) We are confident, I say, and willing rather to be absent from the body, and to be present with the Lord" (2 Cor. 5:6–8); "For the which cause I also suffer these things: nevertheless I am not ashamed: for I know whom I have believed, and am persuaded that he is able to keep that which I have committed unto him against that day" (2 Tim 1:12); "Whose house are we, if we hold fast the confidence and the rejoicing of the hope firm unto the end" (Heb. 3:6); "Now faith is the substance of things hoped for, the evidence of things not seen" (Heb. 11:1—as well as the entire chapter); "Hereby know we that we dwell in him, and he in us, because he hath given us of his Spirit. And we have seen and do testify that the Father sent the Son to be the Saviour of the world. Whosoever shall confess that Jesus is the Son of God, God dwelleth in him, and he in God. And we have known and believed the love that God hath to us"

(1 John 4:13–16); "For whatsoever is born of God over-cometh the world: and this is the victory that overcometh the world, even our faith. Who is he that overcometh the world, but he that believeth that Jesus is the Son of God?" (1 John 5:4–5).

Obviously, Scripture teaches that those who are truly grace-filled will have an absolute conviction of the gospel's truth.

And yet many "religious affections" are not accompanied by this type of conviction. Many ideas that people have, many of their so-called divine revelations, are moving without being convincing. For a little while the people who experience these things may seem to be more persuaded about Christ than they used to be, and they may act as though their lives have been changed. Many of Christ's listeners also believed for awhile, and yet they lacked a thorough and life-changing conviction. This sort of experience makes no lasting change in people, even though they believe they have had a conversion experience. They are still filled with doubts, just as much as ever, and they do not live as though they were always aware of eternity. If they were aware of it, they would not live as they continue to do. Emotionally they have been moved, but they have not experienced a mental conviction of the truth. As a result, their emotions cannot be depended on; they make a big show, the way dry sticks do when they blaze, but they have no enduring heat. Their roots are too shallow for their faith to live long. These people are chasing phantoms, basing their faith on delusion. As a result, their convictions are too weak to last.

But even if religious feeling does come from a deep conviction that Christianity is true, this feeling is still little better than delusion if conviction is not built on reason. By reason I mean real evidence, legitimate, firsthand grounds for belief. We may have a strong belief that the Christian religion is true, but our belief may not be built on our own evidence, but instead on our background, our education, or the opinions of others. We believe merely because our parents did, and their parents before them, and most people in our country also believe in Christianity, and so we do also. All religions foster this sort of secondhand belief; merely because we believe in Christ rather than another god does not make our hearts any better or any truer.

But even if our Christian faith is based on our own reasoning, rather than our family's or our community's or our education's, still something more is required. Reasoning may be an intellectual exercise only, and if it is, our religious feeling will be false. We must not only believe intellectually; we must also believe spiritually. For instance, Judas, without a doubt, believed Jesus to be the Messiah; his conviction was built on the things he had seen and heard firsthand—yet all along he was a devil, and his conviction did not save him. In John 2:23–25, we read of many who believed in Christ's name when they saw the miracles He did, and yet Christ knew He could not depend on them to be true followers. When Simon the sorcerer saw the miracles and signs that the apostles were doing, he also believed, but his heart was still diseased with bitterness, a slave to selfishness (Acts 8:13, 23). Obviously, we can use our human reason to reach the point where we believe in Christ's claims—and yet our hearts will possess no grace.

Spiritual conviction needs the presence of the Holy Spirit. When He actively lives in our hearts, bringing us back to true life, the conviction and belief that we experience will be far different from normal human opinion. The results of this belief will be different, but the belief itself possesses a different quality too, one that can only be experienced by those who are spiritually alive. Scripture confirms this: "They have believed that thou didst send me" (John 17:8); "According to the faith of God's elect, and the acknowledging of the truth which is after godliness" (Titus 1:1); "The Father himself loveth you, because ye have loved me, and have believed that I came out from God" (John 16:27); "Whosoever shall confess that Jesus is the Son of God, God dwelleth in him, and he in God" (1 John 4:15);. "Whosoever believeth that Jesus is the Christ is born of God" (1 John 5:1); "He that believeth on the Son of God hath the witness in himself" (1 John 5:10).

What we said about spiritual understanding also applies to spiritual conviction. When we believe something spiritually, our judgment grows from the illumination of our understanding; we judge things truly because we have a true grasp on reality; our perceptions are clear and accurate. It follows logically that our conviction that the gospel is true comes from our spiritual perception.

Again, Scripture confirms that a saving belief in the gospel depends on the Spirit of God enlightening our minds, causing us to be able to see the gospel's reality; the Spirit unveils the gospel truth, revealing it to our minds so that we can see it clearly: "I thank thee, O Father, Lord of heaven and earth, that thou hast hid these things from the wise and prudent, and hast revealed them unto babes: even so, Father; for so it seemed good in thy sight. All things are delivered to me of my Father: and no man knoweth who the Son is, but the Father; and who the Father is, but the Son, and he to whom the Son will reveal him" (Luke 10:21–22); "And this is the will of him that sent me, that every one which seeth the Son, and believeth on him, may have everlasting life" (John 6:40); in this passage, true faith is the result of a spiritual sight of Christ. We see the same sort of thing elsewhere in the Bible: "I have manifested thy name unto the men which thou gavest me out of the world. . . . Now they have known that all things whatsoever thou hast given me are of thee. For I have given unto them the words which thou gavest me; and they have received them, and have known surely that I came out from thee, and they have believed that thou didst send me" (John 17:6–8). When Christ showed God's name to the disciples, giving them a true grasp of divine things, that was how they knew that Christ's doctrine was divine and that Christ Himself came from God: "Simon Peter answered and said, 'Thou art the Christ, the Son of the living God.' And Jesus answered and said unto him, 'Blessed art thou, Simon Barjona: for flesh and blood hath not revealed it unto thee, but my Father which is in heaven' " (Matt. 16:16–17); "He that believeth on the Son of God hath the witness in himself" (1 John 5:10); "Being more exceedingly zealous of the traditions of my fathers. But when it pleased God, who separated me from my mother's womb, and called me by his grace, to reveal his Son in me, that I might preach him among the heathen; immediately I conferred not with flesh and blood" (Gal. 1:14–16).

Spiritual conviction comes from spiritual understanding, and spiritual understanding, as I have already shown, comes from spiritual enlightenment—a direct spiritual perception of God's glory and excellence. Scripture makes clear that we must see the gospel's reality before we can truly believe it: "But if our gospel be hid, it is hid to them that are lost: in whom the god of this world hath blinded the minds of them that believe not, lest the light of the glorious gospel of Christ, who is the image of God, should shine unto them. For we preach not ourselves, but Christ Jesus the Lord; and ourselves your servants for Jesus' sake. For God, who commanded the light to shine out of darkness, hath shined in our hearts, to give the light of the knowledge of the glory of God in the face of Jesus Christ" (2 Cor. 4:3–6); "But we all, with open face beholding as in a glass the glory of the Lord, are changed into the same image from glory to glory, even as by the Spirit of the Lord." (2 Cor. 3:18). In these passages, Paul tells us plainly that a saving belief in the gospel grows from an enlightened mind—a mind illuminated by divine glory.

This illuminated vision convinces our minds in two ways: The first is direct and the second is indirect.

A view of divine glory convinces the mind, for glory is the direct, clear, and all-conquering evidence of God, especially when it is clearly revealed—or when this supernatural perception is sharp.

When we have been directly convinced by this clear perception of divine glory, our conviction is reasonable; our belief is congruent with our reason, because the divine glory and beauty is in itself a real evidence of divinity, the strongest and most direct evidence. When we see this transcendent, supreme glory, we intuitively know that God is present. This is different from arguing abstractly about God's presence; this is firsthand, direct vision. God's glory is so vastly and inexpressibly different from the glory of any created thing or artificial concept, that if we catch a glimpse of this glory we know that we are perceiving God.

God is God, distinct from all other beings and exalted high above them by His divine beauty, a beauty that is infinitely different from any other. If we see the stamp of this glory somewhere, then we know that we are seeing the divinity's presence there; we are seeing God. That is the way we judge the gospel. We have an intuitive knowledge that God is present in the gospel's message.

This does not mean that we judge the gospel's doctrines without any intellectual argument or deduction at all. It does mean, however, that we do not need the usual long chain of arguments that human judgment requires. There is only one argument needed, and the evidence is direct; our minds only need to take one step to see the gospel's truth. That step lies in the revelation of divine glory.

Rationally, divine things, things that pertain to the Supreme Being, are vastly different from human things. Divine matters are God-like and glorious, so different from human affairs that we cannot express the difference in words. Divine things convince us and satisfy us simply by their very being, and God reveals His nature in those things by which He has chosen to make Himself known.

Human beings reveal their excellence and quality in their words. The writings of Homer, Cicero, Milton, Locke, Addison, and others are far different from the writings of many other intelligent people. Our words reveal who we are; they reveal the ways we are different from all others, and the content of our words conveys our unique excellence. So logically, when God speaks, He too reveals His nature and excellence—but His excellence is as different from ours as ours is from a worm's!

Anyone who has studied humanity can look at the sun and see that it was not artificially made by human hand. And it is reasonable to suppose that when Christ comes at the end of the world, in the glory of His Father, we will only need to look at Him to know that He is divine. God's divinity is beautiful because it is good, and this goodness carries with it its own evidence, reassuring the human heart. In the same way, the disciples were assured that Jesus was the Son of God, for they "beheld his glory, the glory as of the only begotten of the Father, full of grace and truth" (John 1:14).

When Christ appeared in the glory of His transfiguration to His disciples, their physical eyes perceived the external glory that was a sweet and awesome picture of His spiritual glory, and their minds also perceived His spiritual glory itself, so that with good reason they were certain of His divinity. This is clear when Peter refers to his experience: "For we have not followed cunningly devised fables, when we made known unto you the power and coming of our Lord Jesus Christ, but were eyewitnesses of his majesty. For he received from God the Father honour and glory, when there came such a voice to him from the excellent glory, This is my beloved Son, in whom I am well pleased. And this voice which came from heaven we heard, when we were with him in the holy mount" (2 Pet. 1:16–18). Peter refers to the place where the Transfiguration occurred as the "holy mount," because this was the place where they received a full revelation of Christ's holiness—His goodness and wholeness and love. Another of the disciples who was there expressed this same holiness as "his glory, . . .full of grace and truth."

This unique glory of the divine Being demonstrates itself most clearly in the gospel, for the gospel is the direct expression of God's holiness. Now why would we assume that this glory would be invisible? For God to make this glory so that it could not be perceived makes no sense. Granted, some people are incapable of seeing it, but this proves nothing, even if these same people have keen insight when it comes to temporal matters. Common sense tells us that if the gospel's unique quality is spiritual, then only spiritual people can perceive it. The same is true with human works; only a very intelligent person can truly understand the works by authors of great genius. Milton's work may seems boring and lifeless to some, but that is because they lack the discernment and taste to perceive Milton's excellence. And if God has authored a book, then logically we will not be able to see its glories if our hearts are twisted and selfish, alienated from God. When our hearts are dull and stupid, lacking perception and taste, how can we hope to perceive the gospel's moral glory? God, however, is pleased to enlighten us, restoring a holy taste to our hearts, making us whole once more so we can discern and appreciate divine beauties.

Once our eyes are opened so that we can see the beauty of divine things, then we also grasp all the many nuances of doctrine that the gospel contains. These things look strange and obscure to "natural" people, but now we are able to perceive their truth. For instance, we will understand just how hideous sin is, for the same perception that discerns the transcendent beauty of holiness must also see how terribly ugly is its opposite; the same taste that savors the sweetness of true goodness, also tastes the bitterness of evil. This is how we see our own loathsome sinfulness, because now we have the perception to discern it, and so when the Bible speaks of humanity's desperate evil, we understand what it means. We see in a new way the dirtiness in our hearts and the desperate depravity of our natures, for now we can feel the pain of our disease, where before we were numb. This shows us the Scripture's truth when it speaks of humanity's destructive lack, our desperate need of a Savior to bring our hearts back to life. In the same way, we see the truth of all that the Bible says concerning God's glorious majesty. He is the Fountain of all good, our only real source of happiness—and as we see that, we again grasp the meaning of sin's evil. The truth of one reveals the truth of the other, for our wickedness shows us our need for a Savior, and we are able now to see just how beautiful He is. His life and acts were full of dignity and glory, and we comprehend that He is all we need to justify us before God. This is how the Spirit of God reveals the way of salvation through Christ, and this is how we see how appropriate and suitable this way is, how exactly it fits our needs. Now that we perceive divine beauty, we can see the beauty of every part of the gospel plan.

This same new perception also shows us the truth of what the Word of God tells us about our chief happiness—that it consists in enjoying God's holiness. This perception also shows us the truth of what the gospel says about the unspeakable glory of heaven. The prophecies of the Old Testament and the apostles' writings about the glory of the Messiah's kingdom become plain to us now, and we see too where our own duty lies. The truth of all these things are revealed in the Scripture—and many more that I could mention—but only as we receive that new spiritual taste for divine beauty. Without it, we are blind and dull.

Besides this, though, the truth of all these scriptural things is clear to us because we have now experienced them. This convinces our souls that One who knew our hearts better than we know them ourselves, One whose nature was perfect and holy, was the author of the Scriptures. We are persuaded that the gospel shines with divinity.

We can only be convinced that the gospel is true through a reasonable, experiential vision of its internal glory. People who have no knowledge of the Bible at all, who are illiterate or ignorant of the Bible's history, will be unable to have any gripping conviction that it is true if they are forced to depend on the testimony of others. They may be able to believe what others tell them; they may find the testimony of Bible scholars and historians so credible that they decide that in all likelihood the gospel is true. But this type of conviction is not strong enough to inspire them to sell all that they have, to confidently and fearlessly risk everything, counting all things except Christ to be as worthless as excrement. Secondhand historical evidence is just not enough. People who have no knowledge of history cannot possibly grasp the historical arguments that support Christianity's truth. They may believe what scholars tell them, but their belief is not strong enough to bear their entire weight. Some doubts will still linger in their minds, and when trials pinch them, they will say, "How do I know this or that? How do I know when these histories were written? Just because some scholars believe these stories, how do I know that they actually happened? The stories took place a long time ago; what proof do we have that they were ever true?" Endless doubts and questions will lurk forever in their minds.

But the gospel was not given only for scholars. At least nineteen in twenty people—if not ninety-nine in a hundred —are not capable of any sort of scholarly intellectual argument for the Bible's divine authority—and yet Scripture was written for these people just as much as for anyone else. If people have to wait to be educated before they can be convicted by the gospel message, then evangelism becomes an enormously cumbersome task. Many groups of people have recently expressed their desire to learn more about Christianity; how unfortunate for them if they first have to learn the intellectual methods of a scholar!

Why would God force us to depend on probabilities when it comes to the gospel? Why wouldn't He give us explicit proof? He has very carefully provided the assurance we need that we are unconditionally loved, giving us abundant and satisfying evidence of His faithfulness in the covenant of grace; as David says, He "made a covenant, ordered in all things, and sure." Logically, then, at the same time He would not fail to arrange things so that we would have clear evidence that this *is* His covenant, that these promises are His promises—in other words, that the Christian religion is true and the gospel is His Word. Otherwise, all His assurances of His faithfulness would be vain. For the foundation for our faith in the Bible's promises must be first of all, before anything else, the assurance that it *is* His covenant; on this all the scriptural promises stand.

We may conclude then, that God *has* provided us with

the proof we need that this is His covenant with us—proof that is greater than mere probability. We must have some grounds for our assurance, something that is greater than any argument based merely on history or human tradition, something that even illiterate or uneducated people are capable of grasping.

The apostles speak of the same firm assurance that we are describing: "Let us draw near with a true heart in full assurance of faith" (Heb. 10:22), and "That their hearts might be comforted, being knit together in love, and unto all riches of the full assurance of understanding, to the acknowledgment of the mystery of God, and of the Father, and of Christ" (Col. 2:2). Reasonably, we can suppose that God would give the greatest evidence of those things that are the most necessary—so if we are wise and act rationally, the thing we should most long for is this full, undoubting, and perfect assurance. This type of assurance can never be attained merely from arguments built on ancient traditions, histories, and monuments.

When it comes to fact and experience, I find not the smallest reason to suppose that one in a hundred sincere Christians, people who have loved Christ enough to give up everything for Him, have reached their convictions through historical proof. If we read over the stories of the many thousands who died as martyrs for Christ, who cheerfully underwent torture, confident of the gospel's truth, we will see how few of them reached their deep convictions through scholarly study. How could such arguments possibly have given them the solid assurance they needed? Many of these people were physically small and weak, most of them were illiterate, many of them had been brought up in ignorance and darkness, and only recently had come out of it; these people mostly lived and died in times where the great arguments for Christianity's truth were poorly understood. In fact, only lately have these arguments been thought through in any sort of convincing manner, even by scholars—and yet a lack of conviction among many people prevails in our day today, despite the intellectual evidence we have for belief.

Christ's true martyrs did not merely have a strong opinion that the gospel was true; they *saw* its truth. Scripture often refers to these people as "witnesses," and the very word implies that they saw something firsthand. You cannot be considered to be a witness as to the truth of some event if all you have is opinion to back up your statement. Witnesses can only testify if they have actually seen the thing they claim; "We speak that we do know, and testify that we have seen" (John 3:11); "And I saw, and bare record that this is the Son of God" (John 1:34); "And we have seen and do testify that the Father sent the Son to be the Saviour of the world" (1 John 4:14); "The God of our fathers hath chosen thee, that thou shouldest know his will, and see that Just One, and shouldest hear the voice of his mouth. For thou shalt be his witness unto all men of what thou hast seen and heard" (Acts 22:14–15). The true martyrs of Jesus Christ are His witnesses; in the midst of great hardships, their lives declare the type of faith that is the substance of things hoped for, the evidence of things not seen (Heb. 11:1; 12:1). Their actions confirm their total assurance of the gospel's truth and divinity, for they have had their spiritual eyes opened so that they see the unparalleled, inexpressible glory that shines from the gospel; they have seen

God there, and so they can speak as firsthand witnesses. They do not only *think* the gospel is divine; they know it is because they have seen the divinity that shines there.

Without a doubt, Peter, James, and John, after they saw Christ's glory on the mount of the Transfiguration, spoke afterward with the language of eyewitnesses that Jesus is positively the Son of God; this is certainly the claim that Peter makes in 2 Peter 1:16. One day, the Bible tells us, all nations will be able also to make the same positive testimony, for they too will be eyewitnesses to His glory at the day of judgment. On that day, God's glory will be universally seen.

I must point out here, though, that when we consider all the Christians that have a spiritual vision of the gospel's divine glory, they each possess varying degrees of faith—and as a result, their vision's clarity also varies vastly. But all of them have one thing in common: They all have experienced the gospel's truth firsthand; they have internal proof that the gospel is true. God's gospel does not need to go around begging for evidence to prove itself, as some people seem to think, for it contains the deepest and most convincing evidence within itself.

I am not saying that external arguments have no use. This sort of intellectual endeavor should not be neglected but should be highly prized and valued, for arguments like these can work very well to draw the interest of unbelievers, bringing them to seriously consider the gospel. In some ways, these arguments may give birth to a saving faith. Yet what I said before remains true: Spiritual conviction comes only from a grasp of the spiritual beauty and glory of divine things.

As I also said before, this vision of spiritual beauty has a tendency to convince our hearts of the gospel's truth in two ways, either directly or indirectly. We have talked about how this happens directly; let's move on now to my next point: how a glimpse of divine glory convinces us indirectly.

First, it removes our hearts' prejudices against the truth, so that our minds are opened to the truth's full force. The human mind is naturally at odds with the gospel's doctrines, which is a disadvantage to those arguments that prove their truth, causing them to lose their power upon the mind. But when we discover the divine excellence of Christian doctrines, this destroys that natural contrariness; it removes our prejudices, and sanctifies our intellectual capacities, so that they are open and free. Now, we will find these same arguments will be deeply persuasive. This explains the very different effect that Christ's miracles had on the disciples, from the effect they had on the scribes and Pharisees; the disciples were no more intelligent than the Pharisees, but their intelligence was sanctified. The scribes and Pharisees were blind with prejudice, but the disciples could see clearly.

Second, it not only removes the prejudice that hinders our intellectual reason, but it positively helps our reason. Even the speculative ideas become vibrant and life-giving. It directs our intellectual attention to those things that will help us to understand more clearly, and it helps us to perceive the mutual relationships between different concepts. This mental assistance casts light on ideas that would otherwise be dim and obscure, strengthening them so that the mind can better judge them. In the same way, when we see something in the sunlight, we can discern its true shape and location far better than if we look at the same thing by starlight or twilight. Grace-filled emotion is always accompanied by this sharpened sense of judgment.

But before I move on to a new topic, I want to point out some ways that people can be deceived about this matter—and I want to mention several things that are sometimes mistaken for a spiritual and saving conviction, when actually they are something far different.

1. Some degree of conviction can come from natural evidence of God's Spirit.

"Natural" people can have some perception of God's greatness, power, and awesome majesty, and this tends to convince them that the Bible is the Word of a great and terrible God. They may even have a sense of the great guilt that sin against this God brings, and the dreadfulness of His wrath. Because of their guilt and fear, they then tend to believe more readily what the Bible says about the world to come. But this sense of fear and guilt is not enough for a truly spiritual conviction, for these people have no sense of the beauty and sweetness of God's holiness. And yet this fear and guilt are sometimes mistaken for a saving conviction, and the emotions that result are assumed to be a saving feeling of the heart.

2. The sharp impressions that some imaginative people experience, as though they have directly seen visions or heard messages spoken to them, may—and often do—foster a deep conviction in the reality of invisible things.

In the end, however, this sort of experience usually draws people away from God's Word, causing them to reject the gospel. At first, though, these people often have a confident sense that at least some aspects of the gospel are true. For instance, consider a person who imagines he suddenly sees a bright light. Next, he thinks he sees a glorious human shape seated on a throne, looking majestic and beautiful, and then this vision, in a strong, energetic voice, says something remarkable. After this, the person who saw this vision may be confident that the world is full of invisible powers, spiritual beings, for he is certain that he did not create his vision on his own. He may also be confident that Christ is the person he saw and heard speaking, and consequently, he may be confident that Christ is real, and that Christ reigns on a throne in heaven, just as he saw Him; he may also be just as confident that the words he heard the figure speak are true.

But this is all just delusion, and how can delusion lead us toward the truth? Satan may mix some truth with his lies (for instance, even Satan worshippers are convinced that the invisible world is real; unlike the Saduccees, they know that the spirit world is a reality), but when Satan uses this tactic, he does so only to make his lies more convincing.

Many people have been deluded through their imagination in the way I've just describe. They say they know that there is a God, for they have seen Him; they know that Christ is the Son of God, for they have seen Him in His glory; they know that Christ died for sinners, for they have seen Him hanging on the cross, and His blood running from His wounds; they know there is a heaven and a hell, for they have seen the misery of the damned souls in hell, and the glory of saints and angels in heaven—but all the while, what they really mean is that they have experienced some physical image of these things in their imaginations. In the same way, they know that the Bible is the Word of God, and that such and such promises in particular are His Word, for they have heard Him speak them to them; they came to their minds suddenly and directly from God, they suppose, without any effort of their own.

3. People may seem to be deeply convinced about religious matters, when really they are only concerned with the ways that religion meets their own self-interests.

By some means or another, they start out with the confidence that if Christ and heaven are real, then they are there for their own benefit—and this only makes them more disposed to believe any arguments that support their belief. Everything that they hear about religion they apply to their own concerns, and thus they are easily convinced that all the Bible's promises belong to them. After all, it is in their own interest that they be true. Obviously, our judgment is often influenced by our self-interest. That is why a "natural" person may find it very hard to believe in heaven and hell if she thinks that she may be headed toward hell—but she will find it much easier to believe in heaven and hell if she is convinced she is going to heaven. Then she can believe in hell quite easily, and she will complain about others who are too coarse and senseless to escape it; she is confident that she is a child of God, and that God has promised her heaven. As a result, she may seem to possess a strong faith, and she may demonstrate great zeal against anyone who denies her confidence.

But let me move on now to another way that we can tell grace-filled feeling from any other emotion that we experience.

VI. *Grace-filled feeling is accompanied by evangelical humility.*

Evangelical humility is the sense that Christians have of their own utter inadequacy—and their complete dependency on God to meet their need.

We need to clarify the difference between a legal and an evangelical humility. The former is what people experience in their natural state, before grace has entered their hearts, but the latter is what the saints experience. The former comes from God's Spirit at work in the natural world, making particular use of the human conscience, but the latter is from the Spirit's supernatural influence, when He implants divine seeds within the human heart. The former is inspired by a glimpse of God's natural perfections, such as His greatness and awesome majesty, the same qualities that the Israelites saw on Mount Sinai, but the latter grows out of a sense of the transcendent beauty and goodness of divinity. In the former, people sense God's awful greatness and the strictness of His law; they are convinced that they are sinful and guilty and exposed to God's wrath, but they do not truly see their own terrible inadequacy; they do not see how sin has twisted them away from the image they were created to bear. But an evangelical humility grows from the revelation of the beauty of God's holiness. When people are humbled from a legalistic point of view, they may be aware that God is great and terrible, but they do not know how much they need Him; they still see themselves as the center of their universe, and they have no impulse to surrender themselves to God in worship and love. This impulse is given only when we experience evangelical humility, for then our hearts are overcome; we no longer seek only ourselves, for we have seen God's holy beauty. If we are legally humbled, our consciences are convinced, but we lack any spiritual understanding, and so our natures have not been transformed. Legal humility may bring a person to despair, but evangelical humility will induce her to voluntarily renounce herself. The former may subdue people and force them to the ground, but the latter will offer them the freedom and delight of yielding to God's love.

Legal humility has no spiritual goodness about it; it lacks any true virtue, whereas evangelical humility summarizes the Christian's grace and beauty. Legal humility may sometimes serve its purpose, leading to a true evangelical humility, just as we may need natural knowledge before we experience spiritual knowledge. But not all legal humility leads to evangelical. People can fear for their eternal well-being, they can feel terrible guilt and terror, and yet they are still only concerned with themselves; they remain as selfish as ever. With evangelical humility, however, people look at themselves in a whole new way. They no longer think they are the most important thing in the world; instead, they lay themselves down at Christ's feet.

They no longer think only of their own self-interest; instead, they give themselves away.

This humility is essential to true religion. Everything in the gospel's structure, everything that pertains to the new covenant, all that God has done for us to make us whole, all of this was designed to bring this humility into our hearts. This emptiness is the wealth we need, and as long as we lack it, we have no true religion, no matter what we may profess to believe, no matter how deep and intense our religious feeling may be. Habakkuk 2:4 says, "Behold, his soul which is lifted up is not upright in him: but the just shall live by his faith"; in other words, he shall live by his faith in God's righteousness and grace, and not by his own goodness and excellence.

The Bible makes very clear that this humility is necessary if our hearts are to be in the correct relation to God: "The LORD is nigh unto them that are of a broken heart; and saveth such as be of a contrite spirit" (Ps. 34:18); "The sacrifices of God are a broken spirit: a broken and a contrite heart, O God, thou wilt not despise" (Ps. 51:17); "Though the LORD be high, yet hath he respect unto the lowly" (Ps. 138:6); "He giveth grace unto the lowly" (Prov. 3:34); "Thus saith the high and lofty One that inhabiteth eternity, whose name is Holy; I dwell in the high and holy place, with him also that is of a contrite and humble spirit, to revive the spirit of the humble, and to revive the heart of the contrite ones" (Isa. 57:15); "Thus saith the LORD, the heaven is my throne, and the earth is my footstool: . . .but to this man will I look, even to him that is poor and of a contrite spirit, and trembleth at my word" (Isa. 66:1–2); "He hath shewed thee, O man, what is good; and what doth the LORD require of thee, but to do justly, and to love mercy, and to walk humbly with thy God?" (Mic. 6:8); "Blessed are the poor in spirit: for theirs is the kingdom of heaven" (Matt. 5:3); "Verily I say unto you, Except ye be converted, and become as little children, ye shall not enter into the kingdom of heaven. Whosoever therefore shall humble himself as this little child, the same is greatest in the kingdom of heaven" (Matt. 18:3–4); "Verily I say unto you, Whosoever shall not receive the kingdom of God as a little child, he shall not enter therein" (Mark 10:15).

In Luke 7, the centurion acknowledged that he was not worthy that Christ should enter under his roof, and that he was not worthy to come to Him either. The woman who came to Christ in Luke 7:37 had the same attitude: "And, behold, a woman in the city, which was a sinner, when she knew that Jesus sat at meat in the Pharisee's house, brought an alabaster box of ointment, and stood at his feet behind him weeping, and began to wash his feet with tears, and did wipe them with the hairs of her head." She did not think that the hair on her head, which in her day was a woman's natural crown and glory (1 Cor. 11:15), was too good to wipe the feet of Christ. Jesus lovingly accepted her and said to her, "Thy faith hath saved thee, go in peace" (Luke 6:50). The woman of Canaan submitted to Christ when He said, "It is not meet to take the children's bread, and to cast it to dogs"; she did not protest when He spoke to her this way, whereupon Christ said to her, "O woman, great is thy faith: be it unto thee even as thou wilt" (Matt. 15:26–28).

The prodigal son said, "I will arise and go to my father,

and will say unto him, Father, I have sinned against heaven, and before thee, and am no more worthy to be called thy son: make me as one of thy hired servants" (Luke 15:18–19); "And he spake this parable unto certain which trusted in themselves that they were righteous, and despised others: '. . .the publican, standing afar off, would not lift up so much as his eyes unto heaven, but smote upon his breast, saying, God be merciful to me a sinner. I tell you, this man went down to his house justified rather than the other: for every one that exalteth himself shall be abased; and he that humbleth himself shall be exalted' " (Luke 18:9, 13–14); "And they came and held him by the feet, and worshipped him" (Matt. 28:9); "Put on therefore, as the elect of God, . . .humbleness of mind" (Col. 3:12); "I will accept you with your sweet savour, when I bring you out from the people, . . .and there shall ye remember your ways, and all your doings, wherein ye have been defiled; and ye shall lothe yourselves in your own sight for all your evils that ye have committed" (Ezek. 20:41, 43); "A new heart also will I give you. . . . And I will put my Spirit within you, and cause you to walk in my statutes, . . .then shall ye remember your own evil ways, and your doings that were not good, and shall lothe yourselves in your own sight for your iniquities and for your abominations" (Ezek. 36:26–27, 31); "That thou mayest remember, and be confounded, and never open thy mouth any more because of thy shame, when I am pacified toward thee for all that thou hast done, saith the Lord GOD" (Ezek. 16:63); "I abhor myself, and repent in dust and ashes" (Job 42:6).

If we use the Bible as the basis for our thought about true faith, then obviously we need to take a very serious look at the humility that all these passages describe. From this humility springs the self-denial that Christians are asked to practice. This duty consists in two things: first, in a person's denying his worldly inclinations, forsaking and renouncing all temporal objects and pleasure; and, secondly, in his denying his natural desire to put himself at the center of everything, above everything else. This second part of self-denial means that he will renounce his own dignity and glory, and empty himself; freely, with love, he lays himself down and annihilates himself. This is a part of the humility that the Bible teaches, and this is the hardest part of self-denial. Both parts always go together, and one never truly exists without the other, and yet without grace we can come closer to the first part than we can the second.

Many people have abandoned wealth and pleasure and the world's enjoyments, and yet these same people were far from renouncing their own dignity, their sense of their own importance. These people have never actually denied themselves for Christ; instead, they only sold one lust to feed another: they sold a beastly lust to pamper a devilish one, and so they are no better off, but in fact are worse off than they were in the beginning. These people are full of self-righteousness; they are self-exalting, and this is far worse than any natural enjoyment they might have taken in the world's pleasures. They will do anything now to feed and gratify their perverted sense of their own righteousness, for they want to be better than anyone, including God.

This humility that we're talking about can never be achieved by even the most convincing of hypocrites. They may put on a fine show, and they may be quite successful in their own eyes, but in the end they will bungle their act.

They cannot know how to speak and behave humbly; they cannot talk and act in such a way that everything they do breathes the scent of Christ-like humility. A genuine humble spirit is beyond their ability to imitate, for they are not guided from within by the Spirit, nor do they have a genuine spirit of humility within them. All they can do is tell people over and over how humble they are, using lots of expressions to refer to themselves, such as, "I am the least of all saints, I am a poor vile creature, I am not worthy that God should look upon me! Oh, I have a dreadful wicked heart! My heart is worse than the devil! Oh, this cursed heart of mine"—and so on. When they talk like this, though, they do not speak as though their hearts have been broken; they demonstrate none of the heartfelt tears that the woman cried who washed Jesus' feet; they do not act as if they are "remembering and being confounded, and never opening their mouth more because of their shame, when God is pacified," as Ezekiel 16:63 says. Instead, they speak with a light air, with smiles on their face or with a self-satisfied emotion that reminds us of the Pharisees. We have to take their word that they are so deeply humble, for nothing in their behavior tells us so. These people assume that they should talk often about their own failure and inadequacy, and yet they expect that others will look on them as being the most glowing and preeminent of saints. They take this as their due, and they quickly take offense if anyone so much as implies otherwise. They may claim to have a wicked heart plagued by many shortcomings, but if their minister was to take them apart in private and tell them the same thing, they would be quick to inform him that he was not much of a Christian. They would be so injured by his words, that in all likelihood they would begin at once to prejudice others in the church against this minister.

Some people are full of complaints against legal doctrines, legal preaching, and a legal spirit, but they don't really understand what they are protesting. Legalism is more subtle than they imagine; it is far too subtle for them to see. It lurks and operates and prevails in their hearts, and they are apt to be most guilty of it when they are speaking against it the loudest. As long as we have not emptied ourselves of our own righteousness and goodness, in whatever form or shape, we have a legal spirit. If we are proud of our own righteousness, morality, holiness, deep feeling, experience, faith, humiliation, or any goodness of any sort, then a legal spirit possesses us.

Before the Fall, Adam was justified in stating a legal claim to righteousness; technically and legally he had never sinned. But when we try to make the same legal claim, when in reality we are fallen, sinful creatures, we are only demonstrating our spiritual pride. It's a reciprocal relationship: A spiritually proud spirit is a legal spirit; legalism and pride go together. If we are proud of our experiences, thinking that they prove our righteousness, if we shine in our own eyes, then no matter how humbly we talk, speaking of the great things God has done for us, calling upon others to glorify God, we are claiming something for ourselves that is not our due, as though our experiences endued us with some superior worth. We assume that God looks at our worth with the same good opinion we feel; we think our wonderful experiences make us glisten in God's eyes, just as we do in our own—but we are relying on our own inherent value. We think this will be enough to make us shine in God's sight, and this supposed worthiness of ours makes us assume that God will do all sorts of great things for us, blessing us and clothing us with His righteousness. In reality, though, we have turned things around, and we are depending on our own righteousness rather than God's. We would be better off to have no religion at all than to think that we can impress God with our own innate worth. We are living in the world of experience only, basing our concept of reality on a false image, when we should be using our experiences only as proof of God's grace in our lives. We are meant to receive hope and comfort from the world of experience—but we are not meant to build our own worth on it.

Some people insist that works are nothing and faith is everything. They set themselves up as evangelicals who are in opposition to legalists. They put on a good show—and yet in reality they are not truly advancing Christ and the gospel. They do not understand what free grace really means, and they have no concept of true Christian humility.

Some people pretend to be deeply humble, dead to the law and emptied of self—and all the while, they are conceited and elated with themselves. They profess to be totally freed from the law, no longer dependent on any sort of works for their justification, and yet all the while their lives smack of self-righteousness. They think they have totally emptied themselves, and they are confident that they are humbled as low as the dust, but in reality they are full to the brim with the glory of their own self-denial, and they are lifted up to heaven with a high opinion of their own humility. Their humility is the most swollen, conceited, confident, showy, noisy, assuming humility that I have ever seen. Spiritual pride makes them conceited and ostentatious.

For persons to be truly emptied of themselves, to be poor in spirit and broken in heart, is quite another thing, and the results are far different than many imagine. I am astonished by how many people are deceived about themselves this way, imagining themselves humble when they are actually proud. Our hearts more easily deceive us in this area than in any other, and Satan finds us more vulnerable here than anywhere else. Maybe he knows so well how to take advantage of our weakness because it is his own sin too. Experience gives him advantage.

But even though spiritual pride is a subtle and secret sin, one that covers itself with the appearance of great humility, yet two things will always reveal it.

The first thing is this: People who suffer from this disease are apt to compare their spiritual condition favorably to that of others. They think they are the most preeminent of saints. Secretly, inside their hearts, they are always saying, "God, I thank thee, that I am not as other men" (Luke 18:11), or "I am holier than thou" (Isa. 65:5). Therefore, these people are apt to push to the front among God's people, taking the best seats, as it were, as if no one could doubt that these places belonged to them. They always take the highest positions for themselves—and we know how Christ felt about that (Luke 14:7). These people are certain they should be in leadership positions within the church, and they are quick to guide, teach, direct, and manage. "[They are] confident that [they are] a guide of the blind, a light of them which are in darkness, an instructor of the foolish, a teacher of babes" (Rom. 2:19–20). Like the Pharisees, they want to be the teachers or masters of all the rest (Matt. 23:6–7), and they expect that others will yield to their religious guidance.

People who are truly humble, however, are totally different. The Scripture indicates that people like this are apt to believe that their spiritual condition is lower than that of others; they know that they are only the lowest of saints. True lowliness of mind disposes people to think that others are better than themselves: "In lowliness of mind let each esteem other better than themselves" (Phil. 2:3). As a result, they are apt to think the lowest position belongs to them, and their inward disposition naturally leads them to obey that precept of our Savior (Luke 14:10). They do not naturally assume that they should be the teacher of the rest of the church; on the contrary, they usually assume that someone else could do it better than they can, as was true of Moses and Jeremiah (Exod. 3:11, Jer. 1:6). These people are deeply spiritual and possess great wisdom, but they feel more comfortable being taught rather than teaching; they are much more eager to hear and receive instruction, than to dictate to others: "Be swift to hear, slow to speak" (James 1:19). When they do speak, they do not do so with a bold, masterly air, but with gentleness and uncertainty; "When Ephraim spake trembling, he exalted himself in Israel; but when he offended in Baal, he died" (Hos. 13:1). They are not apt to assume authority, nor do they insist on being managers and leaders; instead, they are subject to others; "Be not many masters" (James 3:1); "All of you be subject one to another, and be clothed with humility" (1 Pet. 5:5); "Submitting yourselves one to another in the fear of God" (Eph. 5:21).

Some persons are very impressed by their own experiences; they speak about these experiences, describing how marvelous and extraordinary they were. This can be good; in one sense, every experience of God's saving mercy is a great thing, and we should love to talk about all that He has done for us. The more humble we are, the more awed and amazed we will be at God's wonderful grace. But if we start comparing our experiences of grace to others', finding that ours are always better, deeper, more impressive, then when we say, "God has shown me marvelous mercies," we really mean, "I am the best of all saints, and God has bestowed on me more grace than He has on you." We expect that others will admire us when we describe all our spiritual experiences, but we never consider that we are boasting, for we think to ourselves, "It's not as though I did anything. I'm talking about free grace. God has done so much for me, and why shouldn't others be impressed by all the favors He has shown me?"

The Pharisee thought the same way, as Christ tells us in Luke 18. "God, I thank You," said the Pharisee, "that I am not like other people." Just because they were thanking God for their superiority did not keep them from being full of pride. If they had been truly humble, their religious achievements would not have shone so bright in their own eyes, nor would they have been so filled with admiration for their own beauty.

Christians who are truly spiritual, those who are real saints, the greatest in the kingdom of heaven, humble themselves as a little child (Matt. 18:4). They consider themselves to be like children in their spiritual journey, and they think of their achievements as being as small and simple as a baby's. They are sorry that they do not know more; they are ashamed that they do not love more. Moses, when he had been talking with God on the mountaintop and his face shone so bright that the others were dazzled, did not know that his face shone.

Some people claim to be prominent saints in God's kingdom—but the real saints, the ones who will shine brightest in heaven, are not apt to make such claims for themselves. I doubt there is a true saint in the whole world who would make such an inflated claim for herself. She would be far more likely to say she is the least of all saints, regarding the achievement and experiences of others as far beyond her own. That is the way grace behaves in our hearts; true spiritual light shines on our faults, while our goodness remains invisible to our own eyes. Those who have the most grace will have the most modest image of themselves. This will be clear to anyone who thinks carefully about the following points.

The grace and holiness that we have in our hearts will always seem little compared to the grace and holiness God has available to give us. When we are grace-filled, when our hearts have been illuminated by the Spirit, we realize the fullness of God's bounty—and we see how far short of it we fall. Our souls struggle and reach for this fullness, but God's holiness remains our standard, and we always fall short. When our hearts are ruled by grace, we know that since God gives us everything, we owe Him everything in return; whatever holiness we possess is not enough. We are always working toward a greater commitment to God, making room for more grace within us, and so the grace that we have already never seems like anything worth talking about.

We are like a hungry person who looks down at the small portion on his plate and sees no reason to mention it, for the food is so small compared to his hunger. That is how true grace and spiritual light behave; the more we have, the more we see of what is still to come, the infinite riches that God has available, the infinite dignity of the person of Christ, and the boundless length and breadth and depth and height of the love of Christ.

As grace increases within us, the horizon that lies ahead of us opens more and more to a distant view, until our souls are swallowed up by the vastness of the universe. We are overwhelmed with the need to love this God, this glorious Redeemer, who loved us so much; the love that we have already in our hearts for Him we know cannot possibly be enough. And so the more we comprehend spiritual reality, the smaller our experiences appear in our own eyes, and we assume that others are far beyond us. We are amazed that our own hearts should be so stingy in response to God's infinite bounty, and so we can scarcely believe that such a strange limitation would be true for other spiritual people. How, we wonder, can we be God's children, the recipients of Christ's boundless love, and not be more filled with love? We assume that our failure to love more must be a peculiar problem all our own, for we can only see the outside of other Christians, while we see our own inner beings.

Readers may object at this point, saying that the more we know of God, the more we love Him; why would we *think* our love to be smaller as we grow closer to God, when actually our love is growing also? My answer is this: Yes, our love does grow as our knowledge grows—but our vision of that love is not increased, for our eyes are fixed on God.

We see more and more of His nature, and by comparison our own nature becomes insignificant in our eyes. We have caught a glimpse of something wonderful, and that sight brings with it the strong conviction that a vast abundance lies beyond our ability to see. We are amazed that we should be so blind to such overwhelming reality; from our perspective we know so little of God's infinite nature, and we love Him so little compared to how He loves us. This vision of ourselves in relation to God does not lead to despair and shame, though; at the same time that we become convinced that God has boundless qualities we have failed to grasp, we are also convinced that our own capacity has limitless reaches it has failed to explore. As we look at the infinite spiritual view that lies ahead, we are eager to press forward; we are impatient with anything in ourselves that holds us back, for we long to reach a greater knowledge and a deeper love.

The grace and love of even the best saints in this world is truly very little in comparison to what it ought to be. The highest love ever attained in this life is poor and cold compared to the love we owe. This will be clear to us if we consider two things:

1. The reasons we have for loving God: the demonstrations He has given us of His infinite glory in His Word, in His works, and especially in the gospel of His Son.

2. The capacity we have for love, since God has given us the intellectual faculties to see and understand why we should love God.

The requirements placed on us by these two things makes human love look small indeed! Grace convinces our hearts of this, for grace has the same nature as light, and it brings truth into view. Therefore the more grace we have, the more we will feel the love we owe God and the more we will be convinced that we do not yet love Him enough.

At the same time we have a sharper vision of our own failures, the selfishness and sin that remain in our hearts. When we use God as our measuring stick, rather than other people, our lack becomes apparent, for wherever we fall short of boundless love, that is sin; those are the places where we are still controlled by self. That is the definition of sin: an unwillingness to respond in love as we ought. The more our love falls short, the greater hold sin still has on our hearts. God has infinite goodness held out to us; wherever we lack that goodness, that is sin. It is like a rotten spot, a place where death still rules our hearts, and the more grace we have, the uglier these spots will look to us. How can we still nourish this sort of selfish corruption when Christ loved us with a complete and dying love? We want to thank Him with a greater love than we have yet given Him, a total love; anything else seems like hateful ingratitude.

Grace has a tendency also to make us ultrasensitive to any sin in our lives. Even the smallest selfishness, the tiniest rotten spot in our hearts, seems to outweigh whatever goodness we possess. The reason for this is that the least sin against an infinite God has an infinite deformity in it; if we fall short of God's glory even in the tiniest of ways, we still have fallen short. We have allowed our hearts to be distorted by sin, and thus we cannot possess the completion and perfection of holiness.

God gives us all of Himself, and we owe Him the same in return. Our obligation is infinite—and that makes our failures all the more glaring. If a Being is infinitely lovely, endlessly worthy to be loved by us, then our obligation to love Him is infinitely great. Anything that is contrary to this love possesses infinite iniquity and deformity. And the more we have of true grace and spiritual light, the more we will see reality in this way, for our finite goodness cannot stand up against God's infinite goodness. All that we have is like a drop of water compared to the ocean. This is what spiritual illumination does: It shows us the deformity and distortion in our own hearts—and not in the past only, but in the present. Even our brightest experiences and highest achievements are warped by the selfishness and sin in our hearts, and so the eyes of grace count them as worthless.

I have noticed that many people, however, hide their sense of their own sin with intense religious emotion and revelations. They use these extraordinary experiences to convince themselves and others that all their sin is gone, and to leave them free of any discomfort they might feel about having evil lurk inside them. They can admit their past sins, but not their present ones. When this is the case, this is a sure sign that they are walking in darkness and not the light. Darkness hides our dirt and deformity; but when the light shines in our hearts, it shines in all the secret corners, revealing the dirt and disease, for the light is God's holiness and glory, and it penetrates the deepest dark.

Healing revelations in one sense do conceal our corruption, at least for a time, for they hold us back from acting out of malice, envy, covetousness, or lasciviousness. But they do not stop there, for this healing light continues to search us, revealing the hidden attitudes within us: the places where there is not more love, not more humility, not more thankfulness. For a true saint, it is no longer enough not to act sinfully, for grace allows him to see what is in his heart—and what he sees there weighs him down. That is why he will be certain that he is spiritually thin, full of pride and ingratitude. And if he does actually act out these ugly attitudes, so that selfish behavior mingles with his holy practice, grace will magnify his view of these actions so that in his eyes they look far more hideous and horrible than they do to others around him.

How do you think the angels look at us? Can we rationally supposed that they are impressed by our love and our practice? On the contrary, if they did not look at us through the covering of Christ's righteousness, they could not help but see how full of self and failure we all are. The more grace we have, the more of heaven's light we have in our souls, then the closer will our vision be to that of the angels, who have full access to God's complete glory. The angels look at us through the beams of Christ's abundant glory and love, but how can we suppose our most ardent love and praises appear to them who behold the beauty and glory of God without a veil, without any cloud of darkness? How can our feeble attempts at praise and love look like anything at all to the angels who behold the full light of Christ's reality?

Don't misunderstand me. I am not saying that grace makes the saints on earth constantly miserable, that the more grace they have, the more they will dislike themselves. In many respects just the opposite is true. The saints know that the more grace streams into their lives, the more they are freed from the sinful behaviors that once controlled them. They know when they close themselves off to grace, because they see that sin once more creeps into their actions. Once they have opened themselves again to God's Spirit, they will see why their behavior sank as it did, because grace was not so present in their lives, and they will have a greater sense of guilt for these times of increased sinfulness. Guilt and humility are two different things, though, and it is humility that I have been describing. When grace is present in our lives, we are truly humble; we do not value any accomplishment of our own, for our eyes are fixed on the endless wonder of God. That is why the person who is greatest in the kingdom, or a leader in the church of Christ, is the one who humbles herself as low as the youngest baby. Isn't that what Christ said? (See Matt. 18:4.)

A true saint is aware that grace is present in his life. The more grace he has, the more visible it becomes. But it does not follow that he will become great in his own eyes compared to others. I am not saying that he will have no self-knowledge whatsoever, for he will be aware that grace is real and present in him. But that will not make him think he is superior to others. His own spiritual strength is always off to the side of his vision, almost out of his sight; sometimes he will even need to argue with himself to convince himself that this spiritual quality he does possess is real. After intense rational thought, he may be able to grasp that he is further along in his spiritual journey than others are, but he quickly loses this thought from his consciousness, and it seems unnatural to him to act upon it. But the person who habitually assumes that she is spiritually superior to others is really no saint at all. If the Word of God is true, then this person lacks any true Christian experience at all.

Any experiences we have that tend to make us more conceited about our own spirituality are certainly empty delusions. If we have some revelation that blows us up with pride, then this experience lacks any real spiritual light. The more true spiritual knowledge a person has, the more he is aware of his own ignorance; as is clear in 1 Corinthians 8:2: "And if any man think that he knoweth any thing, he knoweth nothing yet as he ought to know." Also, take a look at Proverbs 30:2–4: "Surely I am more brutish than any man, and have not the understanding of a man. I neither learned wisdom, nor have the knowledge of the holy. . . . Who hath gathered the wind in his fists? who hath bound the waters in a garment? who hath established all the ends of the earth? what is his name, and what is his son's name, if thou canst tell?"

When we are conceited about our spiritual knowledge, the Bible refers to this as being wise in our own eyes: "Be not wise in thine own eyes" (Prov. 3:7); "Be not wise in your own conceits" (Rom. 12:16); "Woe unto them that are wise in their own eyes, and prudent in their own sight!" (Isa. 5:21). People who are wise in their own eyes are some of the least likely to become good. Experience shows the truth of this; "Seest thou a man wise in his own conceit? there is more hope of a fool than of him" (Prov. 26:12).

Some of you may object that the psalmist, who we must suppose was a holy man, speaks of his knowledge as being far greater than anyone else's: "I have more understanding than all my teachers: for thy testimonies are my meditation. I understand more than the ancients, because

I keep thy precepts" (Ps. 119:99–100). Let me answer by saying two things:

1. The Spirit of God can reveal anything He wants to a prophet who is speaking or writing under the influence of immediate inspiration for the good of the church. The Spirit may reveal things that would be impossible for anyone else to think or ever consider. If God can reveal mysteries, that otherwise would be beyond the reach of human reason; or things taking place in a distant place where human eye cannot see; or future events, that human knowledge cannot possibly know—then the Spirit might reveal to David his own deep understanding, so that David would record this revelation and others would be inspired to achieve the same deep knowledge. As he wrote the Psalms, David was under the extraordinary influence of the Holy Spirit; we do not know how he behaved or spoke when he was being guided by the ordinary light of grace. In the same way, we should not assume that God's Spirit would have us curse others and wish the most dreadful misery on them, simply because David, under inspiration, often curses others and prays that misery will come to them.

2. I am not certain that David is speaking here about spiritual knowledge or holiness. He may simply be referring to the great revelations God had given him about the Messiah and His future kingdom, or to the far more clear and extensive knowledge that he had of the mysteries and doctrines of the gospel than

others had in his time. This would then be simply an accurate statement of reality, for God *had* given David extraordinary knowledge, as a reward for his keeping God's testimonies. The Book of Psalms clearly shows that David's knowledge far exceeded all those who had gone before him.

Another infallible sign of spiritual pride is when people think highly of their humility. False experiences are often accompanied by counterfeit humility—fake humility is always conceited. False religious emotions have a tendency, especially when they are intense, to make people think that they are very humble; they become quite proud of being so humble, and admire themselves greatly. But spiritual feeling is just the opposite; it makes us long for greater humility, for what we have attained so far seems like nothing compared to the abominable pride that lingers in our hearts.

People whose humility is counterfeit feel they are stooping from a very great height when they do some humble act, and thus they feel that everyone should admire their great humility. "This is a great act of humiliation," they think, "that I should feel thus and do so." What they mean is, "This is a great humiliation for me, when I am so respectable and superior." They are thinking about how low they have dropped compared to the great height of dignity which is theirs in their hearts. They are quite impressed with themselves for going to such lengths, and they admire themselves immensely.

On the other hand, people who are truly humble do not feel that they have to stoop at all when they do some small loving duty. They look at themselves in relation to

God, rather than in relation to other human beings—and when God is our standard, the difference between His heights and our lowliness is so immense, that the differences between human beings becomes imperceptible. The humble person knows she is nothing compared to God, and as a result the humility she possesses is invisible to her, while her remaining pride seems huge and horrible.

All of us judge humility by looking at a person's actual worldly standing compared to the sort of duties they perform. Thus an act that for one person might take great humility for another requires none, depending on their dignity. For instance, if a world leader was to stop and bend down to tie someone's shoe, we would all be impressed by his humility. But we are not impressed if a mother stops to ties her son's shoe. A truly humble Christian pays no attention to her personal dignity; it is a meaningless concept to her, and so she thinks nothing of performing some menial task for love, any more than a mother thinks twice about tying her children's shoes. The humble person does not think to herself, "My, aren't I humble for doing this lowly thing." Her only thought is that she could never offer enough in return for God's great love for her. She is ready to lie in the dust, as it were, at God's feet.

The same sort of things is true of spiritual conviction. We've all known someone who, when they were under conviction, did not think that they were experiencing any great conviction at all. Their conviction seemed like nothing to them compared to the greatness of their sin. In their eyes, because they were under such deep spiritual conviction, their selfishness and sin seemed so immense that their sorrow and repentance seemed like not enough; from their perspective their degree of conviction fell far short of what was needed. That is because all of us judge our own conviction by two things: first, the sense we have of guilt, and second, the actual degree of real sinfulness present in our lives. Someone who is plainly and notoriously more sinful than anyone else around may judge himself to be the greatest of sinners, but this takes no spiritual conviction on his part, only a realistic self-awareness. But when we are deeply and spiritually convicted, our sensitivity to sin is heightened, and therefore our sin seems greater than anyone else's. The level of our conviction will never seem enough; if it does, then that means that we secretly believe our sins are insignificant, and we are not spiritually or deeply convicted. And humility works the same way in the hearts of the saints; those who possess it the most, are the most unaware of it.

The loftiest saint is not apt to think he is lofty in anything. All his grace and experience looks comparatively small to him in his own eyes, but especially his humility. It is the one thing he cannot see at all. Meanwhile, pride is the one thing invisible to the deluded hypocrite. She notices every humble act she performs, never realizing she is controlled by spiritual pride.

The humble Christian is more apt to find fault with his own pride than with another's. He is apt to put the best construction possible on others' words and behavior, giving them the benefit of the doubt, while he is always severe in his judgment of himself. Meanwhile, the proud hypocrite is quick to discern the speck in her friend's eye, while she is blind to the two-by-four in her own. She is critical of others' pride, finding fault with others' clothing and their way of living; she is affronted ten times as much by her neighbor's jewelry or sense of humor than she is by the filthiness of her own heart.

Hypocrites tend to make a great show of their humility. They use artificial, affected looks, gestures, and manners of speech—or they may dress in some excessively modest style, drawing attention to themselves by making themselves uniquely different from others with their affected humiliations. The false prophets were the same way (Zech. 13:4); so were the hypocritical Jews (Isa. 58:5) and the Pharisees (Matt. 6:16).

True humility does not draw attention to itself in any way, not with an affected style of clothing, nor with a way of life full of outward abasement. This is implied in Matthew 6:17: "But thou, when thou fastest, anoint thine head, and wash thy face" and in Colossians 2:23: "Which things have indeed a shew of wisdom in will worship, and humility, and neglecting of the body." True humility is a quiet thing; it is not noisy and boisterous. Ahab, when he had a visible humility, something that at least looked like true humility, went softly (1 Kings 21:27). A person who is sorry for his sins, filled with true humility, is described by the Bible as being still and silent: "He sitteth alone and keepeth silence, because he hath borne it upon him" (Lam. 3:28); "If thou hast done foolishly in lifting up thyself, or if thou hast thought evil, lay thine hand upon thy mouth" (Prov. 30:32).

Truly spiritual feeling is accompanied by real humility. I have spent so much time describing what real humility looks like, because I consider this to be a matter of great importance. Not only does it help us to discern who is a hypocrite and who isn't, but it also helps us to be careful of our own hearts. The sin of pride and false humility is the sin most hateful to God, according to the Bible, "a smoke in [his] nose, a fire that burneth all the day" (Isa. 65:5).

Readers should not pass over this lightly. If you have ever criticized someone else for thinking better of themselves than they should, then you should probably be examining your own heart for the very sin you are pointing out in another. Our hearts require strict self-examination in this area. If you think to yourself, "No, I do not criticize others for their pride, for it seems to me no one has the problem with this sin that I do," don't be quick to dismiss the matter from your mind. Examine yourself again; do you think highly of yourself for feeling so humble? If you answer yet again, "No, I don't have a high opinion of my own humility; it seems to me that my pride is a horrible thing," still, examine yourself one more time and see whether conceit hasn't risen up under the cover of self-condemnation. You may very well be thinking secretly, "I find my pride so horrible, that I must truly be very humble!"

The difference between true and counterfeit humility gives rise to a vast difference in temperament and behavior as well.

A truly humble person, since she has such a low opinion of her own righteousness and holiness, is poor in spirit. She sees herself as lacking; the contents of her heart, in her own estimation, are small and poor. As a result she acts very much the way a poor person acts, for in her heart she knows her real poverty. "The poor useth intreaties; but the rich answereth roughly" (Prov. 18:23). Humility is spiritual poverty.

We are all beggars at God's gates. The difference between

the hypocrite and the person who is truly humble, however, is this: One is poor in spirit, while the other, who is even more empty and needy, acts as though he is rich, lacking nothing. He is living on imaginary treasure, though. A poor person is modest in her speech and behavior; she is humble and unassuming in her behavior. It is a waste of time for people to pretend they are spiritual, like little children before God's presence, when they are haughty and rude to other human beings. Our humility before God is demonstrated by humble actions toward each other.

The gospel's design is to cut off all self-glorying, not only before God, but also with one another (Rom. 4:1–2). Hypocrites who pretend to feel great humility, while behaving with haughty superiority to those around them, ought to consider these Scriptures: "LORD, my heart is not haughty, nor mine eyes lofty; neither do I exercise myself in great matters, or in things too high for me" (Ps. 131:1); "These . . .things doth the LORD hate; yea, [even] are an abomination unto him: a proud look. . ." (Prov. 6:16–17); "An high look, and a proud heart. . .is sin" (Prov. 21:4); "Thou. . . wilt bring down high looks" (Ps. 18:27); "Him that hath an high look and a proud heart will not I suffer" (Ps. 101:5); "Charity vaunteth not itself, . . .doth not behave itself unseemly" (1 Cor. 13:4–5). A certain modesty and reverence for others grows out of true humility, and this Christian behavior, according to the Bible, should be demonstrated toward those around us: "Be ready always to give an answer to every man that asketh you. . .with meekness and fear" (1 Pet. 3:15); "Fear to whom fear" (Rom. 13:7); "Whilst he remembereth the obedience of you all, how with fear and trembling ye received him" (2 Cor. 7:15); "Servants, be obedient to them that are your masters according to the flesh, with fear and trembling" (Eph. 6:5); "Servants, be subject to your masters with all fear" (1 Pet. 2:18); "While they behold your chaste conversation coupled with fear" (1 Pet. 3:2); "That women adorn themselves in modest apparel, with shamefacedness and sobriety" (1 Tim. 2:9). In this respect, Christians are like little children, little children who behave quietly and respectfully, and their hearts are full of reverence for others.

This same spirit will dispose a Christian to honor everyone: "Honour all men" (1 Pet. 2:17); "Abraham stood up, and bowed himself to the people of the land" (Gen. 23:7). This last passage shows Abraham's remarkable humility and respect for a people whose ways were so different from his own that he was unwilling for his son to marry one of their daughters; and yet he did not consider himself to be superior to them, as this verse clearly shows. Paul also spoke respectfully to his enemy Festus: "I am not mad, most noble Festus" (Acts 26:25); clearly, we are not only to honor other Christians, or only people who treat us kindly, but all people, including our enemies. When Jacob had spent the night wrestling with God—an extraordinary spiritual experience if ever there was one—he did not pride himself on his amazing revelation afterward. Instead, he humbled himself before his brother Esau, the same brother who hated him: "[Jacob] bowed himself to the ground seven times, until he came near to his brother [Esau]" (Gen. 33:3); he called him lord, and commanded all his family to honor Esau in the same way.

All these scripture passages show us clearly what spiritual humility looks like. The humble heart not only honors God, but all creatures. It is not focused on itself, it does not delight itself with self-admiration. Instead, it bows down in reverence and respect to God and those He has created.

Out of this kind of heart all truly holy feeling flows. Christian feeling is like Mary's precious ointment that she poured on Christ's head, so that it filled the whole house with a sweet odor. Her perfume was poured out of an alabaster box, and grace-filled feeling flow out to Christ from a pure heart. Mary could not pour out her ointment until her box was broken, and grace-filled feeling can only flow from a heart that has been broken. The heart-experiences that graces works are also like the ointment Mary Magdalene poured on Jesus' feet (Luke 7), when she had washed them with her tears and wiped them with the hair of her head. All feelings of this nature are a sweet odor to Christ, and brokenhearted love fills our own souls with heavenly sweetness and fragrance. True love, spiritual love, is always humble and brokenhearted. All things that the saints desire, no matter how earnestly and fervently they desire them, are humble desires; in other words, the saints have laid themselves aside, and they no longer desire only what will most suit their own interests. Their hope is a humble hope; and their joy, even when it is unspeakable and full of glory; is a humble brokenhearted joy. None of these spiritual feelings will inflate our hearts; instead, they will leave us all the more poor in spirit, more like a little child, with a greater reverence for others.

VII. You can tell spiritual emotions from others because the feeling that is produced by grace changes our very natures.

Spiritual feeling comes from spiritual enlightenment, from a perception of divine reality, as we have already discussed. But let me go further now. Spiritual revelation, true enlightenment, always transforms our hearts. Not only does it change the way we feel and act, but it changes our very natures: "But we all, with open face beholding as in a glass the glory of the Lord, are changed into the same image from glory to glory, even as by the Spirit of the Lord" (2 Cor. 3:18). This sort of transforming power belongs only to the Spirit of the Lord. Other powers may change the way we feel temporarily; they may affect our transitory emotions. But only the power of our Creator can change our very nature, only He can give us an entirely new nature. And no revelation or enlightenment will have this supernatural effect except if it is divine. The soul is deeply moved by this sort of experience, moved to the point that it is forever changed.

The feelings that we experience during conversion help us to be transformed. Everything that the Bible says about conversion indicates that it changes human nature; it describes this experience with phrases like "being born again," "becoming new creatures," "rising from the dead," "being renewed in the spirit of the mind," "dying to sin and living to righteousness," "putting off the old man, and putting on the new man," "being ingrafted into new stock," "having a divine seed implanted in the heart," "being made partakers of the divine nature," and so on.

So if no great and remarkable lasting change takes place in people's hearts, then although they may imagine that they have been converted—they may even have been deeply moved emotionally—none of it amounts to anything. Conversion means a total change takes place inside the soul, a 180-degree turn from sin to God. Before a person is converted, she may restrain herself from sinning through willpower alone, but after her conversion, she not only refrains from sin, but her very heart and nature are no longer characterized by sin but by holiness. From then on, she has become a holy person, an enemy to sin. Therefore, when a person claims he has been converted, look and see if his disposition and habits are different than they were before. He may be very emotional about his supposed conversion, but if he is still selfish and unloving and dull, then this evidence counts against him, no matter how bright a story he tells. When we are in Christ Jesus, experiences matter little: neither circumcision nor uncircumcision, neither a loud and obvious profession of faith nor a quiet, obscure one, neither a pretty life story nor a broken one, none of it does any good. Christ only cares about who we are on the inside, not what we show to the world—and if we're truly in Him, we will be new creatures.

Sometimes, a person may seem to change for a little while, but then she goes back to being just as she was before. In this case, no real change took place in her nature, for our natures endure; they do not alter from day to day and month to month. A pig whose nature is to be filthy can be washed, but its piggish nature will remain—and a dove whose nature is clean can be soiled, but its nature will remain pure.

So it is with us who have been converted. We must make allowances for our natural temperaments, for conversion does not entirely root them out. Those sins to which we were naturally most disposed before our conversion, will still be the ones that we will be apt to fall into most easily. And yet conversion makes a big difference even with these sins. We do not avail ourselves of all the grace offered us, and so our limited supply does not dig out by the roots our natural temperaments—but the grace we have has great strength and power to help us correct and heal our personal flaws. The change that takes place in conversion is a total change, affecting every part of our being. Grace changes us, touching each sinful part within us; the old person is put off and the new person put on. We are sanctified all the way through our beings, so that we are new creatures; old things are passed away and all things are become new. Sin is put to death, our constitutional sins as well as others.

For instance, if a person before his conversion was naturally inclined to sexual sin, or drunkenness, or cruelty, grace will change these evil tendencies. These are still the sins that will tempt him the most, but they will no longer rule him; they are no longer a part of his very character. In fact, true repentance tends to make us turn against our own chief iniquities more than any others; where we have been most guilty, where we have dishonored God the most, we tend to attack ourselves most fiercely, to be certain that we do not fail our God in the same way again. On the other hand, if we give up most of our sins, but we keep our favorite one, then we are like Saul when God sent him to destroy the Amalekites, telling him to be sure that none were left alive—and instead, Saul killed all the ordinary people, but saved the king.

Some make the foolish argument that their revelations and religious emotions must be real, because when they disappear, they are left lifeless, without any sense of the spiritual world at all; they are just as they were before their extraordinary experiences. These people then assume that this proves that God produced their emotions and not themselves, because (they say) when God left them, all their deep emotions went with Him; they can see and feel nothing, and they are no better than they used to be.

Now, it is true that all grace and goodness in our hearts is entirely from God; we are completely and directly dependent on Him for our supply of grace. But nevertheless the people I've just described are mistaken. God does not communicate Himself and His Spirit, His saving grace, as external objects delivered to the soul. Instead, He gives His Spirit to be united with the soul's faculties, so that He dwells there, changing the very foundation of who we are. We are not merely inanimate receptacles for His grace; we are transfused with grace, receiving it internally so that our natures become totally new. And nature is something that endures. Yes, we are dependent on Christ for a constant supply of grace, but we are not like some lifeless material that can only be moved so long as it is being acted upon by a living agent; His grace communicates life to our hearts. Through Christ's power, we have become inherently as alive as He is, for when Christ has saved us through grace, then He lives forever within us. I am not saying that our soul is a dead thing that only has life because of the life of Christ inside of it, like a dead costume that is given the semblance of life when a living person wears it. No, our souls are also as alive as Christ is alive, because of His power and grace.

When we hold a mirror to catch a sunbeam, we might say that the light in the glass is from the sun, as much as grace in our souls is from Christ. But this metaphor is an imperfect one, for the glass remains unchanged by the sunlight; once we bring the glass indoors, it will no longer shine, for it possesses no quality of light for its own. On the other hand, when our souls receive light from the Sun of Righteousness, our natures become luminous; not only does the Sun shine through us, but we also are little suns, sharing the nature of the Fountain of all light. We are more like lamps than mirrors; we are the lamps in the tabernacle that were lit with heaven's fire and thus became in themselves living burning things. To use yet another metaphor, we not only drink from the water of life that flows from the original fountain, but this water becomes a fountain within ourselves, springing up and flowing out (John 4:14; 7:38–39). Grace could also be compared to a seed planted in the ground; it does not lie unmoving in the soil, to be picked out again later, leaving the soil as it was before. Instead, the seed puts out roots and grows, clinging to the earth and becoming a part of the soil's very nature.

All this is true of spiritual revelations and emotions that are given at a person's original conversion, and this is also true of all subsequent enlightenment and feeling; they are all transforming. Divine power and energy is in each of these experiences just as much as it was in the earliest revelations; and all of them still reach the very bottom of the heart, affecting and altering the soul's nature. This process never stops as long we are alive, for grace works in our hearts to bring us to perfection. That is why the Bible talks about progress of grace in our hearts as an ongoing conversion, a constant renovation of our natures.

That is why the apostle Paul exhorts those who were at

Rome, "beloved of God, called to be saints" (Rom. 1:7), who were subjects of God's redeeming mercies, to "be transformed by the renewing of [their] mind" (Rom. 12:1–2); "I beseech you therefore, brethren, by the mercies of God, that ye present your bodies a living sacrifice. . . . And be not conformed to this world: but be ye transformed by the renewing of your mind." He also wrote to the "saints. . . and to the faithful in Christ Jesus," who were at Ephesus (Eph. 1), that he ceased not to pray for them, that God would give them the "spirit of wisdom and revelation in the knowledge of [Christ]: the eyes of [their] understanding being enlightened; that [they might] know," or experience, what was the "exceeding greatness of [God's] power [towards them] who believe, according to the working of his mighty power, which he wrought in Christ, when he raised him from the dead, and set him at his own right hand in the heavenly places." Paul is talking here about God's glorious power when He converts and renews the soul. That is why Paul exhorts the Ephesians to put off "the old man, which is corrupt according to the deceitful lusts; and be renewed in the spirit of [their] mind; and that [they] put on the new man, which after God is created in righteousness and true holiness" (Eph. 4:22–24).

Some intense emotions come and go without leaving behind any enduring effect. They go off suddenly, like fireworks, shooting from the heights of emotion and rapture directly to totally deadness and dullness. Spiritual emotions are not like this; when they pass, they leave behind a sweet taste and a greater enjoyment for divine things, a stronger bent toward God and holiness. Moses' face not only shone while he was on the mountain, talking with God in an extraordinary way, but it continued to shine after he came down from the mountain. When we have been talking with Christ, the experience will leave us too with a perceptible difference. We will find that there is something remarkable now about our disposition and makeup, and if we trace it to its source, we will find it is because we have been with Jesus (Acts 1:13).

VIII. True grace-filled feeling is different from false, delusional emotions, in that spiritual feeling is accompanied by the lamblike, dovelike spirit and temperament of Jesus Christ; it makes us more like Christ.

In other words, spiritual emotions give birth to the same spirit of love, gentleness, quietness, forgiveness, and mercy, as appeared in Christ.

The evidence for this in Scripture is abundant. In fact, the spirit we have just described might be called the very spirit of the gospel, the Christian spirit that distinguishes it from all others. When some of the disciples of Christ said something that went against this, Christ rebuked them (Luke 9:55), indicating that the natural defensiveness the disciples had displayed was contrary to the spirit of His kingdom. If we are real disciples of Christ, then we will have this spirit in us, and we will live in this way. This is the spirit that will possess and govern our characters.

This is clear in the words of Proverbs 17:27: "A man of understanding is of an excellent spirit." We see the same thing when Christ described the people who are the heirs to His kingdom: "Blessed are the meek: for they shall inherit the earth. Blessed are the merciful: for they shall obtain mercy. Blessed are the peacemakers: for they shall be called the children of God" (Matt. 5:5, 7, 9). This spirit is the special character of those chosen by God: "Put on therefore, as the elect of God, holy and beloved, bowels of mercies, kindness, humbleness of mind, meekness, longsuffering; forbearing one another, and forgiving one another" (Col. 3:12–13). Paul describes this same spirit as "charity": "Charity suffereth long, and is kind; charity envieth not; charity vaunteth not itself, is not puffed up, doth not behave itself unseemly, seeketh not her own, is not easily provoked, thinketh no evil" (1 Cor. 13:4–5). Paul also tells us that the Spirit's fruits in our lives are this same spirit I have described: "The fruit of the Spirit is love, joy, peace, longsuffering, gentleness, goodness, faith, meekness, temperance" (Gal. 5:22–23). The apostle James cautions us that anything contrary to this gentle, loving spirit means we are deluding ourselves if we call ourselves Christ's people: "If ye have bitter envying and strife in your hearts, glory not, and lie not against the truth. This wisdom decendeth not from above, but is earthly, sensual, devilish. For where envying and strife is, there is confusion and every evil work. But the wisdom that is from above is first pure, then peaceable, gentle, and easy to be intreated, full of mercy and good fruits" (James 3:14–17).

Once grace has transformed us, all of our emotions are touched by grace too—but some of these emotions fit better with the spirit of holiness than others. These qualities fit more easily with the gospel message, because they are not contrary to God's own nature which He demonstrated through His Son Jesus. These are the qualities that were so evident in Christ's life while He was here on earth—and

Christ is the direct revelation of who God is, so we can conclude that these qualities are divine. These feelings also are congruent with the drift and design of the work of redemption, and the benefits we receive from it. The feelings match the relationship we have with God and each other.

What are these virtues? Humility, gentleness, love, forgiveness, and mercy. These are what characterize Christians. This loving nature was Christ's, and He is the Head of the Christian church. The Bible speaks of it in both the Old Testament and the New: "Tell ye the daughter of Sion, Behold, they King cometh unto thee, meek, and sitting upon an ass, and a colt the foal of an ass" (Matt. 21:5); "Learn of me; for I am meek and lowly in heart" (Matt. 11:29). This gentle spirit is clear in the very name by which Christ is called: the Lamb. And if these things are true of Christ's character, then they should also be true of ours. To be called a Christian means we are Christ-like; otherwise we don't deserve to bear His name.

"Put on the new man, which is renewed in knowledge after the image of him that created him" (Col. 3:10). All true Christians see the glory of the Lord, as though they were looking in a mirror, and they are changed into the same image, by His Spirit (2 Cor. 3:18). His chosen ones are all predestined to be conformed to the image of the Son of God, that He might be the firstborn among many children (Rom. 8:29). As we have borne the earthly image of the first man, so we must also bear the image of the heavenly Man, for otherwise our natures will remain under the power of earthy limitations—but if we are heavenly, then we will be like those who are in heaven (1 Cor. 15:47–49). Christ is full of grace, and Christians all receive of His fullness, grace for grace; in other words, the grace in our own hearts answers the grace in Christ, in the way that wax answers the seal that presses on it. We shine with His light, the light of the Sun of Righteousness; we illumine the world around us with His shining love and sweetness. The lamps within our spiritual temples are kindled by fire from heaven, and they burn now with the same sort of flame.

The branch of a tree has the same nature as the tree's root; it has the same sap, and it bears the same sort of fruit. The body's members have the same kind of life as the head. All these metaphors show us that it would be strange if Christians lacked the same temperament and spirit that are Christ's, for they are His flesh and His bone, one spirit with Him (1 Cor. 6:17). When they live now, it is not they who live but Christ who lives in them, and a Christian spirit is Christ's mark that He sets upon the souls of His people, His seal on their forehead, bearing His image and inscription.

If we consider ourselves Christians, the followers of Christ, then we must be obedient to the call of Christ: "Come unto me. . .and learn of me; for I am meek and lowly in heart" (Matt. 11:28, 29); we must follow Him: "These are they which follow the Lamb whithersoever he goeth" (Rev. 14:4). True Christians have clothed themselves with the gentle, quiet, and loving temperament of Christ; if we are in Christ, then we have put Him on. In this respect, the church is clothed with the Sun; not only are we free of guilt, clothed with His righteousness, but we are also adorned with His grace (Rom. 13:14). Christ is the great Shepherd, but He is also Himself a Lamb, one of us, for His followers are the lambs: "Feed my lambs" (John 21:15); "I send you forth as lambs among wolves" (Luke 10:3).

Christ's redemption of the church from the power of the devil was foretold when David saved the lamb from the mouth of the lion and the bear.

God's gentle Spirit is further represented by a dove, an emblem of harmlessness, peace, and love. When Christ was anointed by the Father, the Spirit descended on Him like a dove, showing us the real nature of Christ's mission. And the same Spirit that descended on the Head of the church descends on the members as well: "God hath sent forth the Spirit of his Son into your hearts" (Gal. 4:6); "if any man have not the Spirit of Christ, he is none of his" (Rom. 8:9). The whole mystical body, Head, and members have but one Spirit (1 Cor. 6:17; Eph. 4:4). Christ breathes His own Spirit on His disciples (John 20:22). As Christ was anointed, with the Holy Ghost descending on Him like a dove, so Christians also "have an anointing from the Holy One" (see 1 John 2:20, 27). They are anointed with the same oil, the same "precious ointment upon the head, that goes down to the skirts of the garment," a spirit of peace and love: "Behold, how good and how pleasant it is for brethren to dwell together in unity! It is like the precious ointment upon the head, that ran down upon the beard, even Aaron's beard: that went down to the skirts of his garments" (Ps. 133:1–2). Because the church has a dovelike temperament and disposition, the Bible says that she has doves' eyes: "Behold, thou art fair, my love; behold, thou are fair; thou hast doves' eyes" (Song of Sol. 1:15); "Behold, thou art fair, my love; behold, thou art fair; thou hast doves' eyes within thy locks" (Song of Sol. 4:1). The same is said of Christ: "His eyes are as the eyes of doves" (Song of Sol. 5:12); and the church is frequently compared to a dove in Scripture: "O my dove, that art in the clefts of the rock" (Song of Sol. 2:14); "Open to me, . . .my love, my dove" (Song of Sol. 5:2); "My dove, my undefiled is but one" (Song of Sol. 6:9); "Yet shall ye be as the wings of a dove covered with silver, and her feathers with yellow gold" (Ps. 68:13); "O deliver not the soul of thy turtledove unto the multitude of the wicked" (Ps. 74:19). The dove that Noah sent out of the ark, the one that could find no place to perch until she returned, foretold the nature of a true saint.

Gentleness is so great a part of the saint's character, that the words "meek" (or gentle) and "godly" are used as synonyms in Scripture: "Yet a little while, and the wicked shall not be; . . .but the meek shall inherit the earth" (Ps. 37:10–11); "The LORD lifteth up the meek: he casteth the wicked down to the ground" (Ps. 147:6).

This is probably why Christ calls His disciples, the heirs of heaven, little children: "Suffer the little children, and forbid them not, to come unto me: for of such is the kingdom of heaven" (Matt. 19:14); "Whosoever shall give to drink unto one of these little ones a cup of cold water only in the name of a disciple, verily I say unto you, he shall in no wise lose his reward" (Matt. 10:42); "Whoso shall offend one of these little ones. . ." (Matt. 18:6); "Take heed that ye despise not one of these little ones" (Matt. 18:10); "It is not the will of your Father which is in heaven, that one of little ones should perish" (Matt. 18:14); "Little children, yet a little while I am with you" (John 13:33). Little children are innocent and harmless; they do not do much mischief in the world, and no one needs to be afraid of them; they are not dangerous sort of people, and their anger does not last long, for they do not nurse deep resentments and grudges.

So Christians should be like children, free of malice (1 Cor. 14:20). Little children are not sneaky and deceitful, but plain and simple; they are not good at putting on airs and telling complicated lies; they don't know how to make people believe they are something that they aren't. Instead, they are yielding and flexible, not rigid and obstinate; they do not rely on their own understanding, but they trust the instruction of their parents, depending on the superior understanding of adults. As a result, children are another fitting and vivid symbol for those of us who are followers of the Lamb. And the Bible does not only say that these childlike qualities are commendable, something we should all aim toward and which some who are extraordinarily far along spiritually may actually attain; no, the Bible says that a child's spirit is absolutely necessary if we want to enter the kingdom of heaven: "Verily I say unto you, Except ye be converted, and become as little children, ye shall not enter into the kingdom of heaven" (Matt. 18:3); "Verily I say unto you, Whosoever shall not receive the kingdom of God as a little child, he shall not enter therein" (Mark 10:15).

But at this point some of you are probably saying, "But what about Christian fortitude and boldness for Christ? What about being good soldiers in Christian warfare and fighting boldly against the enemies of Christ and His people?"

My answer is this: Without a doubt, the Christian life can be quite aptly compared to a war. The deepest Christians are the best soldiers, fortified with the greatest degree of Christian bravery. We are to be steadfast and vigorous in our opposition to anything that would overthrow the kingdom of Christ. But many people seem to be mistaken about the nature of Christian strength. It is nothing like the brutal fierceness of beasts of prey. True Christian fortitude consists of strength of mind, through grace, and this strength works in two ways: first, to suppress the selfish passions and desires within our own minds; and second, to help us act in love without being hindered by sinful fear or the opposition of enemies.

When hypocrites demonstrate a false bravery for Christ, the same passions that are restrained and controlled by real Christian strength and fortitude are now prominently at work—and they are the exact opposite of the spiritual emotions we have discussed. Spiritual fortitude can be of use when we need to withstand the enemies that are around us—but that is not its ordinary use. For the most part, spiritual strength is needed for resisting and suppressing the enemies that are *within* us; they are our worst and strongest enemies, the ones that have the greatest advantage against us. With great patience and determination, a good soldier of Jesus Christ mentally maintains a holy calm, gentleness, sweetness, and kindness, despite all the storms, injuries, strange behavior, and surprising events of this evil and unreasonable world. The Scripture implies that this is true strength: "He that is slow to anger is better than the mighty; and he that ruleth his spirit than he that taketh a city" (Prov. 16:32).

If we want to be certain what holy strength really is, we need only look at the Captain of all God's hosts, our great Leader and Example, and we will see how His fortitude and valor was clear during His hardest time. This was when He fought the greatest fight every battled with these enemies, and He fought with them all alone, without the support of any of His friends. His power and might were so great that He won this battle with the glorious victory that will be celebrated by all the hosts of heaven throughout all eternity. Now look at Jesus Christ while He was experiencing His last suffering, when His enemies on earth and in hell had made their most violent attack on Him, surrounding Him on every side like roaring lions. Here we see the fortitude of a holy warrior, a champion in God's cause, a fit example for any soldier to follow in his fight against evil.

And how did Christ show His holy valor? Never with fiery passion nor with fierce and violent words. He did not vehemently protest the intolerable wickedness of His opposers, giving them a piece of His mind in no uncertain terms. Instead, He kept His mouth shut when He was afflicted and oppressed, like a lamb going to the slaughter, or a sheep before its shearers. What is more, He prayed that the Father would forgive His enemies because they did not know what they were doing. He never shed others' blood, but with all-conquering patience and love, He shed His own. When Peter, in a burst of pretended boldness for Christ, confidently declared he would sooner die with Christ than deny Him and then began swinging his sword around him, Christ gently rebuked him and healed the wound Peter had given.

Christ's patience, gentleness, love and forgiveness was never more gloriously demonstrated than during His last and greatest crisis. Never did He look so much like a lamb, and never did He show so much of His dovelike spirit. That is why if we see any of Christ's followers who are being violently persecuted and opposed, and yet through it all they maintain the humility and quietness and gentleness of a lamb, the harmlessness and love and sweetness of a dove, we can assume that here is a good soldier of Jesus Christ.

On the other hand, when people are fierce and violent, acting out their sharp and bitter passions, we can assume that they are weak people who lack strength and fortitude: "And I, brethren, could not speak unto you as unto spiritual, but as unto carnal, even as unto babes in Christ. . . . For ye are yet carnal; for whereas there is among you envying, and strife, and divisions, are ye not carnal, and walk as men?" (1 Cor. 3:1, 3).

Some people pretend to be strong and brave for Christ, but their only motive is pride. They may expose themselves to the world's hatred and even provoke its displeasure, all for pride. Pride causes us to seek to be different and unique from everyone else, and people who pride themselves on their spiritual superiority may set themselves up as the opponents of anyone they consider to be sinful. They do so because they want to impress others; they want to feed their own sense of superiority.

But those who are truly brave for Christ are carried beyond any consideration of human approval. They don't care what anyone thinks of them, so long as Christ is pleased with them. They do not even care if their own friends and community admires them, which tells much more about them than if they merely didn't care what their opposers thought. The apostle Paul had this type of indifference to human glory (1 Thess. 2:6). The person who is truly brave for Christ has enough strength to confess her faults openly; she can admit when she is wrong, even to her enemies. This is much better proof of holy bravery than if she had fiercely stood up to her opposers.

Just as some people are mistaken about the nature of true bravery, so others are confused about Christian zeal. It is indeed a flame, but a sweet one. It burns with the heat of divine love and Christian charity, and this is the sweetest and kindest quality that exists in the human heart—or the angelic one, for that matter. Zeal is what gives love's flame its fervor; it makes it ardently and vigorously extend itself as far as it needs to go. Zeal empowers love to withstand any evil that might try to get in its way. Strength against opposition is indeed a part of zeal—or at least a companion of zeal—but this strength works against things and not people. Bitterness against anyone should have no part in our zeal. The warmer true zeal is, the more fervently we feel it, the further we will feel from any bitterness, for we will be that much more full of love for everyone, both for our friends and for our enemies. That is the definition of true Christian zeal: the fervor of holy love. When zeal does help us to overcome opposition, it is mostly the evil that hides in our own hearts that zeal attacks. These are the enemies that the true saint sees most clearly, and these are the enemies he contends with the most, while others' sins seldom trouble his spiritual well-being. That is why true Christian zeal should demonstrate nothing that is contrary to the spirit of gentleness and love, the spirit of a little child, a lamb and dove, that we have already described. True spiritual zeal works hand in hand with this loving spirit, and even encourages it to grow.

I want to add something to what I've said about this Christ-like spirit. The Bible makes plain that three characteristics should be true of every Christian: forgiveness, love, and mercy. Scripture says that each of these three qualities are absolutely necessary.

If we have a forgiving spirit we will be disposed to overlook and forgive injuries. In Scripture, Christ talks about this quality as both a negative and positive evidence: If we possess it, then that is a sign that we are in a state of forgiveness and favor ourselves, but if we lack this spirit, then that is an indication that we are not forgiven of God either. Christ seems to underline this concept several times so that we'll pay attention and never forget how important it is to forgive others: "Forgive us our debts, as we forgive our debtors. . . . For if ye forgive men their trespasses, your heavenly Father will also forgive you: but if ye forgive not men their trespasses, neither will your Father forgive your trespasses" (Matt. 6:12, 14–15). He says the same sort of thing in Mark 11:25–26 and again in Matthew 18:22–35, in the parable of the servant who owed his lord ten thousand talents, but who would not forgive his fellow servant a hundred pence and therefore was punished. When Christ interprets this parable for His listeners, He says, "So likewise shall my heavenly Father do also unto you, if ye from your hearts forgive not every one his brother their trespasses" (Matt. 18:35).

The Bible also makes abundantly evident that true saints are loving and kind. Without love, Paul tells us, though we should speak with the tongues of men and angels, we are as a sounding brass, or a tinkling cymbal; and though we have the gift of prophecy, and understand all mysteries and all knowledge, yet without a loving spirit we are nothing. There is no other virtue or heart-feeling of which the New Testament so often and so expressly insists. Love is the sign for how we can know other Christians, and it is the sign to our own hearts of who we are. Christ calls the law of love

His commandment: "A new commandment I give unto you, That ye love one another; as a I have loved you, that ye also love one another" (John 13:34); "This is my commandment, That ye love one another, as a I have loved you" (John 15:12); "These things I command you, that ye love one another" (John 15:17); "By this shall all men know that ye are my disciples, if ye have love one to another" (John 13:35); "He that hath my commandments [referring to the commandment of love He had already laid down], and keepeth them, he it is that loveth me" (John 14:21).

John, the beloved disciple, had so much of this sweet spirit himself that he emphasized it again and again in his epistles. None of the other apostles talk about love so expressly and insistently as John does: "He that saith he is in the light, and hateth his brother, is in darkness even until now. He that loveth his brother abideth in the light, and there is none occasion of stumbling in him" (1 John 2:9–10); "We know that we have passed from death unto life, because we love the brethren. He that loveth not his brother abideth in death" (1 John 3:14); "My little children, let us not love in word, neither in tongue; but in deed and in truth. And hereby we know that we are of the truth, and shall assure our hearts before him" (1 John 3:18–19); "And this is his commandment, That we should . . . love one another. . . . And he that keepeth his commandments dwelleth in him, and he in him. And hereby we know that he abideth in us, by the Spirit which he hath given us" (1 John 3:23–24); "Beloved, let us love one another: for love is of God; and every one that loveth is born of God, and knoweth God. He that loveth not knoweth not God; for God is love" (1 John 4:7–8); "No man hath seen God at any time. If we love one another,

God dwelleth in us, and his love is perfected in us. Hereby know we that we dwell in him, and he in us, because he hath given us of his Spirit" (1 John 4:12–13); "God is love; and he that dwelleth in love dwelleth in God, and God in him" (1 John 4:16); "If a man say, I love God, and hateth his brother, he is a liar: for he that loveth not his brother whom he hath seen, how can he love God whom he hath not seen?" (1 John 4:20).

Scripture also makes as plain as possible that no one is a true saint who does not do what she can to help those who are not as fortunate as she is, those who are poor and suffering: "The righteous sheweth mercy, and giveth" (Ps. 37:21); "He is ever merciful, and lendeth" (Ps. 37:26); "A good man sheweth favour, and lendeth" (Ps. 112:5); "He hath dispersed, he hath given to the poor" (Ps. 112:9); "He that honoureth [his Maker] hath mercy on the poor" (Prov. 14:31); "The righteous giveth and spareth not" (Prov. 21:26); "He judged the cause of the poor and needy, then it was well with him: was not this to know me? saith the Lord" (Jer. 22:16); "Pure religion and undefiled before God and the Father is this, To visit the fatherless and widows in their affliction" (James 1:27); "For I desired mercy, and not sacrifice; and the knowledge of God more than burnt offerings" (Hos. 6:6); "Blessed are the merciful: for they shall obtain mercy" (Matt. 5:7); "I speak not by commandment, but by occasion of the forwardness of others, and to prove the sincerity of your love" (2 Cor. 8:8); "For he shall have judgment without mercy, that hath shewed no mercy. . . . What doth it profit, my brethren, though a man say he hath faith, and have not works? can faith save him? If a brother or sister be naked, and destitute of daily food, and one of you say unto them, Depart in peace, be ye warmed and filled; notwithstanding ye give them not those things which are needful to the body; what doth it profit?" (James 2:13–16); "But whoso hath this world's good, and seeth his brother have need, and shutteth up his bowels of compassion from him, how dwelleth the love of God in him?" (1 John 3:17). When Christ describes the day of judgment (Matt. 25), He indicates that judgment will be passed on whether we have demonstrated a merciful spirit to others. Christ obviously wanted us to realize that unless we are possessed by love and mercy, we have no chance of being recognized by Him on that day. Scripture indicates that a righteous person and a merciful one are the same thing: "The righteous perisheth, and no man layeth it to heart: and merciful men are taken away, none considering that the righteous is taken away from the evil to come" (Isa. 57:1).

So we can see how clearly Scripture tells us that if we have real grace, we will be controlled by the lamblike, dovelike Spirit of Jesus Christ. This is the essence of Christianity; this is its saving principle, the source of its ability to heal and save us. All the feeling of our hearts should be accompanied by this same spirit. Christ's gentle love should be a part of all our fear and hope, sorrow and joy, confidence and zeal.

Please don't misunderstand me, though; I'm not saying that true Christians have no remains of their original natures. They can be guilty of behavior that is far from loving. But I still affirm—and I will always affirms so long as I continue to believe the Bible—that true Christianity will always be loving and gentle. True Christians have this spirit as an integral part of their characters. Individual behaviors may sometimes step out of line, but love remains the ruling tendency of their hearts.

As a result, ministers and other spiritual leaders have no reason (at least none that Christ gives us) to encourage people whose behavior and character are neither loving nor gentle to think that they have been truly converted. These people tell a good story about their great revelations and enlightenment, but if we use this as the basis for our judgment, we are setting our own wisdom higher than Christ's; we are ignoring a rule that Christ gave us so that we might know who are His disciples.

Many people (especially those who follow some particular religious practices) distort true religion by putting so much emphasis on certain kinds of experiences and emotions, while ignoring the importance of love. When they do so they create a false Christianity that looks very different from the one given in the Scripture. The Bible never talks about any real Christians who are habitually greedy, selfish, cross, and contentious. How silly to think that there is any such thing as a morose, hard-hearted, stingy, spiteful, true Christian! We must learn how to bring people to Christ's rule, and not our rules to people; we must keep ourselves from straining and stretching God's Word to make it consistent with our own behavior (and possibly our friends'), while meanwhile we twist it out of the shape God intended.

Of course we will always have to make allowances for people's natural temperaments—but not allowances big enough to include wolves and serpents as true Christians. Real grace changes our very natures, and the worse we once were, the more conspicuous will be the transformation in our hearts. Some people seem to believe that grace will only control sins like drunkenness or sexual deviation; but this is not a scriptural perspective.

The Bible again and again tells us that the change grace

brings has much more to do with love and gentleness: "The wolf also shall dwell with the lamb, and the leopard shall lie down with the kid; and the calf and the young lion and the fatling together, and a little child shall lead them. And the cow and the bear shall feed; their young ones shall lie down together: and the lion shall eat straw like the ox. And the sucking child shall play on the hole of the asp, and the weaned child shall put his hand on the cockatrice' den. They shall not hurt nor destroy in all my holy mountain: for the earth shall be full of the knowledge of the LORD, as the waters cover the sea" (Isa. 11:6–9). Isaiah 65:25 carries the same message, and in the early church, converts were dramatically changed in this way: "For we ourselves also were sometimes foolish, disobedient, deceived, serving divers lusts and pleasures, living in malice and envy, hateful, and hating one another. But after that the kindness and love of God our Saviour toward man appeared. . .he saved us, by the washing of regeneration, and renewing of the Holy Ghost" (Titus 3:3–5); "In the which ye also walked some time, when ye lived in them. But now ye also put off all these; anger, wrath, malice, blasphemy, filthy communication out of your mouth" (Col. 3:7–8).

IX. Grace-filled feeling softens the heart, making us tender.

False emotion may seem to melt people at first, but in the end it always tends to harden the heart. The delusion that goes along with it finally stupefies the mind, shutting it tight against tenderness and sensitivity. In the end, people become less moved by their present and past sins, less conscientious about future sins, and less concerned about the warnings in God's Word. They are careless about the condition of their hearts, as well as their behavior, and they are less quick to discern what is sinful. When they first were stirred by a legalistic fear of hell, they may have worried about the appearance of evil in their lives, but after a while, having received this and that warm impression, they become convinced that they are justified to have a high opinion of themselves. Since they are no longer worried about hell, they neglect duties that are troublesome and inconvenient. If something in the Bible seems difficult or if it seems to require too much effort and pain, they ignore it, while at the same time they rationalize that various selfish pleasures are harmless.

Instead of embracing Christ as their Savior from sin, these people are actually trusting in Him to help them save their sin. Instead of flying to Him as their refuge from their spiritual enemies, they use Him to defend themselves against God. They turn Christ into the devil's helper, so that they may comfortably continue to sin against God, assuming that Christ will protect them from God's judgment. They trust Christ to allow them the quiet enjoyment of their sins, to be their shield against God's displeasure, and all the while, as they claim to be Christ's children and pretend to press against His heart, they hide their mortal weapons under their clothes. They claim to feel great love for God and great joy in tasting the sweetness of His love for them, but all the while they are hiding death and hatred in their hearts.

The apostle Jude talks about people like this (Jude 4), and God addresses them in Ezekiel 33:13: "When I shall say to the righteous, that he shall surely live; if he trust to his own righteousness, and commit iniquity, all his righteousness shall not be remembered; but for his iniquity that he hath committed, he shall die for it."

The feeling that comes from grace is quite different; it turns a heart of stone more and more into a heart of flesh. Holy love and hope work far better at making us tender and sensitive to sin; love will make us far more watchful and careful than any slavish fear of hell. Grace-filled feeling, as I observed before, flows out of a contrite heart— and "contrite" means a heart that has been bruised, broken with godly sorrow. This makes the heart tender, just as bruised flesh is tender and easily hurt. This godly sorrow has a much greater influence on our behavior than any legalistic sorrow that is motivated only by selfishness.

When Christ compared a newborn Christian to a young child, He was implying this same tenderness of heart, for a child's flesh is very sensitive. The story about Naaman, when his leprosy was cured by his washing in Jordan, foretells what will happen to the soul that is renewed and washed by Christ's regeneration; we are told that "went he down, and dipped himself seven times in Jordan, according to the saying of the man of God: and his flesh came again like unto the flesh of a little child" (2 Kings 5:14). Not only is a child's flesh tender, however, but her mind is sensitive also, for her emotions are easily moved. She cries easily and is worried by others' pain; the Christian should be the same way (John 11:35; Rom. 12:15; 1 Cor. 12:26). A young child melts and begins to cry over the smallest troubles, and so should the Christian's heart be in regard to sin; as a young child is easily scared by that which might threaten her, so should a Christian be alarmed by the appearance of anything that could threaten the soul. A child, when she meets something threatening, does not trust in her own strength but flies to her parents for safety; in the same way, a saint is not self-confident about taking on spiritual enemies, but instead, he flies to Christ. A child is apt to be suspicious of trouble in dangerous places, afraid of the dark, afraid to be left alone or far from home—and the saint is apt to be just as sensitive to spiritual dangers, worried about himself, full of fear when he cannot see the way ahead, afraid to be left alone or at a distance from God.

These childlike qualities are evident in the following Scriptures: "Happy is the man that feareth alway: but he that hardeneth his heart shall fall into mischief" (Prov. 28:14); "My flesh trembleth for fear of thee; and I am afraid of they judgments" (Ps. 119:120); "To this man will I look, even to him that is poor and of a contrite spirit, and trembleth at my word" (Isa. 66:2); "Hear the word of the LORD, ye that tremble at his word" (Isa. 66:5); "Then were assembled unto me every one that trembled at the words of the God of Israel" (Ezra 9:4); "According to the counsel of my lord, and of those that tremble at the commandment of our God" (Ezra 10:3). As a young child approaches people who are bigger than her with awe, so do the saints approach God with holy awe and reverence: "Shall not his excellency make you afraid? and his dread fall upon you?" (Job 13:11).

You can see then that grace-filled feeling does not tend to make us bold, presumptuous, noisy, and boisterous. Instead, we tend to speak with trembling: "When Ephraim spake trembling, he exalted himself in Israel; but when he offended in Baal, he died" (Hos. 13:1). It tends to clothe us with a holy reverence and fear as we interact both with God and others (see Ps. 2:11; 1 Pet. 3:15; 2 Cor. 7:15; Eph. 6:5; Rom. 11:20).

Some of you may be objecting now and saying, "Isn't there such a thing as holy boldness in prayer? This doesn't sound as though we must always approach God with fear and trembling." Well, I have to answer that of course holy boldness is a real quality, one that is often found in the highest saints, people who are filled with faith and love. But this holy boldness is not in the least contrary to reverence, although it is certainly contrary to disunity and servility. Holy boldness abolishes the feelings that arise when we are distant or alienated from God, as a slave is far from his master. Holy boldness assures our hearts that we are now one with God, and we no longer serve Him out of fear. But the angels in heaven cover their faces as they approach the throne of God (Isa. 6:2), showing the same fear and reverence as the lowest and most sinful worm.

The Bible is full of images of this fear and reverence. Rebecca (whose marriage with Isaac foretells the church's role as the bride of Christ), when she meets Isaac, gets down from her camel and covers herself with her veil— and yet she was brought to Issac as his bride, the human relationship that involves the closest, most intimate union of all. Elijah, the great prophet, had a holy familiarity with God, and yet even at times of special nearness to God, even when he talked with Him on the mountain, he wrapped his face in his mantle. He didn't do this because he was terrified with a servile fear. In fact, Elijah doesn't seem frightened at all by the terrible wind, the earthquake, and fire—but after these were all over, and God spoke to him as a friend in "a still small voice" (1 Kings 19:12–13), that was when Elijah hid his face. Moses is another one who spoke with God face-to-face, the way a man speaks with his friend, and yet the Bible says, "Moses made haste, and bowed his head toward the earth, and worshipped" (Exod. 34:8).

Some people demonstrate a most unsuitable and insufferable boldness when they address the great Jehovah. Their familiarity is mere affectation, though, a pretense designed to impress others. If they were ever to catch a glimpse of how far they actually are from God, they would shrink into nothing, consumed by horror and shame. They are like the Pharisee, who boldly spoke to God, confident of his own superiority—but if they grasped their need, they would be more like the publican who "standing afar off, would not lift up so much as his eyes unto heaven, but smote upon his breast, saying, God be merciful to me a sinner" (Luke 18:13).

Sinful creatures like ourselves should approach a holy God with contrition and penitence (but with faith, and without terror). The woman in the seventh chapter of Luke was filled with love for Christ, the sort of love that casts out fear, and yet she approached Christ with such humble reverence and modesty that she stood at His feet and cried, washing his feet with her tears, as though she could not look into His face.

One reason why grace-filled feeling is accompanied by a tenderness of spirit is that true grace, as we have mentioned, tends to increase the conviction of sin. Grace does not anesthetize a person's conscience, but instead makes it all the more sensitive. Grace tends to make us watch our hearts more carefully than any legalistic false spirituality. The heart of someone who is truly sorry is like a burned child who is terrified of the fire. On the other hand, someone who has had a counterfeit repentance, accompanied by false comforts and joys, is like iron that has been suddenly heated and then cooled; it becomes much harder than before. A false conversion puts an end to the prickings of the conscience, and eventually makes the person oblivious to the conscientious legalism that once troubled him.

All grace-filled emotion—not only godly sorrow, but also a spiritual joy—has a tendency to promote this Christian tenderness of heart: "Serve the LORD with fear, and rejoice with trembling" (Ps. 2:11). The same is true of spiritual hope: "Behold, the eye of the LORD is upon them that fear him, upon them that hope in his mercy" (Ps. 33:18); "The LORD taketh pleasure in them that fear him, in those that hope in his mercy" (Ps. 147:11). The greater our hope, the more tender will be our hearts, for once servile fear has been banished, replaced by holy assurance, we feel a proportionate increase of reverential fear. We no longer fear punishment, but instead we fear God's displeasure; we no longer fear hell, instead we fear sin. Our hearts are fixed on God, trusting in Him, and so we have far less worries about external evil and bad news; instead, we worry about our own hearts' strength, wisdom, stability, faithfulness. We have more holy boldness and less self-confidence. We are more certain we will be delivered from hell than others are, but we are more aware that we don't deserve to be. Our faith is less apt to be shaken, but we are more apt to be moved by the troubles of others. We have the firmest comfort, but the softest hearts. Richer than others, we are the poorest of all in spirit: The tallest and strongest saint among us is also like the smallest and most sensitive child.

X. *Another way that holy emotion is different from false feeling is its beautiful symmetry and proportion; in others words, it is well-balanced and consistent.*

Not that this symmetry is perfect in this life. Often it is defective, because we lack grace or proper instruction, because of errors in judgment or some temperamental flaw, because of insufficient education or many other disadvantages that I could mention. Regardless of all these things that can mar spiritual feeling, we never see the strange and wild excesses that we do with false religious feeling.

Truly holy feeling is well-balanced. That is because grace heals our hearts completely, not just here and there. We bear the whole image of Christ; we have put off the old person, and we've put on the new person along with all its parts and members. It pleased the Father to make all fullness, total wholeness, and completion, dwell within Christ; there is in Him every grace; He is full of grace and truth; and we who belong to Christ "of his fulness have all we received, and grace for grace" (John 1:16). We have every grace in us which is in Christ: grace for grace, that is grace answering to grace. Each quality of grace in Christ has its image in us to answer it, and the image we bear is a true image; there is something of the same beautiful proportion in the image as in the original, feature for feature and member for member.

There is symmetry and beauty in God's workmanship.

God made our natural bodies so that they have many members, all in beautiful proportion to one another, and He made our new identity in Christ have the same perfect balance. Many of us were born with a perfect child's body, but disease, weakness, or injury may mar our original perfection. And yet we can still see the beauty that God originally created, despite the present imperfections. The same is true of our hearts.

But the hypocrite is like Ephraim in the Bible, when God was complaining about His people's hypocrisy: "Ephraim is a cake not turned" (Hos. 7:8), half cooked and half raw. His emotions were inconsistent.

Some people are particularly fond of certain religious feelings, while they totally neglect others. As I observed earlier, holy hope and holy fear go together in our hearts (Ps. 33:18; 147:11). But hypocrites enjoy confident hope, while they are void of reverence and caution. Consider the way joy and fear were both at their height in the hearts of the disciples on the morning of Christ's resurrection: "And they departed quickly from the sepulchre with fear and great joy" (Matt. 28:8). But many hypocrites rejoice without trembling; their joy is the opposite of godly fear.

One of the big differences between saints and hypocrites is this, that the saints' joy and comfort is always accompanied by godly sorrow and mourning for sin. The same thing was foretold of God's people when they would come to Canaan, the land of rest flowing with milk and honey: "And ye shall know that I am the LORD, when I shall bring you into the land of Israel, into the country for the which I lifted up mine hand to give it to your fathers. And there shall ye remember your ways, and all your doings, wherein ye have been defiled; and ye shall lothe yourselves in your sight for all your evils that ye have committed" (Ezek. 20:42–43).

A true saint is like a baby in this respect. The saint never had any godly sorrow before she was born again, but now she feels it often; and the baby never cried before he was born while he was in darkness, but as soon as he saw the light, he began to cry and from then on continues to cry often. Although Christ has borne our griefs and carried our sorrows, so that we are freed from the sorrow of punishment and can now sweetly feed upon the comforts Christ has bought for us, that doesn't keep us from the sorrow of repentance. That is why the children of Israel were commanded to always feed upon the paschal lamb with bitter herbs. True saints are spoken of in Scripture not only as those that have mourned for sin, but as those that do mourn, who continue to mourn: "Blessed are they that mourn: for they shall be comforted" (Matt. 5:4).

And not only do hypocrites have unbalanced religious emotions, but they also demonstrate the emotions they do have in a strange, patchy way. For instance, they may say that they love Christ with all their hearts—and all the while they are being moved with such raptures of affection for God, they are filled with contention, envy, revenge, and backbiting toward the human beings around them. Oh, how they love Jesus—but they've been nursing an old grudge in their hearts toward a neighbor for the last seven years. In all their dealings with others, they are obviously not observing the rule of "doing to other as they would have them do to them." On the other hand, other people are kind to their fellow humans, acting good-natured and generous, while they demonstrate next to no love for God.

Other hypocrites love some people but not others. They are full of affection for one group of people, while they have nothing but bitterness for another. They like their own group—the people who look like them and act like them and believe like them—but they hate anyone who is different from themselves. What does Jesus say about this? "Be the children of your Father which is in heaven: for he maketh his sun to rise on the evil and on the good. . . . For if ye love them which love you, what reward have ye? do not even the publicans the same?" (Matt. 5:45–46).

Then there are the people who are very kind and loving to their neighbors, admiring the company of God's children, and behaving very sweetly whenever they are away from home—when they are inside their own houses, they are rude and inconsiderate to their wives, neglect their children, and treat the people closest to them poorly.

Others may feel a great distress about one particular sinner; they may do all they can to win that person, agonizing over his condition. Meanwhile, they care nothing about all the others who are living equally miserable lives. Their feelings are all out of proportion. Of course, it is true that grace may fix our minds more on one particular person at a particular time than another. The Holy Spirit may lay this person on our hearts for a particular reason, so that we feel as though we are in labor, suffering to bring them forth spiritually. But this happens for particular circumstances; as a rule, we should not suppose that grace will draw our hearts toward only one person while ignoring all the others. Grace would have us feel fervent love and compassion toward humanity in general.

Another form of imbalance can be seen when people demonstrate love for only one part of a human being; for instance, they are concerned about people's external condition, and do all that they can to help their physical circumstances, giving their money and sharing whatever they have, but all the while they care nothing about the spiritual or emotional condition of these same people. Other people go just the opposite; they pretend to be very concerned about people's souls, while they care nothing about their physical well-being. After all, making a great show of love, pity, and distress for souls costs them nothing; but they must part with money from their pockets if they want to pretend to care about more than people's souls. True Christian love includes both souls and bodies, and this is the way Jesus Christ loved. He showed mercy to human souls by preaching the gospel to them—and He also showed mercy to their bodies by going about doing good, healing all sorts of sickness and disease among the people. In Mark 6:34 we have a remarkable instance of Christ's compassion for humanity's entire being: "And Jesus, when he came out, saw much people, and was moved with compassion toward them, because they were as sheep not having a shepherd: and he began to teach them many things." Here we see His compassion for their souls. And in the sequel we see His compassion for their bodies, when He feeds five thousand of them with five loaves and two fishes. If the compassion of professing Christians toward others does not work in the same way, then it is not real Christian compassion.

Another sign that our emotions are out of proportion and unbalanced is if we are very troubled by the sins of others, while we are numb to our own defects and selfishness.

A true Christian may be concerned about the condition of another's heart, he may even mourn over another's coldness, but at the same time, he is not apt to be as worried about the badness of anybody's heart as much as he is his own. After all, he can see his own heart most clearly. But the opposite kind of imbalance can be seen as well, where a person worries about her own problems all the time and never seems to notice the troubles of others.

At this point, I want to point out that as a general rule a sure sign of hypocrisy is when people pretend they have very deep spiritual accomplishment, when all the while they haven't reached even the most basic spiritual level. For instance, a person may claim that he is living a deeply spiritual and divine life, but really he is not even a moral person. Or another person may say she trusts God to save her for eternity, and yet meanwhile she doesn't trust Him enough to share her money with others. These people are like travelers who assume that they have almost reached their destination, when really they've barely begun their journey—or like a mountain climber who thinks he's nearly to the top, when he hasn't even climbed halfway yet. But all this is off my topic.

All that I've said about the feeling of love can also be applied to the other "religious affections": true spiritual feeling extends itself in its appropriate proportion to the various things that are its due, while false feeling is usually oddly out of proportion. For instance, religious desires and longings: The saints desire things that are spiritual, and the intensity of their longing is in some proportion to their actual need for these things. With false longing, though, a person's desires run after all sorts of strange things with an impatient insistence; sometimes she craves something that is relatively unimportant while she neglects things that are obviously of far greater importance. For example, she may feel an urgent need to talk about all her experiences to others, spending a great amount of time in conversation—and yet at the same time she feels relatively little need to spend time in prayer, pouring out her soul before God in secret, asking for His help in living in greater conformity to Him and more to His glory. Scripture speaks far more often, though, of "groanings that cannot be uttered," of "soul-breakings for the longing it hath," and of "longings, thirstings, and pantings" than it does of a desperate need to talk to another person.

Hatred and zeal can also be grossly imbalanced. When they are truly spiritual feelings, they are felt against sin in some proportion to the degree of sinfulness: "I hate every false way" (Ps. 119:128, 104). But false hatred and zeal against sin is felt for one particular sin only. A person may be zealous against people who swear and dress in fancy clothes—and all the while, he is notorious for covetousness, stinginess, backbiting, envy toward his superiors, rebellion and hatred for political leaders, and deep-rooted ill will to all who have injured him. False zeal is felt against the sins of others, but the person who has true zeal feels it for her own sins more than anything else.

Unbalanced emotions are also evident when a person's emotional condition varies a great deal from day to day. Of course, all of us, even the deepest of Christians, experience emotional ups and downs, but beneath this surface fluctuation, we should have a basic steadiness. The righteous person is said to be one whose heart is fixed, trusting in God (Ps. 112:7), whose heart is established with grace (Heb. 13:9), who keeps going on the way he has chosen: "The righteous also shall hold on his way, and he that hath clean hands shall be stronger and stronger" (Job. 17:9).

When a person's faith is unsound, she is apt to be religious by fits and starts. One moment, her emotions are as high as the clouds, and the next moment they've dropped to the earth; one day, she is fascinated with religion and emotional about her spiritual practice, but the next day, she is careless and selfish. If she believes she has been blessed in some extraordinary or conspicuous way, she may be greatly moved emotionally, but soon her interest wanders back to her own selfish concerns. She is like the children of Israel in the wilderness, who were excited about what God had done for them at the Red Sea, where they sang His praise—and then soon fell right back into craving the "fleshpots" of Egypt; then again, when they came to Mount Sinai and saw God's great demonstration of Himself there, they were once more excited about their covenant with God. They said, "All that the Lord hath spoken will we do, and be obedient"—and almost immediately made themselves a golden calf to worship.

People like this are controlled by false emotions. They are like the waters of a flash flood, when after a sudden rain fills up a stream bed with water—and then the water disappears and the stream bed is once more dry and empty until the next shower. A true saint is like a stream from a living spring; rainfall may increase the stream and drought may diminish it, but it never runs dry; "The water that I shall give him shall be in him a well of water springing up" (John 4:14). Jeremiah gives us another image: "Blessed is the man that trusteth in the LORD, and whose hope the LORD is. For he shall be as a tree planted by the waters, and that spread-eth out her roots by the river, and shall not see when heat cometh, but her leaf shall be green; and shall not be careful in the year of drought, neither shall cease from yielding fruit" (Jer. 17:7–8).

Hypocrites are like comets that appear for awhile with a mighty blaze, but their motion is unsteady and irregular (that is why they are called "wandering stars" [Jude 13]), and their blaze soon disappears; in fact, they only appear once in a great while. But true saints are like the fixed stars, which, though they rise and set, and are often clouded, are still fixed and steady in their orbits, shining with a constant light.

Just as false emotions show a strange unevenness at dif-ferent times, they also are unsteady in different places. Some people seem to be greatly moved by spiritual concerns whenever they are with other people, but in private they feel nothing close to what they demonstrate in public. When they are alone in secret prayer, talking privately with God, their hearts are numb and lifeless. The true Christian with-out a doubt will delight in religious fellowship and Chris-tian conversation; she can't help but find her heart moved by the fellowship of others—but she also delights in spend-ing time all alone with God.

These private, solitary times are necessary if our hearts are to be truly fixed on God. True religion makes us want to spend time alone in meditation and prayer. We read that this was true for Isaac (Gen. 24:63). Even more important, we read in the Gospels that Christ too needed to be alone with His Father. Concealing deep feeling is difficult, and yet grace-filled feeling is often more silent and private than that which is counterfeited.

The same is true of spiritual sorrow. The Bible foretells that religious mourning will be done in private: "And the land shall mourn, every family apart; the family of the house of David apart, and their wives apart; the family of the house of Nathan apart, and their wives apart; the family of the house of Levi apart, and their wives apart; the family of Shimei apart, and their wives apart; all the families that remain, every family apart, and their wives apart" (Zech. 12:12–14). Even the sorrow we feel for the sins of others is best experienced privately, when we are alone rather than when our emotions are on public display: "If ye will not hear it, my soul shall weep in secret places for your pride; and mine eye shall weep sore, and run down with tears, because the LORD'S flock is carried away captive" (Jer. 13:17).

The joy grace gives is also greatest when we are alone; the Bible speaks of it as "hidden manna" (Rev. 2:17) and the psalmist implies that his sweetest comfort is to be had when he is alone: "My soul shall be satisfied as with marrow and fatness; and my mouth shall praise thee with joyful lips: when I remember thee upon my bed, and meditate on thee in the night watches" (Ps. 63:5–6). Christ calls His bride to come away from the world into a place of solitude where He can give her His sweetest love: "Come, my beloved, let us go forth into the field; let us lodge in the villages. . . . There will I give thee my loves" (Song of Sol. 7:11–12).

Scripture shows us that the saints' greatest spiritual experiences always took place when they were alone. Abraham saw God and talked with Him when he went off into the wilderness by himself—not when he was surrounded by his large family. Isaac received the special gift God gave him—his wife, Rebekah—when he was walking alone, meditating in the field. Jacob had gone off by himself apart from his family for some private prayer when Christ came to him, and he wrestled with Him and obtained the blessing. God revealed Himself to Moses in the bush, when he was alone in the desert (Exod. 3). And after that, God showed him His glory and admitted him into the most intimate communion with God while he was alone on the mountain — and Moses went so far as to spend forty days and forty nights alone (except for God's presence), and when he came down, his face was shining. God talked to Elijah and Elisha when they were by themselves. And when Jesus Christ had His future glory poured out on Him at the Transfiguration, it was not when He was in the middle of the crowd, or even when He was with the twelve disciples, but when He had gone into a place of solitude on a mountain with His three closest friends. When the angel Gabriel came to Mary, and when the Holy Ghost came upon her and the power of the Highest overshadowed her, she was apparently alone; even her closest and most intimate earthly friend, Joseph, knew nothing of what had happened to her until she told him. The woman who was the first to know the joy of Christ's resurrection was alone with Christ at the sepulcher (John 20). And when John, the beloved disciple, was favored with those wonderful visions of Christ and the future of the church and the world, he was alone on the island of Patmos.

I'm not saying that the saints were not also clearly blessed when they were with others. And obviously, we all find our hearts refreshed by Christian conversation and public worship. But I am trying to show that although true grace does delight in demonstrating itself within community, yet it reveals itself uniquely and intimately when we are alone. That is why if people seem to spend most of their time on social religion, and hardly any time alone with God, when they are deeply moved in public, but unaffected when they have no one to talk to but God, then we should suspect that their faith is not sincere

XI. Another way we can tell spiritual "affections" from others is that the deeper our spiritual feeling, the more we long for even more of God. In other words, our spiritual appetites are increased when our emotions are stirred. On the other hand, false emotions inspire us to go no further with God; we tend to be satisfied with the experience we have had and seek nothing more.

The more a true saint loves God, the more she wants to love Him, and the more uneasy she is with her lack of love for Him; the more she hates sin, the more she wants to hate it more, and regrets that she is still so attached to it; the more she mourns for sin, the more she wants to mourn for sin; the more her heart is broken, the more she longs for it to be broken still more; the more she thirsts and longs after God and holiness, the more she wishes she could breathe out her very soul in longing for God. When spiritual emotions are kindled, it is like lighting a flame; the higher the flame leaps, the more ardent it is, and the more it burns, the more vehemently does it seek to burn still more. In the same way our spiritual appetite for holiness is sharper when we have more holiness and grace in our hearts.

The person who is spiritually newborn will naturally thirst for holiness, just as a newborn baby will naturally thirst for his mother's breast: "As newborn babes, desire the sincere milk of the word, that ye may grow thereby: if so be ye have tasted that the Lord is gracious" (1 Pet. 2:2–3). In this world, all we get is a taste of the future glory that will be poured out in all its fullness in eternity; we only receive a down payment on our future inheritance (2 Cor. 1:22; Eph. 1:14). Even the strongest saints are only children compared with what they will be one day, and that is as it should be (1 Cor. 13:10–11). No matter how far we go with God in this world, how deep spiritually, we will never be satisfied, we will always long to go still further, still deeper. Paul makes this attitude clear when he says, "Forgetting those things which are behind, and reaching forth unto those things which are before, I press toward the mark. . . . Let us therefore, as many as be perfect, be thus minded" (Phil. 3:13–15).

The reason why all this is true is that the more holy emotions that we have, the greater is our spiritual taste (I'm referring to the faculty I have already described that perceives spiritual excellence and holiness). And the more grace we have, while we are here in this state of imperfection, the more we see our imperfections and need, the distance we are from completion, and so we realize how much more grace we need—and as I demonstrated earlier, this leads to evangelical humility.

Besides, grace before it reaches perfection is a thing that is always growing, just as living things continue to grow until they reach their perfection—and the healthier they are, the more they grow. Therefore the cry of true grace is always, "Lord, I believe; help thou my unbelief" (Mark 9:24). And the more we receive of spiritual revelation and deep holy feeling, the more we are earnest beggars for more grace and spiritual food, so that we can grow. And we don't merely sit around idly wishing we had more grace, but we seek it actively, doing whatever we can to pursue it in our hearts.

Some of you may be saying, "But aren't spiritual pleasures soul-satisfying?"

I may sound as though I'm being inconsistent, when I answer that yes, they are—but it depends what you mean by soul-satisfying. Certainly, spiritual joy is not cloying in nature, so that once we have tasted it we have no desire for more. But spiritual joy is soul-satisfying in the following ways:

1. It is designed to match our need and capacity. Once we have tasted it, we have no desire for other pleasures. Instead, we sit down fully contented with what we have; we stop wandering out searching for something that will please us. Our souls never feel surfeited by it, never wearied by it, but instead we give ourselves over to this joy forever. We want nothing besides this joy—but that does not mean that we don't want more of it.

2. Spiritual joy is also satisfying in this respect, that it meets the expectation of our appetites. When we pursue selfish pleasures, we expect to find great satisfaction, and yet we are always disappointed. Spiritual joy never disappoints.

3. The gratification that spiritual joy gives us is permanent. Selfish enjoyment is far different. When we satisfy our selfish appetites, we may feel temporarily glutted—but that feeling soon disappears, and we are left feeling as empty as we did before.

4. Spiritual joy is an infinite ocean. If we are not satisfied with the amount we have, all we need to do is open up our mouths a little wider, and we will be fed.

But because spiritual joy is so satisfying, our souls crave more and more of it—and just as gravity's pull is stronger the closer an object gets to the earth, so are our hearts pulled toward the spiritual world the closer we come to God's Spirit. This is the way spiritual emotions work—the deeper they are, the greater our appetite will be for grace and holiness.

But with counterfeit religious emotions the story is far different. Before these false experiences, the person may have had a desire for true grace—but afterward, that desire is diminished. Especially when false feeling is very intense, it puts an end to his longing for grace and holiness. Instead of seeing himself as a poor needy creature, he now considers himself rich; he cannot imagine that he could possibly be any better off than he is now, and so he no longer seeks for any higher experience of God.

A person like this behaves as though he has already reached perfection, while he lives the rest of his life on his one and only religious experience. True saints, though, are continually challenged to go higher and deeper with God; "Seekers after God" is one of the names that Scripture gives to godly people: "This is the generation of them that seek him, that seek thy face, O Jacob!" (Ps. 24:6); "Let not those that seek thee be confounded for my sake" (Ps. 69:6); "The humble shall see this, and be glad: and your heart shall live that seek God" (Ps. 69:32); "Let all those that seek thee rejoice and be glad in thee: and let such as love thy salvation say continually, Let God be magnified" (Ps. 70:4).

The Bible nearly always speaks of a Christian's work and seeking beginning *after* her conversion, and her conversion is merely the starting point of her journey. The New Testament refers to people "giving earnest heed to themselves, running the race that is set before them, striving and agonizing, wrestling not with the flesh and blood but principalities and powers, fighting, putting on the whole armor of God, and standing, pressing forward, reaching forth, continuing instant in prayer, crying to God day and night"—and it is referring to the saints, not to people who were never converted. Today, though, many people have gotten in the habit of assuming that once we become Christians, we no longer have to wrestle and strive spiritually; instead, they think we can sit back and relax, enjoying spiritual laziness. But the Lord "hath filled the hungry with good things; and the rich he hath sent empty away" (Luke 1:53).

Some people who have experienced only false spiritual feeling may crave more of these experiences. But they want more only because these impressions and revelations tend to make them look important to others—or because they want to be reassured that they really are the important saints they had originally supposed. This is different from the healthy hunger for more and more holiness that the true saint experiences. Holiness is like meat and drink to the spiritual appetite: "My meat is to do the will of him that sent me, and to finish his work" (John 4:34). The saints desire the sincere milk of the Word, not so much because they are insecure about God's love for them, but because they are hungry to grow deeper in holiness. Grace is their treasure (Isa. 33:6: "The fear of the LORD is his treasure"), and godliness is the gain that they are greedy for (1 Tim. 6:6). Hypocrites long for revelations only because they inflate their self-image.

But I have reached my last point, the last distinguishing quality of truly spiritual feeling that I will mention.

XII. Grace-filled and holy feeling demonstrates itself in Christian practice—in other words, in loving acts and practical kindness.

I mean by this that spiritual feeling makes us live differently, so that Christian practice is now the very business of our lives.

This implies three things:

1. That our behavior or practice in the world will be completely directed by Christian rules.

2. That we put our Christian practice ahead of all other responsibilities, so that it becomes the guiding principle of our entire lives, the business that transcends all other work we do.

3. That we persist in this practice until the end of our lives; it is not merely our business at certain times, for instance on Sundays, or for certain circumstances that may last a month or a year or even seven years. No, it is our business forever, through all the changing seasons of our lives.

The necessity of each of these is clearly taught in the Word of God.

I. It is necessary that all of our behavior be completely directed by Christianity's rules.

"Every man that hath this hope in him purifieth himself, even as he is pure. . . . And ye know that he was manifested to take away our sins; and in him is no sin. Whosoever abideth in him sinneth not: whosoever sinneth hath not seen him, neither known him. . . . He that doeth righteousness is righteous, even as he is righteous. He that committeth sin is of the devil" (1 John 3:3, 5–8); "We know that whosoever is born of God sinneth not; but he that is begotten of God keepeth himself, and that wicked one toucheth him not" (1 John 5:18); "Ye are my friends, if ye do whatsoever I command you" (John 15:14). If one part of our life alone is sinful, and we do not cut it off, it will carry our entire life to destruction (Matt. 5:29–30).

I want to stress here that in order to be completely and absolutely obedient to God, we must not only avoid wicked practices, consisting in sins of commission, the negative side of religion (the things we must not do), but we must also completely and absolutely practice the positives of our religion. Sins of omission are as much breaches of God's commands as sins of commission. Christ, in Matthew 25, speaks out strongly against the positive things we may have failed to do: "I was an hungred, and ye gave me no meat. . . ." A person should not be considered to be obedient to Christ merely because she isn't a thief or a liar, she doesn't oppress others or get drunk or riot, she isn't engaged in sexual perversion and she doesn't swear. All this alone is not enough, and a conversion that goes this far and no farther is a false one. A true Christian must also be devout, humble, gentle, forgiving, peaceful, respectful, kind, merciful, and charitable. Without qualities like these, she does not obey the laws that Christ said were the most important of all.

II. Our Christian practice must be the guiding principle of all the business of our lives, the work we do that transcends all other responsibilities.

All Christ's people not only do good works, but they are zealous about doing good works (Titus 2:14). We cannot serve two masters at once, and if we are God's true servants, we will make His service our whole work, throwing all our hearts and all our strength into it; in other words, as Paul said, "This one thing I do" (Phil 3:13). We are not called to idleness, but to labor in God's vineyard, and all true Christians comply with this call. Lazy people are not "followers of them who through faith and patience inherit the promises"; "And we desire that every one of you do show the same diligence to the full assurance of hope unto the end: that ye be not slothful, but followers of them who through faith and patience inherit the promises" (Heb. 6:11–12).

III. We will persist in this service throughout our whole lives, through all the changing circumstances that happen, until we die.

Scripture is full of examples of saints who endured in their Christian practice throughout their entire lives; the passages are too many to list here. All of these biblical saints, however, endured various trials, and yet they continued to faithfully act out their holiness.

By trials, I mean those things that make our Christian walk harder. They may be things that tempt us from our duty, things that appear enticing and attractive; or they may be things that frighten us away from our duty, things that make our Christian walk look too painful and terrible for us to bear. All of us who are Christians can expect to endure various kinds of trials during our lives. Not only are they a part of natural life, but, as I have already discussed, God uses these trials to prove ourselves and others are in true relationship with Him.

True saints may be guilty of some backsliding; they may fall into sin now and then when they yield to temptation, and they may even commit great sins against God. But still they never completely fall away from God so much that they are tired of religion or habitually hate God's service and neglect it permanently. We see this principle in many Scripture passages (Gal. 6:9; Rom. 2:7; Heb. 10:36; Isa. 43:22; Mal. 1:13). They can never backslide so far that they are habitually more engaged in other things than they are in the business of religion. If we have experienced a true conversion, then we have been transformed; our very natures have been changed, as we have already discussed, and thus we can never backslide back into our old identities.

We who are alive will never be lifeless again. And that is why holy feeling has such power in our lives. A statue may look very much like a real person, a beautiful person, in fact. It may resemble a strong and active human being—but yet it lacks an inner source of life and strength. It does nothing, it can do no work; it is only good to look at, for it can accomplish nothing. False emotions and revelations do not go deep enough to be sources of action; they never reach the deepest point in us from which our behavior springs. The seed that fell on stony ground did not have enough earth, and the root could not bring forth fruit—but spiritual holy feeling goes to the very bottom of the heart, taking hold of the inmost springs of life and activity.

This is the greatest strength of true godliness: It changes the way we act. This is what the apostle Paul was talking about when he spoke of the power of godliness (2 Tim. 3:5). This power acts first within the soul, stirring our hearts to experience a living and active spiritual feeling. But the power of godliness does not remain secret, hidden within our hearts; it is a practical power, that helps us conquer our will and selfish cravings. It carries us on our spiritual journey toward holiness, through all the temptations, difficulties, and opposition that we face along the way.

If we are only pursuing religion as a way to meet our selfish interests, then we are unlikely to find our behavior much changed by it, because we will only be interested in those parts of religion that meet our own ends. Anything that would demand a change in our behavior does not suit us. In the same way, if we seek a spiritual life for selfish reasons, we will not tend to stick with it throughout our entire lives. As our lives change from year to year, our faith will demand different things of us. If we were only pursuing our own private interests all along, somewhere along the line we will give it up as it no longer serves those interests. True faith, however, is invariable; it its always the same, at all times and through all the changes in our lives; it never alters in any respect.

As we have discussed before, spiritual feeling gives us a taste for the excellence of divinity. Since we have that taste, it only follows that we will seek to conform our behavior to the same standards of excellence. Holiness makes us inclined to practice holiness—in other words, to practice everything that is holy. That which we love, we long to possess; that which we admire, we seek to adorn ourselves with. The action that delights our hearts in God and others, we will seek to practice. As we have already said earlier, God's Spirit gives us a taste for holiness and a disgust for everything that falls short of the complete nature God intended.

We observed earlier that spiritual emotion convinces us of the divine reality. If we were never convinced of this reality, why would we bother to change the way we live? But if we are absolutely certain that God and His gospel are real, then we cannot help but change the way we live.

Again, though, without a change in our nature, our behavior will not be thoroughly changed. Until the tree is healed, the fruit will not be good. We do not pick grapes from thorns, nor figs from thistles. The pig can be cleaned up for a little while, but unless you change his nature, he will still wallow in the mire. Nature can be violently restrained for awhile, but in the end it is more powerful than anything that opposes it, the way a river at flood time will either burst through a dam or go around it and find a new channel. When a "natural" person denies his selfish cravings and lives a strict religious life, appearing humble, painful, and earnest in his religion, it is not natural; everything he does is a force against nature. You can throw a stone up in the air, opposing gravity's natural strength, and the more force with which you throw it, the higher it will go—but eventually, all the force you used will be spent, and nature's force will remain: The stone will drop back to the ground. In the same way, as long as our selfish nature is not put to death but left as the living center of our hearts, we are wasting our time if we expect it not to rule our lives. But if the old nature is killed, replaced by a new and heavenly nature, then we can reasonably expect that we will walk in newness of life—and continue to do so to the end of our days.

Because true saints are humble, as we have described, they are willing to do whatever they are told by the One they serve, and this is another reason why their behavior will be changed so radically. We have also already mentioned the lamblike, dovelike spirit that the saints possess in Christ. This spirit is yet another reason why their faith demonstrates itself practically, for Christ's gentle spirit expressed itself by doing good. The saints are sensitive to moral evil, as I have said, dreading any hint of rotten selfishness within their hearts, and this too tends to make them act with love and kindness to others. One reason that this behavior is consistent, not demonstrated at one time and not another, or at one place and not another, is because, as we have said, true spiritual feeling is well balanced; always and everywhere it has a beautiful symmetry and proportion. And yet again, the spiritual appetite which we have also already discussed makes the saints persevere in their holy practice with an ever greater fervency.

Clearly, then, each of the qualities of spiritual feeling that we have already discussed tends to lead us toward an active and practical Christian lifestyle.

If we consider the way the Bible asks us to make a complete choice for God, then this only illustrates and confirms my point. If we deny ourselves whenever our own interests and Christ's are in competition, then our behavior will be quite different than it once was. If our hearts belong completely to Jesus, then our actions will belong to Him too. We cannot do one without the other, and this total commitment will cause us to endure all the trials life brings us with patience and perseverance.

True grace is not an inactive thing; in fact, nothing in heaven or earth is more active, for grace is life itself, spiritual and divine life. It is not a barren thing, for nothing in the universe is more fruitful. Grace within our hearts has the same direct relation to our external actions as a fountain has to a stream, or as the sun has to sunbeams, or as life has to the beating of our pulse, for the very nature and definition of grace is that it is a source of holy action.

Regeneration, the work of God that infuses grace into our hearts, has a direct relation to practice; for practice is the end of regeneration, the purpose for which the whole work was wrought. This is why Christ died: "Who gave himself for us, that he might redeem us from all iniquity, and purify unto himself a peculiar people, zealous of good works" (Titus 2:14); "According as he hath chosen us in him before the foundation of the world, that we should be holy and without blame before him in love" (Eph. 1:4); "Created in Christ Jesus unto good works, which God hath before ordained that we should walk in them" (Eph. 2:10). Holy practice is as much the end of all that God does with us, as fruit is the end of all that the farmer does with his fields (Matt. 3:10; 13:8, 23, 30–38; 21:19, 33–34; Luke 13:6; John 15:1–8; 1 Cor. 3:9; Heb. 6:7–8; Isa. 5:1–8; Song of Sol. 8:11–12; Isa. 27:2–3). Every spiritual activity in a true

Christian is calculated to reach this end. Every revelation, every grace, every blessing leads directly to this fruit.

You will gather from what I have said so far that Christian practice, or a holy life, is a clear sign of true and saving grace. But I will go even further and assert that it is the greatest of all the signs of grace, both as evidence of the sincerity of others and also as proof to our own consciences.

But you need to understand exactly what I mean by that. Therefore, I want to make the following point:

Christian practice and holy life is a sign of sincerity to others.

The Word clearly tells us that in this respect this is the main evidence of grace. Christ, who knew better than anyone how we should judge others, said: "Ye shall know them by their fruits" (Matt. 7:16); "Wherefore by their fruits ye shall know them" (Matt. 7:20); "Either make the tree good, and his fruit good; or else make the tree corrupt, and his fruit corrupt" (Matt. 12:33). He seems to be saying, in other words, that it makes no sense for the fruit to be different than the tree, since the fruit tells us what the tree is like; "For the tree is known by his fruit." The fruit is the proof that distinguishes one tree from another; "Every tree is known by his own fruit" (Luke 6:44).

Christ doesn't say, "You shall know the tree by its leaves or flowers—or you shall know what people are like by their talk, or you shall know them by the good story they tell of their experiences, or you shall know them by the way they speak, their emphasis and feeling, or by how much they talk, or by how fond or emotional you feel as you listen to them." No, by their fruits you shall know them; the tree is known by its fruit.

And just as this is the evidence that Christ told us to look for in others, when we judge them, so it is evidence that Christ told us to give to others, so that they can judge us. "Let your light so shine before men, that they may see your good works, and glorify your Father which is in heaven" (Matt. 5:16). Christ tells us here to demonstrate our godliness to others.

Godliness is like a light that shines inside the soul. Christ tells us that this light should not only shine inside us, but that it should shine out where others can see it too. But how can we do this? By our good works.

Christ does not say that others will hear your good works, your good story, or your moving expressions; no, He says, that others "may *see* your good works, and glorify your Father which is in heaven." Doubtless, if Christ gives us a rule for making our light shine where others can see it, then His rule will be the best we can find.

The apostles also indicate that Christian fruits are the best proof of true faith. In the sixth chapter of Hebrews, the apostle Paul speaks of people who have common illuminations and have been "enlightened, and have tasted of the heavenly gift, and were made partakers of the Holy Ghost, and have tasted the good word of God, and the powers of the world to come" (v. 4), that afterwards fall away, and are like barren ground, that is "nigh unto cursing, whose end is to be burned" (v. 8); and then he adds in the ninth verse (speaking of his love for the Hebrew Christians who have the saving grace that is better than all these "common illuminations"), "But, beloved, we are persuaded better things of you, and things that accompany salvation, though we thus speak." And then, in the next verse, he tells them the reason he had such good thoughts of them; he does not say it was because they had given him a good account of what God had done in their souls, or because they had talked very emotionally, but it was their work and labor of love: "For God is not unrighteousness to forget your work and labour of love, which ye shewed toward his name, in that ye have ministered to the saints, and do minister." Paul also speaks of faithful practical service as the best evidence that people love Christ more than anything else, even themselves: "For all seek their own, not the things which are Jesus Christ's; but ye know the proof of him, that, as a son with the father, he hath served with me in the gospel" (Phil. 2:21–22).

The apostle John expresses the same ideas as the basis of his good opinion of Gaius: "For I rejoiced greatly, when the brethren came and testified of the truth that is in thee" (3 John 3). How did the brethren testify of the truth that was in Gaius? And how did the apostle determine that the truth was in him? It was not because he talked right and used Christian language. Instead, he walked in the truth: "Even as thou walkest in the truth. I have no greater joy than to hear that my children walk in truth. Beloved, thou doest faithfully whatsoever thou doest to the brethren, and to strangers; which have borne witness of thy charity before the church" (3 John 3–6). In the same passage John seems to be telling Gaius how he should judge others; in verse 9, he mentions Diotrephes, who did not behave himself well, and led away others with him, and then in the eleventh verse, John directs Gaius to beware of such people and not to follow them; says the apostle, "Beloved, follow not that which is evil, but that which is good. He that doeth good is of God: but he that doeth evil hath not seen God."

I want to point out also that the apostle James expressly states that the best way to show our faith to others is through our actions: "Yea, a man may say, Thou hast faith, and I have works: shew my thy faith without thy works, and I will shew thee my faith by my works" (James 2:18). If we try to demonstrate our faith without acting it out, then we are merely talking. As James says in verse 14, "What doth it profit, my brethren, though a man say he hath faith?"

We can demonstrate our hearts to our neighbors in two ways: by what we say and by what we do. But James clearly prefers the latter as the best evidence. Certainly we can reveal ourselves through our words, describing our conversion experiences and the steps we went through and all the revelations that accompanied it, and this does show others our faith. But James assures us that all these verbal professions fall far short of an active demonstration of our faith through our works.

Just as Scripture plainly teaches that practice is the best evidence of sincere Christianity, so our reason tells us the same thing. Logically, our actions tell more about who we are than our words can. This is common sense, and all humanity, through all ages and nations, teaches that the human heart can be judged best by the person's practice. This is how we tell if someone is a loyal subject, a true lover, a dutiful child, or a faithful servant. If someone claims to love us a great deal and be our best friend, we all know that this does not mean as much as the person who is faithful and constant to us through both prosperity and adversity, who is ready to lay down herself, and deny herself, for our sake. If we are wise, we will trust such evidences of sincere friendship far more than a thousand pretty promises and affectionate verbal expressions. Equally, it makes sense that our behavior is the best proof of our friendship with Christ. Reason will tell us the same thing that Christ said in John 14:21: "He that hath my commandments, and keepeth them, he it is that loveth me."

So if we see a person whose life imitates Christ's, who denies himself for Christ in order to promote His kingdom, reason tells us that this is more dependable evidence of love for Christ, than if he only says he loves Christ, and talks of the inner experiences he's had and what strong love he feels—but meanwhile his behavior is nothing like Christ's and he hesitates to put himself out in any way to promote Christ but instead is full of excuses. A person may talk about self-denial and the world's emptiness, but meanwhile her life shows how attached she is to material things and how hard it is for her to give to others. Meanwhile, another Christian may not say a great deal, yet his behavior shows how ready he is to forsake the world, whenever it stands in the way of his duty, and he is free to part with anything that will promote religion and the good of his fellow creatures. Logically, the second person gives a more credible demonstration of a heart weaned from the world.

If a person walks humbly before God and others, if she is patient through affliction, and gentle to others, this is a better evidence of humility than if she only talked about how great a sense she has of her own unworthiness. She may say she has thrown herself in the dust, that she has emptied herself, that she is filthy and abominable—but all the while she acts as if she considers herself to be the first and best of saints, the Christian leader of the entire town; she is self-willed, and impatient; she cannot bear to be contradicted or opposed. We can be sure in this case that her behavior springs from a lower place in her heart than her verbal profession. But if another Christian is always compassionate to people in trouble, if she is ready to bear their burdens with them, willing to spend what she has for them, and to be inconvenienced in order to promote the good of others' souls and bodies, this is a more credible demonstration of a spirit of love. A person can talk all he wants about the love and pity and anguish he feels for others, but what if meanwhile his behavior shows he is selfish and greedy, unable to share with others? When people are overwhelmed with emotion, they may think they are willing to do great things and to suffer much; they may talk earnestly and confidently about their plans, but really their hearts are still selfish. Passing emotions easily produce words, and words are cheap; godliness is more easily feigned in words than in actions. Christian practice is a costly, laborious thing, and the self-denial that is required of Christians must be practiced, not just talked about. Hypocrites can much more easily talk like saints than act like saints.

Plainly then, Christian practice is the best demonstration of true godliness. Given that, however, I must make the following clarifications:

First, I want to point out that when the Scripture speaks of Christian practice as the best proof of sincerity, that does not mean that all professions of faith should be ruled out. This rule applies to Christ's followers who *have* made a profession of faith, so that their sincerity and truthfulness can be determined. The early church needed a guideline for deciding who should be a part of their community. But this guideline was not intended for those who made no claims of being Christians. When Christ says in the seventh chapter of Matthew, "By their fruits ye shall know them," He was talking about those who professed to be Christians, false prophets, "which come to you in sheep's clothing" (Matt. 7:15). The apostle James says, "Shew me thy faith without thy works, and I will shew thee my faith by my works" (James 2:18). Both of these passages imply that they refer to people who call themselves Christians. A profession of Christianity is plainly presupposed.

In the Bible references we've discussed, this profession is not the main thing in the evidence, yet it is necessary and prerequisite, just as having an animal body is a necessary prerequisite of being a human being. If someone plainly states that he is not a Christian, that he does not believe that Jesus is the Son of God, then these rules given to us by Christ and His apostles do not oblige us to look upon this person as a sincere Christian, no matter how lovingly he behaves. These rules were given us to judge professing Christians only. Fruits must come from open flowers.

The obvious question here, however, is this: How does a person profess Christianity? I have two answers.

1. In order for a person to claim to be a Christian, she must lay claim to all that is necessary for being a Christian, the essence of Christianity. Whatever makes Christianity what it is, that is what is necessary to a true profession. If we take only a part of

Christianity, and leave out a part that is essential to it, then what we take is not Christianity, because some part of its essence is lacking. So if we say we believe only a part, and leave out an essential part, that which we profess is not Christianity. In other words, in order to profess Christianity, we must say that we believe Jesus is the Messiah, because this belief is essential to Christianity. We also must profess, either expressly or implicitly, that Jesus paid the price for our sins, and other essential doctrines of the gospel, because belief in these things is also essential to Christianity. But there are other things that are just as essential to religion as orthodox doctrine; for instance, we need to repent of our sins, renounce all sin, embrace Christ as our only Savior, love Him above all, be willing for His sake to forsake all, and give up ourselves to Him entirely and forever. These things belong as much to the essence of Christianity as belief in any of the gospel's doctrines—and therefore we must profess them if we call ourselves Christians.

This doesn't mean that in order to be professing Christians we must explicitly lay claim to every individual thing that pertains to Christian grace or virtue—but certainly we must either expressly or implicitly indicate our belief in the essence of religion. Our profession of faith should be guided by the precepts in God's Word, or by scriptural examples of public professions of religion.

In the Bible, when people first asked for entrance into Christianity, they confessed their sins, demonstrating their sorrow for sin (Matt. 3:6). The baptism they were baptized with was called the baptism of repentance (Mark 1:4). John, when he baptized them, exhorted them to bring forth fruits suitable for repentance (Matt. 3:8); he encouraged them that if they did so, they should escape the wrath to come and be gathered as wheat into God's garner (Matt. 3:7–12). So the apostle Peter says to the Jews, "Repent, and be baptized" (Acts 2:38), which shows that visible repentance is a qualification necessary for baptism, and therefore ought to be publicly professed. When the Jews returned from captivity and entered publicly into covenant with God, they did so with public confession of their sins (Neh. 9:2). Philip, in order to baptize the eunuch, required that he should profess that he believed with all his heart; and they that were received as visible Christians, at the great outpouring of the Spirit that began at the day of Pentecost, appeared gladly to receive the gospel: "Then they that gladly received his word were baptized: and the same day there were added unto them about three thousand souls" (Acts 2:41). The Bible foretells that all nations will one day publicly make this profession: "Look unto me, and be ye saved, all the ends of the earth: for I am God, and there is none else. I have sworn by myself, the word is gone out of my mouth in righteousness, and shall not return, That unto me every knee shall bow, every tongue shall swear. Surely, shall one say, in the LORD have I righteousness and strength: even to him shall men come; and all that are incensed against him shall be ashamed. In the LORD shall all the seed of Israel be justified, and shall glory" (Isa. 45:22–25). People who claim to be a Christian must profess to give themselves up entirely to Christ, and to God through Him, as the children of Israel did when they publicly recognized their covenant with God: "Thou hast avouched the LORD this day to be thy God, and to walk in his ways, and to keep his statutes, and his commandments, and his judgments, and to hearken unto his voice" (Deut. 26:17). They ought to claim to be willing to embrace religion with all its difficulties, and to walk in obedience to God, universally and perseveringly (Exod. 19:8; 24:3, 7; Deut. 26:16–19; 2 Kings 23:3; Neh. 10:28–39; Ps. 119:57, 106). They ought to state that all their hearts and souls are the Lord's, forever available to serve Him (2 Chron. 15). When God's people swear by His name or to His name (which seems to mean that they solemnly offer themselves up to Him in covenant, vowing to receive Him as their God, to be entirely His, and to obey and serve Him), the Bible speaks of it being a duty to be performed by all God's visible people (Deut. 6:13; 10:20; Isa. 19:18; 45:23–24; compare these verses with Rom. 14:11; Phil. 2:10–11; Isa. 48:1–2; 65:15–16; Jer. 4:2; 5:7; 12:16; Hos. 4:15; 10:4).

Therefore, in order for people to be considered true Christians by the rest of the Christian community they must visibly live a holy life, either expressing or plainly implying all the things we've just mentioned. We are to know them by their fruits. That means that by their fruits we will know whether they are what they profess to be. It does not mean that we are to know by their fruits that they have something in them they don't even pretend to possess.

2. If people are to make a true profession of faith, then they must understand the meaning of what they profess; that is, they must have been instructed in

the principles of religion, with an ordinary capacity to understand the meaning of what is expressed by their profession. For sounds have no meaning and tell us nothing, if the speaker has no sense of those sounds' meaning.

But nothing in Scripture indicates that for a person to be accepted by the rest of the Christian community, he must be able to spell out step by step the theological ramifications of all that the Holy Spirit did in his heart; in fact, he need not even be aware of all that the Spirit has done. There is no trace in Scripture of any of the apostles or early ministers requiring such knowledge in order for the person to be lovingly received as a Christian brother. The early church never required a written exam as part of their initiation process. They did require a profession of the things the Spirit had done—but they never insisted on a theological understanding of just how the Spirit accomplished these things. Nor is there the smallest hint in Scripture of any such custom in the church of God from Adam to the death of the apostle John.

I am far from saying, however, that people don't need to give any sort of account of their experiences to their Christian family. But if they profess to believe the essence of Christianity, then that is the same as saying that they have experienced those things. In other words, if they claim to believe the gospel of Christ, if they profess to cleave to Him with their whole souls, as the refuge and rest of their souls, and the fountain of their comfort, if they say that they repent of their sins, and utterly renounce all sin, giving themselves up wholly to Christ, subjecting themselves to

Him as their King, if they renounce all enjoyment of this empty world and claim to comply with every command of God, even the most difficult and self-denying, and devote their whole lives to God's service, and if they say they have forgiven those who have injured them and they are filled with love for others, then—if they solemnly profess all these things—this is the same as professing that they have experienced all these things in their hearts.

Nor do I suppose that we will totally disregard all verbal professions of faith. Especially with our spiritual leaders, we are justified in asking them to state their beliefs verbally. What a person says also helps us to know if she really understands just what she is professing.

In order for us to accept a profession of Christianity, we must have good reason to think that the person is not merely complying with some prescribed form, using words without any real meaning, speaking ambiguously. Instead, he must honestly speak of that which he feels in his own heart; otherwise his profession has no meaning. It's simply empty noise.

I don't suppose either that just because a person can go into great detail about the circumstances of her Christian experience, telling a coherent, chronological story, that this proves anything. Being able to tell a good story doesn't mean that her experience is any more real, but it does help us to decide that her story seems believable. Still, Scripture never insists that a person outline her Christian experience in consecutive steps. Other things are vastly more important and essential.

Moving on now, we need to look at the ways that Christian

practice is visible to others. Being an honest person or a moral person is not enough. Just because we have never been charged with any particular transgression is not enough to make our light shine before others. This is not the labor of love that persuaded the apostle that the Hebrews were sincere (Heb. 6:9–10). Christian goodness is not merely a negative concept, as in the absence of evil; it is a positive concept: the definite presence of holiness as a visible behavior.

Christians must live a life devoted to the service of God: They must appear to follow the example of Jesus Christ, and measure up to those excellent rules in the fifth, sixth, and seventh chapters of Matthew, the twelfth chapter of Romans, and many other parts of the New Testament. They must demonstrate their love for God and their love for others, both their friends and their enemies; they must be gentle and forgiving; they must share what they have and live lives of moderation and selflessness; they must control their tongues, ruling their words with kindness. And they must do all these things all the time and everywhere—at church, with their families, among their neighbors, on Sundays and every day, in business and in conversation, with friends and with enemies, with superiors, inferiors, and equals. All this is the only real proof of sincere Christianity; no other evidence can measure up to this.

Undoubtedly, Christians demonstrate their sincerity with varying degrees of evidence in their life and practice, just as some people speak more clearly of their experiences than others do. Nevertheless, the living demonstration of a Christian spirit is vastly beyond the prettiest and brightest story that was ever told about the particular steps in a faith experience.

But yet, outward appearances and external demonstrations are never infallible evidences of grace. The behaviors that I've described are the best we can do; when we see them, we are obliged to embrace others as saints, and love them and rejoice in them as God's children. This external proof is all we need in this world. But nothing that we see in each other is ever enough to make us absolutely certain concerning the state of one another's souls. We cannot see each other's hearts, nor can we even see all our external behaviors. Much of what we do is in secret, hid from the world's eye. We can never know for sure how far someone may go to put up a good front, imitating grace. Undoubtedly, though, if others could see as much as what our own consciences see, that might be infallible proof of our state, as will be clear in the next part of this discussion.

Now that we've demonstrated that Christian practice is the best evidence of sincerity, let me move on to observe that Scripture also speaks of Christian practice as a sure evidence of grace to people's own consciences. This is clear in 1 John 2:3: "Hereby we do know that we know him, if we keep his commandments." The testimony of a good conscience is spoken of as that which may give us assurance of our own godliness: "My little children, let us not live in word, neither in tongue; but in deed and in truth. And hereby we know that we are of the truth, and shall assure our hearts before him" (1 John 3:18–19). The apostle Paul, in Hebrews 6, speaks of the work and labor of love of the Hebrew Christian as that which not only persuaded him that they were truly illuminated by grace, but also proved to him that they too had a deep assurance of hope concerning themselves: "But, beloved, we are persuaded better things of you, and things that accompany salvation, though we thus speak. For God is not unrighteous to forget your work and labour of love, which ye have shewed toward his name, in that ye have ministered to the saints, and do minister. And we desire that every one of you do shew the same diligence to the full assurance of hope unto the end" (Heb. 6:9–11). When we practice our faith, we can rejoice in our own happy state: "Let every man prove his own work, and then shall he have rejoicing in himself alone, and not in another" (Gal. 6:4); "Then shall I not be ashamed, when I have respect unto all thy commandments" (Ps. 119:6); in other words, then I shall be bold, assured, and steadfast in my hope. When Jesus said, "Every tree that bringeth not forth good fruit is hewn down, and cast into the fire. Wherefore by their fruits ye shall know them" (Matt. 7:19–20), He followed this rule for judging others, with words that clearly indicate that He intended this rule to apply to ourselves too: "Not every one that saith unto me, Lord, Lord, shall enter into the kingdom of heaven; but he that doeth the will of my Father which is in heaven. Many will say to me in that day, Lord, Lord, . . .and then will I profess unto them, I never knew you: depart from me, ye that work iniquity. Therefore, whosoever heareth these sayings of mine, and doeth them I will liken him unto a wise man, which built his house upon a rock. And everyone that heareth these sayings of mine, and doeth them not, shall be likened unto a foolish man, which built his house upon the sand"(vv. 21–26). When we follow Christ's commandments, this assures our own consciences that we are Christians. This is the best proof of our own sincerity.

I want to note here that when the Scripture speaks of good works, good fruit, and keeping Christ's commandments, we cannot reasonably assume that it refers only to our external actions, the motion and behavior of our bodies, without including the aim or intention behind these behaviors. Otherwise, if our understanding and will count for nothing, then they are no more good works or acts of obedience than are the regular motions of a clock. Physical actions, looked at from this perspective, are neither acts of obedience nor disobedience, any more than are the physical motions during a convulsion. But the obedience and fruit of which the Bible speaks is the obedience and the fruit of the entire person; not only the acts of the body, but the obedience of the soul, the acts and practice of the soul.

I don't suppose, however, that when the Bible speaks of works and fruit and practice, it includes all inner piety and holiness of heart, both the source and its expression, both spirit and practice; if it did include all this, then there would be no difference between root and fruit. The inner reality and the external proof would be one and the same thing, which would make no sense. No, what the Bible is saying is this: Grace-filled behavior and holy actions indicate a person's heart. Grace works in our hearts in many ways, but the Bible refers here to an active holiness, an act of grace that is expressed by our outward obedience. Our hearts have been changed, and as a result our behavior has changed too.

I want to clarify here that grace works in two ways.

1. What some people call immanent acts—that is, when acts of grace remain within our souls, beginning and

terminating there, without any direct relation to any outward action or practice.

During contemplation, grace behaves this way. Whatever takes place in the heart does not directly end up as anything beyond the mind's thoughts. This sort of act of grace, however, as with all acts of grace, will immediately affect the way we live.

2. Other acts of grace are more strictly called practical, because they directly cause action to be taken.

They are the acts of grace that command acts of our wills, directing our external actions—for instance, when a saint gives someone a cup of cold water or voluntarily endures persecution, because of his deep love for Christ. These external actions are produced by grace; these acts of grace are practical and productive, not only because their nature is productive (for all true acts of grace are productive), but because they produce action. Grace acts on our wills, changing the practice of our souls.

Our physical behavior is shaped by the union between our souls and our bodies, a union fixed and maintained by God. From our souls' perspective, the change wrought by grace in our souls and the change in our behavior are one and the same; our actions are the soul's good work. Those things that our wills decide are indeed our actions.

In other words, the aim and intention of the soul is part of our good works. For not only can we not do justice or distribute alms mechanically, but neither can we call certain behaviors Christian if the person doing them has never heard of Christ or any of His commands. The acts of obedience and good fruit spoken of in the Bible are not mere motions of the body, but acts of the soul.

That is why we must consider the motives for our actions, the goal we were shooting toward; if we are not directing our behaviors as offerings to God, then they are not acts of denial of ourselves, or obedience to God, or service to Him, but something else instead. The martyrs experienced these acts of grace, and all true saints live a life full of acts of grace such as these. Their good works are caused by grace at work in their souls, and this is the obedience and fruit at which God looks. He looks at the soul more than the body, for our souls govern our bodies. God is concerned with the soul's behavior, and God can see the soul, for "the LORD seeth not as man seeth, for. . .the LORD looketh on the heart" (1 Sam. 16:7).

And that is why obedience, good works, and good fruits prove to our own consciences that grace lives in our hearts, for these good works include the soul's practice that precedes and governs the body's actions. When Scripture speaks of our works as the main evidence to others of our sincere Christianity, then it refers to what is visible to others, but when it speaks of our works as proof of our sincerity to our own consciences, then it refers to that which is visible to our own hearts, not only the motion of our bodies, but the activity of our souls that directs that motion. We can see this internal activity even more directly than we can see our physical acts.

Scripture makes plain this variation in meaning. At the conclusion of Christ's Sermon on the Mount, He speaks of our practice as the best sign of our being true disciples; without this disciplined behavior, He says we are like a man who built his house on the sand, but with it, we are like a man who built his house on a rock. Jesus is speaking here not only of our outward behavior, but of our internal discipline as well. This meaning becomes clear when we look at His words in context, for before the parable of the wise man and the foolish man, He says this: "Blessed are the poor in spirit; . . .blessed are they that mourn; . . .blessed are the meek; . . .blessed are they that do hunger and thirst after righteousness; . . .blessed are the merciful; . . .blessed are the pure in heart; . . .whosoever is angry with his brother without a cause; . . .whosoever looketh on a woman to lust after her; . . .love your enemies; . . .take no thought for your life," and other passages like this. All this implies inner activity. When Christ says, "He that hath my commandments, and keepeth them, he it is that loveth me" (John 14:21), He evidently has in mind the command that He repeated several times in the same discourse, that we should love one another as He loved us (see John 13:34–35; 15:10–14). This command is acted out externally, but it has more to do with the activity of the heart. When the apostle John says, "Hereby we do know that we know him, if we keep his commandments" (1 John 2:3), he was plainly thinking of this same command, as is clear in the verses that follow (1 John 2:7–11, and 2 John 5–6).

When the Bible tells us that in the end humanity will be judged according to their works, and that everyone will receive what their physical actions have earned, the Bible is not referring to our external behaviors only. Why else would the Bible speak so often of God searching the hearts and trying the reins that He may "render to every man according to his deeds"? For example: "And all the churches shall know that I am he which searcheth the reins and hearts: and I will give unto every one of you according to your works" (Rev. 2:23); "I the LORD search the heart, I try the reins, even to give every man according to his ways, and according to the fruit of his doings" (Jer. 17:10). If when the Bible says "his ways" and "the fruit of his doings," it means only physical actions, why would God need to search the heart and reins in order to know those actions? Hezekiah claims God's favor, based not only on his outward actions, but on what was in his heart: "Remember now, O LORD, I beseech thee, how I have walked before thee in truth and with a perfect heart" (Isa. 38:3).

Our inner activity is most important, yet our external activity is included, since this is the visible effect of grace in our hearts. No one, however, can pretend to be holy when their external lives are full of wickedness. Our soul's inner practice commands our physical practice; we cannot separate our physical activity from our soul's. Soul and body are one. If a person claimed that his heart longed to be in church but his feet carried him to a brothel, that person would be just as ridiculous as another person who said she wanted to give a coin to a beggar but her hand refused to let go of it.

I want to go on now to show that when we are assured of our own hearts' sincerity by the proof of our actions, that proof is far better than any revelation, spiritual enlightenment, or contemplation. (One Bible scholar reminds us that John, Christ's beloved disciple and intimate friend, did not justify his confidence with the fact that he was personally acquainted with Jesus. On what did he base his proof? "Because we keep his commandments" [1 John 2:3].) I will demonstrate this with the following arguments:

Argument I

Common sense tells us that what our hearts desire will be shown by our actions. If we are sincere about our faith, then we will choose God before all other things; we will be willing to give up everything for Christ. But our actions tell what our hearts truly choose. For instance, when God and other things stand in competition, God set before us on one hand, and our worldly interests or pleasures on the other (as so often happens in the course of a person's life), whatever we choose, however we act, means we have committed ourselves to one and forsaken the other. This is the real proof of that which we prefer. Sincerity means we forsake all for Christ; but to forsake all for Christ in our hearts is the very same thing as actually forsaking all for Christ. Only when Christ and other things are in actual competition, when we must actually and practically choose one and forsake the other, only then do we know if our hearts' commitment is truly sincere.

Following Christ with our desires is the same as desiring to follow Christ. Denying our desires for Christ is the same as desiring self-denial for Christ. Our behavior expresses our hearts. Godliness is not a heart that *intends* to do the will of God, but a heart that does it. The children of Israel in the wilderness intended to do God's will, as we read in Deuteronomy 5:27–29, "Go thou near, and hear all that LORD our God shall say: and speak thou unto us all that the LORD our God shall speak unto thee; and we will hear it, and do it. And the LORD heard the voice of your words, when ye spake unto me; and the LORD said unto me, I have heard the voice of the words of this people, which they have spoken unto thee: they have well said all that they have spoken. O that there were such an heart in them, that they would fear me, and keep all my commandments always, that it might be well with them, and with their children for ever!" The people intended to keep God's commandments, but this was not enough for God. He needed their behavior to reflect their hearts' intentions.

How silly then for someone to pretend they have a good heart, while they live a wicked life. Obviously, such people do not love God above all; no one can argue against plain fact and experience. People who live in sin and yet claim to be holy act as though they think they can trick God. But they can't. The apostle Paul says, "Be not deceived; God is not mocked: for whatsoever a man soweth, that shall he also reap" (Gal. 6:7). In other words, "Do not deceive yourself with an expectation of eternal life if you do not sow the Spirit here; it is useless to think that you can make a fool of God or that He will be tricked and baffled by shadows instead of substances, with empty pretense instead of the good fruit He expects. Your pretense is plain to Him."

The meaning of the word *mock* in Scripture is clear in these verses: When Delilah said to Samson, "Behold, thou hast mocked me, and told me lies" (Judges 16:10), that is, "You have baffled me, intending to make a fool of me, as if I might be easily satisfied with pretense instead of truth." Lot, when he told his sons-in-law that God would destroy that place, "seemed as one that mocked unto his sons-in-law" (Gen. 19:14), that is, he seemed to want to play games with them, as though they were so credulous as to believe such a silly story.

But the great Judge, whose eyes are as a flame of fire, will not be mocked or baffled by any pretenses. If in His name people have prophesied and wrought miracles, if they have had faith so that they could remove mountains and cast out devils, if their religious feeling has been deep and intense, and they have seemed to have had grace, yet if they were workers of iniquity, they will not be able to hide their hypocrisy from their Judge, though their hiding places have been so dark and deep that no human search could find them. "There is no darkness, nor shadow of death, where the workers of iniquity may hide themselves" (Job 34:22).

Would a wise prince let himself be fooled and baffled by a subject, who only pretended that she was a loyal subject? The subject might talk loud and often about how much she loved the prince, but meanwhile she would be living in rebellion against him, following a pretender to his crown, stirring up sedition against him. Would the prince stand for this? Or would a master allow himself to be gulled by a servant who pretended to feel deep love and honor toward him in her heart, and a great sense of the master's worthiness and kindness, while at the same time she refused to obey him or do anything at all for him?

Argument II
When circumstances force us to make an active, practical choice between God and our own interests, Scripture refers to these occasions as "trials." They are called trials, because

these events try and prove Christians' true natures, revealing whether they are really what they profess to be. Furthermore, these circumstances expose the reality of God's supreme love to the test of experiment and fact. They prove to us just what reality is, both in our own natures and in God's.

Scripture gives us many instances of this concept that trials are proof: "And thou shalt remember all the ways which the LORD thy God led thee these forty years in the wilderness, to humble thee, and to prove thee, to know what was in thine heart, whether thou wouldst keep his commandments, or no" (Deut. 8:2); "I also will not henceforth drive out any from before them of the nations which Joshua left when he died: that through them I may prove Israel, whether they will keep the way of the LORD" (Judges 2:21, 22; see also Judges 3:1, 4; Exodus 16:4). "My brethren, count it all joy when ye fall into divers temptations; knowing this, that the trying of your faith worketh patience" (James 1:2–3); "Ye are in heaviness through manifold temptations: that the trial of your faith, being much more precious than of gold. . .might be found unto praise and honour and glory" (1 Pet. 1:6–7). The apostle Paul says that giving to the poor is proof of the sincerity of Christians' love (2 Cor. 8:8). Scripture often refers to our trials as a furnace that tries the purity of gold and silver: "Thou, O God, hast proved us: thou hast tried us, as silver is tried. Thou broughtest us into the net; thou laidst affliction upon our loins" (Ps. 66:10–11); "And I will bring the third part through the fire, and will refine them as silver is refined, and will try them as gold is tried" (Zech. 13:9). Something that looks like gold is put into the furnace to see whether it is real gold or not, and difficulties in our lives are called trials, because they try us, revealing whether we are what we appear to be—real saints.

If we put true gold into the furnace, we will find its great value and preciousness; in the same way, our value is revealed when we undergo these trials: "That the trial of your faith, being much more precious than of gold that perisheth, might be found unto praise and honour and glory" (1 Pet. 1:7). True and pure gold will come out of the furnace weighing as much as it did when it went in, and true saints, when tried, come forth like gold (Job 23:10). Christ distinguished true grace from counterfeit by this, that it is gold tried in the fire (Rev. 3:17–18).

Clearly, then, Scripture calls these difficult circumstances "trials" because they reveal our sincerity better than any other test. Our response to trials makes known our true natures.

When God proves us this way, to see what is in our hearts and whether we will keep His commandments or not, we shouldn't think that He does this for His own information, as though He could not see the truth any other way. God knows our hearts already—but He allows us to be tried so that we may know them too.

Thus, when God proved Israel through the difficulties they met with in the wilderness and in Canaan, to show what was in their hearts, whether they would keep His commandments or not, we must understand that He did this to reveal them to themselves, that they might know what was in their own hearts. So when God tried Abraham with that difficult command of offering up his son, it was not for God's satisfaction, but for Abraham's, so that he might have a deeper understanding of who he was in relation to God. When Abraham was proved faithful under this trial, God said to him, "Now I know that thou fearest God, seeing thou hast not withheld thy son, thine only son from me" (Gen. 22:12). This clearly implies that Abraham's response to this trial gave him a clearer vision of his grace than ever before. God tested him, so that he would know for certain who and what he was.

We find that Christ from time to time used the same method to convince the consciences of those who pretended to be friends with Him, showing them to be what they were. This was the method He used with the rich young man (Matt. 19:16–22). This man seemed to show great respect to Christ; he came kneeling before Him, calling Him "good Master," professing to obey all the commandments, but Christ tried him, by telling him to go and sell all that he had, and give to the poor, and come and take up his cross and follow Him, telling him that then he should have treasure in heaven. Similarly, Christ tried someone else in Matthew 8:19–20. This person said to Christ, "Master, I will follow thee whithersoever thou goest." Christ immediately put his friendship to the proof by telling him that the foxes had holes, and the birds of the air had nests, but that the Son of Man had nowhere to lay His head. And Christ is likely to try His followers today in the same general way, through His providence. The seed is sown in every kind of ground— stony ground, thorny ground, and good ground—and it all looks alike when it first springs up. But when it is tried by the sun's burning heat, the reality is soon clear.

Since these are the things God uses to try us, certainly the best way for us to judge ourselves is by these same things. These trials of His are not for His information, but for ours; therefore, we ought to make use of the information they provide us. The clearest way to know our gold is to look at it and examine it in God's furnace. If we want to know if a building is strong or not, we must look at it when the wind blows. If we want to know whether something that looks like wheat is really wheat or only chaff, we must observe it when it is winnowed. If we want to know whether a staff is strong or a rotten, broken reed, we must watch it when it is leaned on and it bears weight. If we would weigh ourselves accurately, we must weigh ourselves in the scales that God uses.

The trials we encounter on our spiritual journeys are like balances in which our hearts are weighed; Christ and the world—or Christ and His competitors in our hearts—are put into opposite scales, and then we can see which has more weight in our hearts. This is the same as when we reach a fork in our path; one way leads to Christ, and the other leads to something that we selfishly crave. We must choose one or the other; we cannot go both ways at once, and the path we choose will reveal the direction of our hearts. This is simply another metaphor for laying Christ and the world in two opposing scales; one side will sink, the other will rise.

Therefore trials measure the true quality of our hearts as accurately as scales compare the weight of two opposing substances.

Argument III

Another argument that supports this concept that holy practice is the strongest evidence of grace in our hearts is this: Grace, according to Scripture, is made perfect in action; in other words, it comes to its completion. The apostle

James says, "Seest thou how faith wrought with his works, and by works was faith made perfect [or finished, as the original word means]?" (James 2:22).

The love of God is also said to be made perfect, or finished, when we keep His commandments: "He that saith, I know him, and keepeth not his commandments, is a liar, and the truth is not in him: but, whoso keepeth his word, in him verily is the love of God perfected" (1 John 2:4–5). The commandment of Christ that John is referring to here is that great commandment of His that tells us to love each other, and again, the love of God is perfected in the same sense: "If we love one another, God dwelleth in us, and his love is perfected in us" (1 John 4:12). Without a doubt, John is still talking about loving one another in the same way that he explained in the preceding chapter, where he says that loving one another is a sign of God's love: "Whoso hath this world's good, and seeth his brother have need, and shutteth up his bowels, . . .how dwelleth the love of God in him? My little children, let us not love in word, neither in tongue; but in deed [or in work] and in truth" (1 John 3:17–18). By loving in work this way, John says, "The love of God is perfected"—or completed.

Holy practice is the natural effect of grace; the tendency and design of grace produces acts of love. Only then is its operation completed and crowned. The tree is made perfect by the fruit; it is not perfected when the seed is planted in the ground; it is not perfected when the seed sprouts; nor is it perfected when it comes up out of the ground, nor when it grows leaves, nor even when it blossoms. Only when it has produced good ripe fruit, is it perfected or completed. Fruit is its end; the design of the tree is now finished; all that belongs to the tree is completed and brought to its proper effect.

Grace is made perfect, or finished, when it produces fruit —active love; sin, however, produces a different type of fruit: "When lust hath conceived, it bringeth forth sin: and sin, when it is finished, bringeth forth death" (James 1:15). The process has three steps: First, sin begins when we selfishly desire something. Second, we become obsessed with this desire, consumed by it. And last of all, the fruit is produced, and we actively do some evil deed to bring about our desire. This is what James calls the completion or perfecting of sin; the word, in the original, is the same that is translated *perfected* in the earlier references.

Certainly, then, if grace is made perfect by its fruit, if a practical active grace is its proper effect and end, its completion and crown, this must be the strongest evidence of grace, above anything else. If we want to see the proper nature of anything, and see how it is different from other things, we have to look at its ending, its completion. The apostle James says that by works faith is made perfect; he is arguing to prove that works are the chief evidence of faith, whereby faith's sincerity is demonstrated (James 2). And the apostle John, after he had once again told us that love is made perfect by keeping Christ's commandments, observes that "perfect love casteth out fear" (1 John 4:18), meaning that when love has matured to completion, there will be no more room for fear in our hearts.

Argument IV
Another thing which makes clear that holy practice is the

principal evidence for judging both our own and others' sincerity, is that this is what the Bible tells us. Even the most minimal knowledge of Scripture is enough to show us that this is true throughout the Scripture, from the beginning of Genesis to the end of Revelation. And in the New Testament, where Christ and His apostles expressly spell out the signs of true godliness, this is almost the only evidence given.

Christ and His apostles again and again say things like, "By this you shall know that you know God. . .By this are the children of God revealed. . .Hereby we shall assure our hearts. . .He is the man that loveth Christ," and so on. But I can find no place where either Christ or His apostles say that Christian practice is the only thing we need. In many of these places, love for each other is spoken of as a sign of godliness; and, as I have observed before, love is the best sign of true grace. But Scripture makes clear that we must put our love into action. The apostle John, who, more than anyone else, insists on love for each other as a sign of godliness, explains himself this way, "We know that we have passed from death unto life, because we love the brethren. He that loveth not his brother abideth in death. . . . But whoso hath this world's good, and seeth his brother have need, and shutteth up his bowels of compassion from him, how dwelleth the love of God in him? My little children, let us not love in word, neither in tongue; but in deed [i.e., in deeds of love] and in truth. And hereby we know that we are of the truth, and shall assure our hearts before him" (1 John 3:14, 17–19).

When Scripture insists on our loving each other as a sure sign of godliness, it does not mean the emotional fondness we feel for each other, as much as that we express our love actively and practically, laying aside our own needs in service to each other; this is real love (see Rom. 13:8–12; Gal. 5:14; Matt. 22:39–40).

Scripture clearly tells us that our behavior is the best proof of our hearts. If we doubt that holy practice reveals true holiness, then we might as well say that Christ and His apostles did not know what they were talking about. But, if we make the Word of Christ our rule, then we should try our own hearts by the same instrument Christ and His disciples used: Do we practice love? And certainly spiritual leaders should also value what Christ valued. To ignore the scriptural rule and insist on entirely different sets of rules, as many ministers do, is dangerous practice; it is going out of God's way, judging ourselves and guiding others in an unscriptural manner. God knew the way for leading and guiding souls that was safest and best for them; He insisted so much on this rule of love because He knew they needed it—and He left other things alone, because He is wise and He knew it would not be good for us to put too much emphasis somewhere else.

As the Sabbath was made for humanity, so the Scriptures were made for us too; they are, by God's infinite wisdom, custom-made for our use and benefit. We should, therefore, make them our guide in all things, in our thoughts of religion and of ourselves. For us to emphasize something that Scripture minimizes, or for us to minimize something that the Scripture stresses, tends to give us a warped idea of religion. It leads us indirectly and gradually away from a healthy realistic view of ourselves and into delusion and hypocrisy.

God again and again speaks in His Word about the importance of Christian practice: "He that hath my commandments, and keepeth them, he it is that loveth me" (John 14:21). Christ gives this rule to the disciples, not so much to guide them in judging others, as to apply it to themselves for their own comfort after His departure. Christ repeats the same message again and again; verse 15: "If ye love me, keep my commandments"; verse 23: "If a man love me, he will keep my words"; verse 24: "He that loveth me not keepeth not my sayings"; chapter 15:2: "Every branch in me that beareth not fruit he taketh away: and every branch that beareth fruit, he purgeth it"; verse 8: "Herein is my Father glorified, that ye bear much fruit; so shall ye be my disciples"; verse 14: "Ye are my friends, if ye do whatsoever I command you"; John 8:31: "If ye continue in my word, then are ye my disciples indeed"; and in 1 John 2:3: "Hereby we do know that we know him, if we keep his commandments"; verse 5: "Whoso keepeth his word, in him verily is the love of God perfected: hereby know we that we are in him"; chapter 3:18–19: "Let us love . . .in deed and in truth. And hereby we know that are of the truth." What is translated *hereby* could have been translated more literally from the original, *by this* we do know. Holy practice is spoken of as the thing that separates the children of God and the children of the devil; the same chapter, verse 10: "In this the children of God are manifest, and the children of the devil"; verses 6–10: "Whosoever abideth in him sinneth not: whosoever sinneth hath not seen him, neither known him. Little children, let no man deceive you: he that doeth righteousness is righteous, even as he is righteous. He that committeth sin is of the devil. . . . Whosoever is born of

God doth not commit sin. . . . Whosoever doeth not right-eousness is not of God"; 2 John 6: "This is love, that we walk after his commandments" (in other words, following Christ's commandments proves our love); 1 John 5:3: "This is the love of God, that we keep his commandments"; James 1:27: "Pure religion and undefiled before God and the Father is this, To visit the fatherless and widows in their affliction, and to keep himself unspotted from the world."

We hear the same message in the Old Testament: "And unto man he said, Behold, the fear of the LORD, that is wisdom; and to depart from evil is understanding" (Job 28:28); "Did not thy father eat and drink, and do judg-ment and justice? . . . He judged the cause of the poor and needy; . . .was not this to know me? saith the LORD" (Jer. 22:15–16); "Come, ye children, hearken unto me: I will teach you the fear of the LORD. . . . Keep thy tongue from evil, and thy lips from speaking guile. Depart from evil, and do good; seek peace, and pursue it" (Ps. 34:11, 13–14); "Who shall abide in thy tabernacle? who shall dwell in thy holy hill? He that walketh uprightly" (Ps. 15:1–2); "Who shall ascend into the hill of the LORD? or who shall stand in his holy place? He that hath clean hands, and a pure heart" (Ps. 24:3–4); "Blessed are the undefiled in the way, who walk in the law of the LORD" (Ps. 119:1); "Then shall I not be ashamed, when I have respect unto all thy com-mandments" (Ps. 119:6); "The fear of the LORD is to hate evil" (Prov. 8:13).

The Bible is more emphatic about this rule than any other. "Be not deceived; God is not mocked: for whatsoever a man soweth, that shall he also reap" (Gal. 6:7); "Be not deceived: neither fornicators, nor idolaters. . .shall inherit the kingdom of God"(1 Cor. 6:9–10); "For this ye know, that no whoremonger, nor unclean person. . .hath any inheritance in the kingdom of Christ and of God. Let no man deceive you with vain words" (Eph. 5:5–6); "Little children, let no man deceive you: he that doeth righteousness is righteous, even as he is righteous. He that committeth sin is of the devil" (1 John 3:7–8); "He that saith, I know him, and keepeth not his commandments, is a liar, and the truth is not in him" (1 John 2:4); "If we say that we have fellowship with him, and walk in darkness, we lie, and do not the truth" (1 John 1:6); "If any man among you seem to be religious, and bridleth not his tongue, but deceiveth his own heart, this man's religion is vain" (James 1:26); "If ye have bitter envying and strife in your hearts, glory not, and lie not against the truth. This wisdom decendeth not from above, but is earthly, sensual, devilish" (James 3:14–15); "As for such as turn aside unto their crooked ways, the LORD shall lead them forth with the workers of iniquity" (Ps. 125:5); "An highway shall be there, . . .and it shall be called The way of holiness; the unclean shall not pass over it" (Isa. 35:8); "And there shall in no wise enter into it any thing that defileth, neither whatsoever worketh abomination, or maketh a lie" (Rev. 21:27). In many places Christ also said, "Depart from me, I know you not, ye that work iniquity."

Argument V
Another thing that shows us that holy practice is the greatest sign of sincerity, not only to the world, but to our own consciences, is that this evidence is used before the judgment

seat of God. God's judgment is not based on His opinion, as when a human judge must make up his mind whether to be merciful or not; no, God's judgment is based on reality. God knows this reality without any proof on our part, but perhaps on that day the evidence will be given for our benefit: "And I saw the dead, small and great, stand before God; and the books were opened: . . .and the dead were judged out of those things which were written in the books, according to their works. And the sea gave up the dead which were in it; and death and hell delivered up the dead which were in them: and they were judged every man according to their works" (Rev. 20:12–13); "For we must all appear before the judgment seat of Christ; that every one may receive the things done in his body, according to that he hath done, whether it be good or bad" (2 Cor. 5:10).

Our behavior, our external practice, is the only evidence that the Bible ever mentions when it speaks of the future judgment (Matt. 25:31–46; Rom. 2:6–13; Jer. 17:10; 32:19; Job 34:11; Prov. 24:12; Rev. 22:12; Matt. 16:27; Rev. 2:23; Ezek. 33:20; 1 Pet. 1:17). On that day we will not be asked to tell our stories or explain our theology; instead, all of our actions will be shown to us, each thing that we did both privately and publicly: "For God shall bring every work into judgment, with every secret thing, whether it be good, or whether it be evil" (Eccl. 12:14). The balance used then will be the same balance that is being used now in our lives, for by each trial that comes into our life, we are being weighed in the same way that we will be on the Judgment Day.

Therefore, we can undoubtedly infer that our works (as I have already defined them) are the best indication of who we are. Since God places such absolute importance on them, we would do well to do the same. "He that hath my commandments, and keepeth them, he it is that loveth me" (John 14:21).

Not that we don't see grace at work in our lives in other ways also. When we engage in contemplation, meditating on God's nature, grace may work in very satisfying ways within our hearts. But the fact remains that grace can best be seen in active, practical ways. You may be able to identify a fig tree by its leaves or its bark or its shape—but the best evidence is that it actually bears figs.

If a person hears of a great treasure in a far land, and she sells all that she has and gives up everything at home, so that she can journey to this land to seek the treasure, then everyone who knows her will know—and she herself will be certain—that she has truly committed herself to this treasure. She did not merely feel a passing interest in it, nor did she simply talk about the treasure all the time; no, she has given up everything else for it. However, she herself is conscious of why she is going to such great effort, or otherwise her body's motion proves nothing. In the same way, Christian practice proves the saving value of the pearl of great price and the treasure hid in the field.

We prove the strength of any tool by its use, just as we prove the strength of our arms by their ability to fight and work. Most of the everyday objects around us are useful for some purpose, for example, a saw, a string, a chain, an ax, a foot, a tooth, and so on. If any of these things are too weak to bear the pressure we put on them, then they are worthless. That is the way it is with all the mind's virtues. We prove their strength by using them in the midst of the temptations and trials that God allows in our lives. If they can hold up under the pressure, we know they are real and serviceable. Knowledge that makes us whole and happy, will also be practical: "If ye know these things, happy are ye if ye do them"(John 13:17); "To depart from evil is understanding" (Job 28:28).

Holy practice is real proof of repentance. When people professed their repentance to John the Baptist, he told them, "Bring forth therefore fruits meet for repentance" (Matt. 3:8). Holy practice is also real proof of a saving faith, as is clear in James 2:20–26, where James tells us that if our faith is living, it will be practical and active. Furthermore, practice is real proof of a saving belief of the truth: "I rejoiced greatly, when the brethren came and testified of the truth that is in thee, even as thou walkest in the truth" (3 John 3). Practice is the real proof too of a living trust in Christ. The apostle Paul trusted in Christ, and committed himself to Him, venturing his entire life on the ability and faithfulness of his Redeemer: "For the which cause I also suffer these things: nevertheless I am not ashamed: for I know whom I have believed, and am persuaded that he is able to keep that which I have committed unto him against that day" (2 Tim. 1:12). What is more, practice is real proof of love for God and others, just as it is proof of true humility; "He hath shewed thee, O man, what is good; and what doth the LORD require of thee, but to do justly, and to love mercy, and to walk humbly with thy God?" (Mic. 6:8). And our practice proves our reverence for God as well; "Come, ye children, hearken unto me: I will teach you the fear of the Lord. . . . Keep thy tongue from evil, and thy lips from speaking guile. Depart from evil, and do good; seek peace, and pursue it" (Ps. 34:11, 13–14). Our practice proves that we are really thankful to God, and it proves where our desires lie: "One thing have I desired of the LORD, that will I seek after" (Ps. 27:4); "O God, thou art my God; early will I seek thee: my soul thirsteth for thee, my flesh longeth for thee in a dry and thirsty land, where no water is; to see thy power and thy glory" (Ps. 63:1–2). Christian practice is the evidence of our hope: "Every man that hath this hope in him purifieth himself, even as he is pure" (1 John 3:3). And if we act out our faith cheerfully, this is the best evidence of the joy that lives in our hearts: "Thy testimonies have I taken as an heritage for ever: for they are the rejoicing of my heart. I have inclined mine heart to perform thy statutes alway, even unto the end" (Ps. 119:111–112); "The abundance of their joy. . .abounded unto the riches of their liberality" (2 Cor. 8:2). What is more, our behavior proves our courage (1 Cor. 9:25–27, 2 Tim. 2:3–5). All these spiritual emotions are proved by the active practice of our faith.

Any supernatural revelation should also be proved by the degree that it influences a person's behavior. Of course we must make allowances for a person's natural temperament, but even an ill-tempered person's behavior will be noticeably changed for the better by the touch of true grace.

All of this supports my argument that Christian practice is the greatest sign of saving grace. Before I conclude this book, I want to briefly answer two objections that some of you may possibly have.

Objection I
Some of you may be saying, "Don't most Christians agree

that they should judge their relation to God mostly by their inner experience? Aren't these spiritual experiences the best proof of true grace?"

I'd have to answer that this is undoubtedly true: We *should* judge our relationship with God mostly by experience. But this does not contradict what I have just said about Christian practice. Christian practice *is* spiritual practice; it is not simply physical movement and external actions. A human is one being, spirit and body together, and spiritual practice for all of us who are human is the practice of the spirit and the body together. The spirit animates, commands, and actuates the body to which it is united, and therefore, the main thing in this holy practice is the holy action of the mind, directing and governing the motions of the body.

These external physical motions belong to Christian practice only secondarily, for they are dependent on the acts of the soul. Our inner experience of grace within our souls is expressed outwardly through our bodies. The fact that these inner exercises have external behaviors directly connected to them does not diminish them in any way, or make them less spiritual. For example, our love for God is not less of a spiritual thing because it is expressed with practical, observable acts of self-denial.

Admittedly, all Christian experience is not appropriately called practice, but all Christian practice is appropriately called experience. To speak of Christian experience and practice as if they were two separate things is to make a distinction that is not based on reason. If we make this distinction, it is not merely unreasonable but also unscriptural, as we have seen: "This is the love of God, that we keep his commandments" (1 John 5:3); "Come, ye children, . . .I will teach you the fear of the LORD. . . . Depart from evil, and do good" (Ps. 34:11, 14).

And not only does the most important and obvious part of Christian experience lie in spiritual practice, but nothing else can be so appropriately referred to as experiential religion. Active love for God and others is the Christian experience that allows us to see whether we have the heart to do God's will, forsaking all things for Christ, or not. Experimental philosophy tests various opinions and ideas to see if they are facts, and experimental religion, a religion based on experience, brings religious "affections" to the test.

An external religious practice that lacks inner experience is good for nothing. And experience that is not expressed in practice is worse than nothing. Real spiritual light directs both our hearts and our hands. Religion is mostly love, but true religion is not merely warm feelings; it must be expressed by practical, active love. In the same way, friendship between earthly friends is mostly love, but it is the sort of love that carries them through fire and water for each other.

Nothing that I have said contradicts what some theologians say about the only sure sign of grace being acts of grace. Why should grace be limited to the invisible world? Aren't these active, practical demonstrations of grace also acts of grace, perhaps the highest acts of grace? And the more of these trials we experience, where each time grace is tried and proved, the more the evidence is heightened. The disciples, when they first saw Christ after His resurrection, had good evidence that He was alive, but when they spent the next forty days with Him, while He showed Himself to them with many infallible proofs, they had even greater evidence.

In the midst of trials, the Spirit gives our hearts the clearest evidence possible that we are truly God's children. This is clear in Scripture: "If ye be reproached for the name of Christ, happy are ye; for the spirit of glory and of God resteth upon you" (1 Pet. 4:14); "We. . .rejoice in hope of the glory of God. And not only so, but we glory in tribulations" (Rom. 5:2, 3). In the same way, Christ revealed Himself to Shadrach, Meshach, and Abednego in the furnace. And Paul speaks of a similar comfort in the midst of tribulation in Romans 8:18: "For I reckon that the sufferings of this present time are not worthy to be compared with the glory which shall be revealed in us." Revelation's promise of the white stone and the new name to him that overcomes (Rev. 2:17) makes clear that Christ will give us special comfort and blessing as we overcome the trial in that day of persecution.

Objection II
Some of you may say that by putting so much emphasis on Christian practice, I am creating a legalistic doctrine, one that magnifies works and tends to lead people to exaggerate the importance of their own actions, while diminishing the glory of free grace. This perspective, you may say, is inconsistent with the gospel doctrine of justification by faith alone.

But this objection also lacks a foundation in reason. Why is it inconsistent with free grace that holy practice is a sign of it? I am not saying that God's grace is bought by our works, but only that they are proof of grace. When a beggar looks at the money in his hands as a sure sign of the kindness of the person who gave it to him, this does not take away from that person's kindness. If the beggar had to have money in his hand before he could be given anything, that would mean that the gift was not free—but I am saying just the opposite.

Nothing we can do makes us deserve God's grace. Free grace means that it is bestowed on the unworthy and the unlovely; we have no excellence in ourselves that merits God's grace, but the excellence is all in God. Grace flows from the fullness of His nature, from the fullness of the Fountain of good, regardless of our condition. This is the doctrine of justification without works that the Bible teaches: That nothing we do can earn His love, and yet He bestows it on us freely anyway, through the righteousness of Christ rather than our own righteousness. We are justified by our faith, not our works. But our works are the fruit of our faith. If we say that works are not important simply because we are not justified by them, we might as well say that nothing in our religion is important, not even faith or hope or love, for none of them justify us in God's eyes.

Scripture is not afraid to link God's total grace with the necessity of divine practice, as we see in these passages: "Let the wicked forsake his way, and the unrighteous man his thoughts: and let him return unto the LORD, and he will have mercy upon him; and to our God, for he will abundantly pardon" (Isa. 55:7); "Wash you, make you clean; put away the evil of your doings from before mine eyes; cease to do evil; learn to do well; seek judgment, relieve the oppressed, judge the fatherless, plead for the widow. Come now, and let us reason together, saith the LORD: though your sins be as scarlet, they shall be as white as snow; though they be red like crimson, they shall be as wool" (Isa. 1:16–18).

What I have said about the importance of holy practice as the greatest sign of sincerity is not derogatory of the freedom and sovereignty of gospel grace; it is not legalistic, nor does it clash with the gospel doctrine of justification by faith alone without the works of the law. And it certainly does nothing to lessen the glory of the Mediator and our dependence on His righteousness. Careful consideration of all that I have said makes this clear. So if you find you are still objecting, then I suspect you are experiencing merely a sort of knee-jerk reaction to the word *works,* when you have no real reason in the world for reacting so negatively. You might as well have the same sort of reflex to the words *holiness, godliness, grace, religion, experience,* and even *faith* itself, for none of these can make us righteous either, and if we claim they can, then our doctrine is just as legalistic as if we claimed we were justified by our works.

We hurt our religion when we dismiss what Scripture insists is most important, while we emphasize revelations and emotional impressions. We don't want to be legalistic, we say, nor governed by the old covenant, and so we spend all our time analyzing our emotional experiences, thinking that we will find the evidence of grace here in these extraordinary signs and wonders. We pride ourselves on our discernment and wisdom, but all this is actually darkness and delusion. Remember what Scripture says: "Every word of God is pure: he is a shield unto them that put their trust in him. Add thou not unto his words, lest he reprove thee, and thou be found a liar" (Prov. 30:5–6).

We should not trust our own discernment of others' hearts, for we can only see a little way into the depths of the human heart. Our emotions can be moved by many things without any supernatural influence, and their natural springs are varied and secret. Many things may affect them jointly at once: the imagination, our natural temperament, education, circumstances, malicious spirits, and so on. No philosophy or science will ever be exact enough to guide us safely through the labyrinth and maze of our own hearts.

Our only hope is to follow the clue which God has given us in His Word. God knows what He has created; He knows our nature and what will be most healthy for us. He understands all the complicated interactions of cause and effect that are woven through our natures. And therefore we will be wise if we trust His wisdom rather than our own, stressing those elements of the spiritual journey that He has told us are essential for proving the truth.

If we do anything else, then it's no wonder if we are bewildered, confounded, and fatally deluded. But if we make a habit of looking at things the way Christ and His disciples did, than we will be able to judge ourselves and others realistically and reliably, freeing our religion from delusion.

If we were all to make this our practice, then perhaps it would become fashionable for us to show our Christianity with our love and kindness rather than with our loud and ostentatious stories. We might find we all practice our faith with more energy, serving God not with our tongues, but by serving those around us. Christians who are intimate friends would talk together of their experiences and blessings with more humility and modesty, aiming for each other's profit;

their tongues would not go running ahead of them, but instead their tongues would follow their hands and feet (2 Cor. 12:6). Spiritual pride would be cut off by this sort of practice, shutting the devil's largest door into our hearts.

If all this was to happen, our religion would be lived out in such a way that those who saw us would not be cynical spectators, leaning toward infidelity and atheism. Instead, our practice would tend to convince them that there is a living reality in religion, a reality that would wake them up and win them over. In this way our light would shine before the world, so that others, seeing our good works, would glorify our Father who is in heaven.

THE ESSENTIAL CHRISTIAN LIBRARY

Books That Stand the Test of Time. . .
Priced as if Time Were Standing Still

Essential reading for every Christian, these hardbound, time-tested classics will form a priceless collection of Christian writing that will bring inspiration and encourage devotion to God for years to come. Beautifully bound, affordably priced at $9.97 each!

Best of Andrew Murray on Prayer, The
Christian's Secret of A Happy Life, The by Hannah Whitall Smith
Faith's Great Heroes, Volume One
Great Sermons, Volume One
God Calling edited by A. J. Russell
Hiding Place, The by Corrie ten Boom
Hinds' Feet On High Places by Hannah Hurnard
In His Steps by Charles M. Sheldon
Morning & Evening by Charles H. Spurgeon
My Utmost for His Highest by Oswald Chambers
Pilgrim's Progress, The by John Bunyan
Prison to Praise by Merlin Carothers
Riches of Bunyan, The
Search for Holy Living, The

Available wherever books are sold.
Or order from:

Barbour Publishing, Inc.
P.O. Box 719
Uhrichsville, OH 44683
http://www.barbourbooks.com

If you order by mail, add $2.00 to your order for shipping.
Prices subject to change without notice.

ISBN 1-57748-525-4

9 781577 485254